DOUBT TRUTH T

The Law of Non-Contradiction has been high orthodoxy in Western philosophy since Aristotle. The so-called Law has been the subject of radical challenge in recent years by dialetheism, the view that some contradictions are indeed true. Many philosophers have taken the Law to be central to many of our most important philosophical concepts. In *Doubt Truth to be a Liar*, Graham Priest mounts the case against this. Starting with an analysis of Aristotle on the Law, he discusses the nature of truth, of rationality, of negation, and of logic itself, and argues that the Law is inessential to all of these things. The book takes off from Priest's earlier book, *In Contradiction* (a second edition of which is also published by OUP), developing its themes largely without recourse to formal logic.

The book is required reading for anyone who wishes to understand dialetheism; (especially) for anyone who wishes to continue to endorse the old Aristotelian orthodoxy; and more generally, for anyone who wishes to understand the role that contradiction plays in our thinking.

Graham Priest is Boyce Gibson Professor of Philosophy at the University of Melbourne, and Arché Professorial Fellow at the University of St. Andrews.

Doubt Truth to be a Liar

GRAHAM PRIEST

CLARENDON PRESS • OXFORD

OXFORD
UNIVERSITY PRESS

Great Clarendon Street, Oxford OX2 6DP

Oxford University Press is a department of the University of Oxford.
It furthers the University's objective of excellence in research, scholarship,
and education by publishing worldwide in

Oxford New York

Auckland Cape Town Dar es Salaam Hong Kong Karachi
Kuala Lumpur Madrid Melbourne Mexico City Nairobi
New Delhi Shanghai Taipei Toronto

With offices in

Argentina Austria Brazil Chile Czech Republic France Greece
Guatemala Hungary Italy Japan Poland Portugal Singapore
South Korea Switzerland Thailand Turkey Ukraine Vietnam

Oxford is a registered trade mark of Oxford University Press
in the UK and in certain other countries

Published in the United States
by Oxford University Press Inc., New York

British Library Cataloguing in Publication Data

Data available

Library of Congress Cataloging in Publication Data

Priest, Graham.
Doubt truth to be a liar / Graham Priest.
p. cm.
Includes bibliographical references (p.).
1. Truth. 2. contradiction. 3. Logic. I. Title.
BC171.P76 2006   121′.6–dc22   2005020197

Typeset by Laserwords Private Limited, Chennai, India
Printed in Great Britain
by
Biddles Ltd., King's Lynn, Norfolk

ISBN 978–0–19–926328–8 (Hbk.)   978–0–19–923815–4 (Pbk.)

1 3 5 7 9 10 8 6 4 2

Doubt thou the stars are fire;
Doubt that the sun doth move;
Doubt truth to be a liar;
But never doubt I love.

(*Hamlet*, II. ii. 115)

For Minou

Preface

In Contradiction, which was first published in 1987, provided a sustained argument for and defence of dialetheism. My thoughts on the topic have continued to evolve since that time, however. A general discussion of the evolution can be found in the second edition of that book, which is a companion volume to this one. One particular area of development concerns the implications of dialetheism for certain key philosophical notions, such as truth and rationality—and vice versa. That is what this book is about.

The book draws on papers that I have published since 1987. In particular, it draws on the following material, which, however, has been refashioned in some places—at some points substantially—in the cause of coherence:

Chapter 1: 'To Be *and* Not to Be—that is the Answer: Aristotle on the Law of Non-Contradiction', *Philosophiegeschichte und Logische Analyse*, 1 (1998), 91–130.

Chapter 2: 'Truth and Contradiction', *Philosophical Quarterly*, 50 (2000), 189–95.

Chapter 3: 'Perceiving Contradictions', *Australasian Journal of Philosophy*, 77 (1999), 439–46; and 'Could Everything be True?', *Australasian Journal of Philosophy*, 78 (2000), 189–95.

Chapter 4: 'What Not? A Defence of a Dialetheic Account of Negation', in D. Gabbay and H. Wansing, (eds.) (1999), *What is Negation?*, Dordrecht: Kluwer Academic Publishers, 101–20.

Chapter 5: 'Boolean Negation and All That', *Journal of Philosophical Logic*, 19 (1990), 201–15.

Chapter 6: 'Can Contradictions be True? II', *Proceedings of the Aristotelian Society*, suppl. vol. 67 (1993), 35–54; and 'Rational Dilemmas', *Analysis*, 62 (2002), 11–16.

Chapter 7: 'Why it's Irrational to Believe in Consistency', in B. Brogard and B. Smith (eds.), *Rationality and Irrationality, Proceedings of the 23rd International Wittgenstein Symposium*, Vienna: öbv&hpt Verlagsgesellschaft mbh & Co. (2001), 284–93.

Chapter 8: 'Paraconsistent Belief Revision', *Theoria*, 68 (2001), 214–28.

Chapter 9: 'Inconsistency and the Empirical Sciences', in J. Meheus (ed.) (2002), *Inconsistency in Science*, Dordrecht: Kluwer Academic Publishers, 119–28.

Chapter 10: 'On Alternative Geometries, Arithmetics and Logics: A Tribute to Łukasiewicz', *Studia Logica*, 74 (2003), 441–68.

Chapter 11: 'Validity', in A. Varzi (ed.) (1999), *The Nature of Logic*, Stanford: CSLI Publications (*European Review of Philosophy*), 183–206.

Chapter 12: 'Logic: One or Many?', in J. Woods and B. Brown (eds.), *Logical Consequences: Rival Approaches*, Oxford: Hermes Scientific Publishers Ltd. (2001), 23–38.

I am grateful to the editors, professional associations, and publishers in question for permission to reuse the material.

Footnotes in those papers thanked all those whose constructive criticism helped in their production. These included by name: Jonathan Adler, Diderik Batens, JC Beall, Paddy Blanchette, Andrew Brennan, Deb Brown, Stewart Candlish, Max Cresswell, Nick Denyer, André Fuhrmann, André Gallois, Jay Garfield, Len Goddard, Bill Grey, Ian Hinckfuss, Colin Howson, Dominic Hyde, Arnie Koslow, Roger Lamb, Julian Lamont, Isaac Levi, David McCarty, Gary Malinas, Joke Meheus, Winston Nesbitt, Daniel Nolan, Thomas de Praetere, Greg Restall (several times), Hans Rott, Steve Schiffer, Hartley Slater, Timothy Smiley, Roy Sorensen, Göran Sundholm, Richard Sylvan, Koji Tanaka, Ellen Watson, Peter Woodruff, Peter Unger, Achille Varzi, and Byeong Yi.

A version of the whole book was given in a series of Arché seminars in the Department of Logic and Metaphysics, University of St Andrews, Candlemas term, 2004. I am grateful to all the people who provided helpful comments and criticisms there, too; and especially to Ross Cameron, Roy Cook, Neil Cooper, Hud Hudson, Daniel Nolan, Agustin Rayo, Stephen Read, John Scorupski, Stewart Shapiro, Robbie Williams, Crispin Wright, Elia Zardini. Collective thanks go to Arché and the University of St Andrews for the congenial atmosphere they provide, to the University of Melbourne for their graciousness in allowing me to take periods of research leave there, and to my colleagues at the University of Melbourne for their never-failing support and stimulation. Finally, my thanks go to the staff of Oxford University Press, particularly Peter Momtchiloff for his thoughtful guidance with the book, and to Peter Milne, who read the penultimate draft of the book for the Press, and gave detailed and perceptive comments which much improved the final product.

GP

Melbourne
2005

Contents

PART II: NEGATION

PART III: RATIONALITY

PART IV: LOGIC

Introduction

Dialetheism is the view that some contradictions are true: there are sentences (statements, propositions, or whatever one takes truth-bearers to be), α, such that both α and $\neg\alpha$ are true, that is, such that α is both true and false.[1] Dialetheism is what this book is about.

There are many questions that one might ask about the view. One—perhaps the most obvious—is why one might suppose it to be true. *In Contradiction*[2] gives a number of reasons for supposing it to be so. These concern the paradoxes of self-reference, motion and change, and the conflict of norms, particularly legal norms. Doubtless there are other reasons. But that is not what this book is about.

Another question one might ask is as to the history of the view. The short answer is that in Western philosophy it flies in the face of orthodoxy, in the shape of the so-called "Law of Non-Contradiction". The long and more adequate answer is a complex one. But this book is not about that either.[3]

Yet another question is that of how dialetheism bears on the history of philosophy in general. Philosophers often seem to be pushed into the inconsistent despite themselves. The situation suggests itself as a prime locus of the relevance of dialetheism. It arises, in particular, when the issue of the limits of thought or language is broached. Think of Kant's problem with speaking of noumena, or Wittgenstein's problem of saying the unsayable (in the *Tractatus*). *Beyond the Limits of Thought*[4] discusses that situation. This book is not about that either.

One more question that one might ask about dialetheism concerns the details of a formal logical theory appropriate for the view. It is clear that a paraconsistent logic is required, but how does it work? Though the book alludes to details of this kind occasionally, it is not about that either.[5] (Some knowledge of formal logic is certainly required to read parts of the book; but I have deliberately omitted from it any heavy-duty logic.)

What this book *is* about is the relation of dialetheism to certain core philosophical notions. Since dialetheism is the view that some sentences and their negations are true, it obviously concerns truth and negation explicitly. The first part of the book is about the first of these, truth; the second is about the second, negation. Dialetheism, as defined, does not require it to be rational to believe some contradictions. However, the view would be of limited significance if it were never rational to believe contradictions.[6] Hence, rationality is also intimately connected with dialetheism. The third part of

---

[1] The notion was coined in this way by Priest and Routley. See p. xx of Priest, Routley, and Norman (1989). Note that I use 'false' simply to mean 'has a true negation'.

[2] Priest (1987). In the rest of this book, I will refer to this simply by its name.

[3] The matter is taken up in Priest (2007).   [4] Priest (1995*a*).

[5] For a full discussion of the details of paraconsistent logic as they bear on dialetheism, see *In Contradiction* and the relevant chapters of Priest (2001*a*).

[6] As Sainsbury (1994), 135, in effect, notes.

the book is about this. For Aristotle, the "Law of Non-Contradiction" was a principle of metaphysics, not logic. Since at least Leibniz, however, it has been taken to be a logical principle, indeed a central such principle. Dialetheism now, therefore, bears on the nature of logic. The final part of the book concerns this. The contents of each part of the book, in more detail, are as follows.

PART I: TRUTH

The only major defence of the "Law of Non-Contradiction"—and so the only major critique of dialetheism—in the history of Western philosophy was given by Aristotle in book Γ of the *Metaphysics*. The defence is highly problematic. It is not clear what, exactly, his arguments are meant to establish, or how, exactly, they are meant to establish it. Chapter 1 of the book is a commentary on the relevant passage, as well as on some arguments that other commentators have claimed to find in it. As we will see, none of the arguments in question succeeds in discrediting dialetheism. The chapter also raises a number of issues that are taken up in subsequent chapters. Chapter 1 is the longest chapter of the book, and detailed analysis of texts is not to everyone's taste. If one is keen to get on to matters of more philosophical substance, this chapter can be skipped, or read fast, provided one is prepared to accept that Aristotle's defence of the law—and its modern descendants—are badly flawed. However, since Aristotle's is the canonical defence of the law, a detailed analysis of the whole text is necessary, lest I be thought to be hiding something.

If contradictions *can* be true, what does this tell us about truth: what must truth be like if contradictions are such that they may be true? This is the topic of Chapter 2. The answer is, perhaps surprisingly, 'pretty much any way one likes'. As we will see, all the standard accounts of truth are compatible with dialetheism; indeed, a number of them actually lead in its direction.

Once one has conceded that some contradictions can be true, though, what is there to stop us supposing that all contradictions are true? This is the topic of Chapter 3. That question might, in fact, be understood in different ways. One is as the question: how does one know that not all contradictions are true? Another is as to how one would go about arguing with someone who held all contradictions to be true. Both questions are addressed in the chapter.

PART II: NEGATION

Just as one may ask what truth must be like if contradictions can be true, so one may ask what negation must be like if contradictions can be true. But in the case of negation, unlike that of truth, the answer cannot be so liberal. In particular, if some and only some contradictions are true, negation must not be explosive: a sentence and its negation cannot imply everything. Is there a credible account of negation according to which it is like this? The answer to this question is 'yes', as Chapter 4 shows.

But even if that is right, is there not a perfectly good notion of negation which is explosive, and so, for which, at least, dialetheism is ruled out? It is standardly assumed that there is, in the shape of "Boolean negation". This assumption is taken up and rejected in Chapter 5.

And speaking of rejection, it is, again standardly, assumed that there is a close connection between negation and rejection: to negate is to reject. The first part of Chapter 6 investigates the connection between negation, rejection, and the closely related notion of denial. These notions *are* connected, but the connection is by no means as simple-minded as the orthodox assumption has it. The chapter also takes up the connection between rejection and truth—or, more accurately, untruth. This will take us into the territory of rationality, in the shape of a discussion of rational dilemmas.

PART III: RATIONALITY

Chapter 7 takes up squarely the question of rationality. Again, we may ask what rationality must be like if contradictions are such that some of them may be believed rationally. This chapter provides an answer. Though it is frequently assumed that belief in a contradiction is the nadir of rationality, an account of rationality that allows for the possibility of this is not so far from orthodox accounts, as we will see.

We do not only believe or not believe things rationally, we revise or fail to revise our beliefs rationally. And it is often assumed that consistency is the fulcrum of this procedure: rational belief-revision is a form of consistency-maintenance. This is not, in fact, correct. As Chapter 8 shows, belief-revision works perfectly intelligibly in the environment of inconsistency.

Discussions of the belief of inconsistencies, and so of their rational belief, are often carried out in the domain of the *a priori*, and specifically in the domain of conceptual paradoxes of certain kinds. What of the domain of the *a posteriori*? Do the same considerations obtain in the empirical sciences? Chapter 9 returns an affirmative answer to this question.

PART IV: LOGIC

It is sometimes thought that consistency is integral to a coherent account of logical validity. The lie to this is already given by formal paraconsistent logics, which provide a coherent notion of validity allowing for inconsistency. Such logics are not (currently) orthodox, though. In other words, orthodox beliefs concerning validity must be revised to make way for this possibility. Can views about logic be revised? Not only *can* they be, they *have* been, as Chapter 10 demonstrates. But what, then, must logic be like if belief about it is rationally revisable? Chapter 10 answers that question. Logic, it will turn out, is simply a fallible theory about crucial notions such as validity.

But what, then, is validity? Chapter 11 returns an answer to that question. It provides a schematic account of validity on which all logicians, paraconsistent and non-paraconsistent, deductive and non-deductive, may agree.

Finally, if logical theories may be revised, it is clearly possible for there to be different theories that vie for acceptance, that is, for there to be rival theories. But what, exactly, does rivalry in logic amount to? And must there be a uniquely correct logic, or might more than one logic be correct? The issue of logical monism and logical pluralism is the topic of Chapter 12.

By the end of the book we will have an integrated and coherent account of the connections between dialetheism and the notions of truth, negation, rationality, and validity, together with a number of closely associated notions. The account is perfectly general, in the sense that it may be subscribed to by dialetheist and non-dialetheist alike. But if the account, or something like it, is correct, it has particular significance for dialetheism. Many philosophers have taken consistency to be a *sine qua non* of the notions in question. Hence, it might well be supposed—and many philosophers have supposed—that the behaviour of these notions rules out the very possibility of dialetheism, the view that some truths are false. The supposition is, then, mistaken. These core notions of philosophy provide no ground to doubt that the conjunction of all truths is also false, that is, to doubt truth to be a liar.

PART I
TRUTH

1

Aristotle on the Law of Non-Contradiction

1.1 INTRODUCTION

A number of the Presocratic philosophers endorsed explicitly contradictory views. In book Γ of the *Metaphysics*, Aristotle took these in his sights, and defended what was to become known as the Law of Non-Contradiction. This was a crucial moment in the history of philosophy. With the exception of Hegel and his fellow-travellers, and whilst Aristotle's opinion on nearly every other matter has been overturned—or at least challenged—nearly every Western philosopher and logician has accepted the authority of Aristotle on this matter. There is hardly a defence of the Law since Aristotle's, worth mentioning.

Of recent years, things have taken a novel twist. For developments in contemporary logic itself have made it possible to countenance, if not the old Presocratic views, at least others that endorse the truth of some contradictions. It therefore becomes crucial to recharge the debate that has lain dormant for over two millennia, and ask: did Aristotle settle the matter? Addressing this question is the aim of this chapter.

The matter has already been addressed by a few commentators in the last hundred years.[1] Some have come out in Aristotle's favour; others against. All the commentators so far, however, believed that Aristotle's conclusion was correct, even if his arguments were incorrect.[2] I do not. The following confrontation of views will therefore be a real one, not merely an academic exercise.

I will proceed by producing a commentary on Aristotle's text, with suitable inter-polations where appropriate. But the analysis does not pretend to be a scholarly one; I am not competent to do this, and there are already excellent scholarly commentaries available, e.g. Ross (1924), Kirwan (1993), De Rijk (2002). What interests me is not so much the niceties of exegesis as whether there is *any* interpretation of what Aristotle says that will establish what he wishes. As I warned in the Introduction, this chapter is the longest and, in some ways, most detailed in the book. Those who are not interested in textual commentary may read the chapter quickly, or skip over it and come back to parts of it if or when necessary.

---

[1] For example, the pioneering Łukasiewicz (1910), and the delightful Dancy (1975). Both are insightful and required reading for anyone interested in this text. The end of Łukasiewicz' essay is a little disappointing, though. After demolishing Aristotle's arguments, he nonetheless seems to think that Aristotle was justified in entrenching the law as 'unassailable dogma', for the sketchiest of reasons. See n. 22.

[2] There is one exception. Łukasiewicz (1910), sect. 19, following Meinong, held that it failed for impossible objects, such as the round square.

1.2 THE LAW OF NON-CONTRADICTION (5^b 18–22)

Our text, then, is *Metaphysics* Γ, 1003^{a}21–1012^{b}34 (future references are abbreviated). The arguments we are concerned with occur largely in chapter 4, but let us start with a quick look at the whole book. In the first three chapters Aristotle explains that there is a study whose job is to investigate the most fundamental features of 'being *qua* being', i.e. the properties that all entities have merely in virtue of being entities. It turns out that these are the Laws of Non-Contradiction (LNC) and Excluded Middle (LEM). Chapter 4 contains arguments against those who would violate the LNC. Chapters 5 and 6 attack the arguments that were supposedly given by various Presocratics for violating the Law. Chapter 7 defends the LEM; and chapter 8 deals with both laws, but adds essentially no new arguments concerning the LNC.[3]

Let us now pick up the text towards the end of chapter 3. Apparently following Plato,[4] Aristotle states the LNC thus (5^{b}18–22):[5]

For the same thing to hold good and not hold good simultaneously of the same thing and in the same respect is impossible (given any further specifications which might be added against dialectical difficulties).

Two comments are in order here. First, the principle, as stated, says that it is not possible that there is an object, *a* and property, *F*, such that $Fa \land \neg Fa$. This is obviously not the most general form of the law, which would be more like: it is not possible for there to be a proposition, α, such that $\alpha \land \neg\alpha$. Aristotle appears to be ignoring those cases where α is of something other than simple subject/predicate form. I do not think that this is the case, however; Aristotle is simply assuming that the general case can be reduced, in some way or other, to this one. Indeed, in a later chapter he states the Law in what would appear to be the more general form: 'opposite {i.e. contradictory} assertions are not simultaneously true' (11^{b}14).

Secondly, Aristotle realizes that there are many apparent violations of the LNC: a top is moving (has angular velocity) and not moving (has no linear velocity); the Channel Tunnel is in England (at one end), but also in France, and so not in England (at the other); capitalism is private production (in that the means of production are privately owned), but public production (in that the means are worked communally). But these apparent violations are due to the fact that we have not spelled out the object or the property finely enough: once we say which part of the object we are referring to, and in what respect the property is claimed to apply, the apparent violations disappear.

[3] The contents of chapter 4 are also swiftly summarized, without adding anything essentially new, in book 9 (K), ch. 5. The authorship of this book is uncertain. See Ross (1924), pp. xxv ff.

[4] 'It is obvious that the same thing will never do or suffer opposites in the same respect in relation to the same thing and at the same time.' *Republic*, 436, b (translation from Hamilton and Cairns (1961)).

[5] All quotations from the *Metaphysics* are taken from Kirwan (1993). Square braces [. . .] indicate his insertions; my insertions in all quotations in this chapter are marked with curly braces {. . .}.

Aristotle is rather vague about what qualifications may be made to save the Law from apparent counter-examples. And given a putative counter-example, it is always possible for a defender of the Law to try to disarm it with suitable qualifications. For example, some have tried to solve the Liar Paradox by arguing that the relevant sentence is true in one context, false in another, or true in one tokening and false in another.[6] These suggestions have to be taken on their individual merits (and demerits). Note, however, that there is no reason to suppose that such a device will always work, unless, in advance, one *assumes* the LNC. That this device is sometimes available does not, therefore, constitute a defence of the LNC.[7] Aristotle pursues the matter no further.

1.3 THE FIRMEST OF ALL PRINCIPLES (5^b22–35)

After stating the LNC, Aristotle goes on, next, to argue that the LNC is the 'firmest' of all principles since no one can believe anything of the form $\alpha \wedge \neg\alpha$ (5^b22–27). This is, *prima facie*, a rather strange thing to say. After all, Aristotle takes up the challenge to defend the LNC precisely because some people appear to believe things of this form. And whether or not they did, I certainly do. I believe, for example, that the Russell set both is and is not a member of itself.[8] Aristotle points out that what people say, they may not necessarily believe. This is quite true, but hardly sufficient to show that people such as I do not believe contradictions. People are not infallible about what they believe, but that someone sincerely asserts something (and is clear that what they assert is what they mean) is *very* strong *prima facie* evidence that they believe it. And someone who would fly in the face of this evidence had better have pretty good reasons.

Aristotle does go on to give such a reason (5^b28–33). Essentially it goes as follows. If someone believes $\alpha \wedge \neg\alpha$ then they believe α and they believe $\neg\alpha$; but if they believe $\neg\alpha$ then they don't believe α (believing α and believing $\neg\alpha$ are contraries). Hence it follows that they both believe and do not believe α—a violation of the LNC. This is a hopeless argument. For a start, it will work only if it is impossible to have violations of the LNC of a certain form—something still moot at this stage of the argument; more importantly, it begs the question against someone who claims that they believe contradictions. Such a person will not accede to the claim that believing α and believing $\neg\alpha$ are contraries. In the absence of further considerations, their beliefs simply refute this.[9]

---

[6] See, e.g. Priest (1995*a*), ch. 10.

[7] Nagel (1944) suggests that the Law is normative, in the sense that whenever we find an apparent counter-example, we should *introduce* respects in which each of the contradictories holds, to 'institute appropriate linguistic usage' (p. 214). Unfortunately, it is not clear that one *can* always do this; and Nagel provides no argument at all as to why we *must* do this, or be "inappropriate".

[8] See, e.g. *In Contradiction*.

[9] The further considerations could be that a contradiction of the form '*x* believes α and *x* does not believe α' could be true. In this case, the argument might be sound, but now the conclusion that *x* does not believe that $\alpha \wedge \neg\alpha$ does not rule out that *x* *does* believe it. For further comments on

There are arguments in chapter 4 that can be interpreted as attempts to show that one cannot believe a contradiction. We will come to these in due course. For the present, there appears to be no reason to believe that I do not believe what I believe I believe.

The chapter closes (5^b33–35) by Aristotle claiming that the LNC is the most fundamental principle of demonstration: 'it is, in the nature of things, the principle of all the other axioms . . .'. What this means is not entirely clear. There are many principles of demonstration that do not depend on the LNC in any obvious sense. For example, in the semantics for some paraconsistent logics, sentences are allowed to be both true and false, and so the LNC fails. Yet many other things hold as logical truths (e.g. the LEM) or as valid inferences (e.g. $\alpha \vdash \alpha \vee \beta$). Aristotle even recognizes this elsewhere. In the *Posterior Analytics* (A11, 77^a10 ff.) he says:

The impossibility of joint affirmation and denial is presupposed in no proof (syllogism) unless the conclusion itself was also to have demonstrated such. Then it is demonstrated insofar as one accepts that it is true to predicate the major term of the middle term and not true to deny it. But as far as concerns the middle term and likewise the minor term, it makes no difference to hold that it is and is not.[10]

Aristotle's point is simply illustrated: if all *A*s are *B*s and all *B*s are *C*s, it follows that all *A*s are *C*s, even if some *A*s are also not *B*s. After all, they are still *B*s as well, and so *C*s.

Maybe, then, what Aristotle meant by the claim that the LNC is the principle of all the other axioms was not that each of the others presuppose it, but that the very notion of (deductive) inference presupposes it.[11] The best argument for this that I can construct goes as follows. If it is logically possible for a contradiction to be true, then it is logically possible for anything to be true. But the inference $\alpha \vdash \beta$ is valid iff it is impossible for $\alpha \wedge \neg\beta$ to be true. Hence the inference is not valid. This argument fails, however. First, if contradictions may be true then, even if $\alpha \wedge \neg\beta$ is possible, it may be impossible also, and hence the inference $\alpha \vdash \beta$ may *still* be valid (even if invalid as well).[12] Secondly, the definition of validity is tendentious anyway. A more adequate modal definition of validity is that the inference $\alpha \vdash \beta$ is valid iff, necessarily, if α is true then β is true. The suggested definition reduces to this if (and only if) one accepts (an incorrect) material account of the conditional. One might argue that even without this account, since $\alpha \wedge \neg\beta$ entails $\neg(\alpha \rightarrow \beta)$, $\Diamond(\alpha \wedge \neg\beta)$ entails $\Diamond\neg(\alpha \rightarrow \beta)$ (and so $\neg\Box(\alpha \rightarrow \beta)$)), but both of these inferences are problematic once the possibility of

this passage, see Łukasiewicz (1910), sect. 5–7. Barnes (1967) endorses a version of this argument, but this employs a notion of disbelief that simply slides ambiguously between not believing and believing that not. See also Nuttall (1978). Upton (1982–3) endorses the claim that the LNC is a psychological law on the grounds of introspection. The unsatisfactoriness of trying to establish psychological laws in this way hardly needs to be laboured. In any case, my introspection tells me something quite different.

[10] The translation is taken from Łukasiewicz (1910), 503 of the first English translation cited, where the matter is further discussed.

[11] According to Dancy (1975), 9, Leibniz held something like this view.

[12] It is worth noting that there is nothing wrong about using an invalid form of inference: every inference is of the form: *p*, therefore *q*; which is invalid. A good inference is one for which there is some valid form which it instantiates.

inconsistency arises. For example, the second fails in the semantics of chapter 6 of *In Contradiction*.[13]

1.4 ARISTOTLE'S OPPONENTS

Before we turn to chapter 4 itself, it will be important to take note of who Aristotle's opponents are. As Aristotle stated the LNC, anyone who thinks that some contradictions are true, a simple dialetheist, like me, is an opponent. However, it is clear that often Aristotle is attacking opponents with stronger views, who hold *all* contradictions to be true. Two such groups are mentioned explicitly: Herakliteans and Protagoreans.

Aristotle's views concerning the beliefs of these two groups can be extracted from what he says, and particularly the arguments he marshals against them in chapters 5 and 6. It is clear that he draws heavily on Plato's account of both views in the *Theaetetus*. Whether his views are historically correct is a moot point.[14] This is not important here, however, since our concern with these matters is only as an aid to understanding Aristotle's arguments in chapter 4.

Herakliteans, according to Aristotle, thought that everything about the physical world was in a state of flux, and that the way to describe this was in a contradictory way. A change from α to $\neg\alpha$ was thus to be described by the contradiction $\alpha \wedge \neg\alpha$. It would seem that this state was *sui generis*. In particular, it was not an amalgam of the states described by α and $\neg\alpha$ separately; and hence both the conjuncts were simply false of the transition state. (See, *Theaetetus* 157, a, b, which can be interpreted as attributing such views to Herakliteans.[15]) Such Herakliteans must therefore have rejected the law of conjunction elimination: $\alpha \wedge \beta \vdash \alpha$ (and β). It is worth noting that Aristotle himself may well have rejected this law. At *Prior Analytics* 57^b3 Aristotle argues that contradictories can't both entail the same thing. Now suppose that $\alpha \wedge \neg\alpha$ entails α and $\neg\alpha$. Then by contraposition (which Aristotle endorses immediately before this), $\neg\alpha$ and $\neg\neg\alpha$ each entail $\neg(\alpha \wedge \neg\alpha)$. Łukasiewicz (1957), 49 f., discussing this passage, argues that Aristotle was simply making a logical mistake. There may well be more to it than this, however, as we shall see in 1.13.

Some Herakliteans, such as Cratylus, held an even more extreme view: *all things*, including even meanings, are in a state of flux. And if this is so, then it makes it very difficult to say *anything* determinate about the world at all. Hence, for such people, even the contradiction $\alpha \wedge \neg\alpha$ could describe a situation only in an unsatisfactory and indeterminate way. (See, e.g. *Theaetetus* 183, a, b.) Cratylus, indeed, came in the end to the view that nothing could be said, and so gave up speech all together (10^a10–15).

---

[13] For further discussion of the text in this section, see Dancy (1975), ch. 1.

[14] For a modern account, see, e.g. Barnes (1979).

[15] Certain interpreters of Marx and Hegel have espoused similar views. See, e.g. Havas (1981). I do not, myself, think this a correct interpretation. It seems to me that a "one-sided" description is better viewed as conversationally misleading than as false. See Priest (1989–90), 397.

Protagoreans, again according to Aristotle, were rather different. They held everything to be true, and *a fortiori*, every contradiction. In fact, assuming conjunction-elimination, these two claims are equivalent. Aristotle argues that Protagoreans are committed to every contradiction in chapter 5 (9^a9): '. . . if everything that is thought or imagined is true, it is necessary that everything should be simultaneously true and false.' This strikes me as quite unfair to Protagoras—even Aristotle's Protagoras. For a start, Protagoras thought that whatever someone believes is true *for them*, not true *simpliciter*. Arguably, at least, he thought that *nothing* was true *simpliciter* (a view Aristotle attacks in chapter 8). More importantly, even ignoring this distinction, that everything is true follows from Protagoras' views if (but only if) everything is believed by someone. This is an empirical premise, which I see no reasons to believe to be true.

For these reasons, I will not call the people Aristotle has in mind here 'Protagoreans'. I will call the view that everything is true 'trivialism'; and I will call someone who believes everything a 'trivialist'. The principle that not everything is true I will call the Law of Non-Triviality (LNT). Trivialism clearly entails dialetheism. If a contradiction entailed everything, then dialetheism would entail trivialism, and hence these two views would not be distinct. However, I, for one, do not accept this entailment; and as far as I am aware, there is no textual evidence to suggest that Aristotle did either. Indeed, there is evidence that he did not.[16]

It is not clear that anyone has ever endorsed trivialism, as such;[17] but the question of what one can say against it is an interesting one for dialetheism: for a dialetheist cannot argue that triviality is impossible simply on the ground that inconsistency is impossible. Hence, in what follows, we will also consider the import of what Aristotle has to say for trivialism.

A couple of observations about trivialism should be made straight away. For a start, we know that the world is not trivial. This is a necessary truth whose proof is as follows. If the world is trivial it is not trivial (since everything follows). Hence the world is not trivial (by the LEM or *consequentia mirabilis*).

More interestingly, one may argue that one ought to reject the view that the world is trivial as follows. If the world is trivial then everything follows. In particular, it follows that it is irrational to believe that the world is trivial. Hence, if one believes that the world is trivial then one should believe something and, at the same time, believe that it is irrational to believe it. This is irrational. One ought to reject something if it is irrational to believe it.[18]

---

[16] For a start, 'Socrates is a man; Socrates is not a man; hence Aristotle is a cow' is a fallacy of four terms for Aristotle. More importantly, in the *Prior Analytics* (63^b31–64^a16), Aristotle tells us explicitly that contradictions entail certain conclusions in some syllogistic moods but not in others. Historically, the first argument to the effect that a contradiction entails everything, that I am aware of anyway, was given by the twelfth-century logician William of Soissons. See Martin (1986). One might also try to extract this consequence from some Stoic and Megarian accounts of the conditional—but only with difficulty. On all this, see Priest (2007), 2.1.

[17] Though maybe Anaxagoras is one possible candidate. He held that, at least at one time, everything was all mixed up so that no predicate applied to any one thing more than a contrary predicate (7^b25–6). This view is consistent with nothing being true, though.

[18] This form of argument, though not its application, is due to Littman (1992). We will meet it again in sect 6.5.

One might object to the last step, on the ground that one ought not to reject something irrational if it is also rational to believe it.[19] Whether or not this is so is beside the point here. For it is not rational to believe that the world is trivial. There is no evidence, there are no reasons, to believe that the world is trivial (or even the much lesser claim that I am a frog). And it is not rational to believe that for which there is no evidence. Thus, one ought to reject the claim that the world is trivial.

Of course, the trivialist can accept all these conclusions—after all, they accept everything. The trivialist is a slippery protagonist, and there will be a lot more to be said about them in Chapter 3. This will do for the present.

1.5 DEMONSTRATION BY REFUTATION (5^b35–6^a28) ch.4

Let us now turn to chapter 4 itself. This contains a number of arguments for the LNC. Ross and Kirwan both isolate seven different arguments, though they cut the cake slightly differently. I will follow Ross's enumeration. Of these seven, the first is the most complex, and takes up as much space as the other six put together. But before we discuss the arguments we need to get clear about what, exactly, they are supposed to demonstrate.

At the start of chapter 4 (5^b35–6^a10), Aristotle claims that the LNC is so fundamental that it is impossible to demonstrate it. By 'demonstration', here, he means something quite specific. A demonstration is a deductive argument from "first principles". The principles are both more certain than that which is to be demonstrated, and also, in some sense, explain it. Even granting this notion of demonstration, it is not clear that the LNC cannot be demonstrated, since it is not clear that it *is* a first principle. Consider, for example, the Law of Identity, $\Box(\alpha \rightarrow \alpha)$. Though nothing is completely uncontentious, there is hardly *any* disagreement about the correctness of this Law.[20] And given this, $\neg\Diamond(\alpha \wedge \neg\alpha)$ follows from one application of the rule of inference: $\Box(\alpha \rightarrow \beta) \vdash \neg\Diamond(\alpha \wedge \neg\beta)$.

One might object that the principle of inference here simply presupposes the LNC. This is moot: it is valid, for example, in the semantics of *In Contradiction*, chapter 6, according to which contradictions may be true. But whatever one says about this particular case, the point remains: it is not at all obvious that no proof of the LNC in Aristotle's sense is possible.

This is all a side issue, though. For the point of this paragraph is to distinguish this kind of proof of the LNC from the kind of proof that Aristotle thinks he *can* give. Aristotle calls it a 'proof by refutation'. Someone who disbelieves the LNC can be refuted 'if only the disputant says something' (6^a12); and if they will not, they are 'similar to a vegetable' (6^a16). Presumably, this is directed at the mature Cratylus. The point, presumably, is not just to abuse him, but to note that if someone refuses to say anything, then debate is pointless. We are close to one of Aristotle's later arguments at this point, so I will take up the issue at the appropriate juncture. The important question here is what kind of proof Aristotle thinks he can give against an opponent

---

[19] See the discussion of rejection in sect. 6.5.   [20] As Łukasiewicz (1910), sect. 9, notes.

who will speak. And here we meet the first exegetical problem: what, exactly, is a proof by refutation? For the moment, let us stick with the first refutation. We will come to the others later.

Clearly, a demonstration by refutation would seem to be some kind of *reductio* argument. But there are many things that can go by this name. For a start, *reductio ad absurdum* can simply be a principle of inference of the following form: from a proof that α entails $\beta \wedge \neg\beta$, infer $\neg\alpha$. In standard logic it is deductively valid, and though it is not a valid syllogism, Aristotle recognized it as a legitimate mode of inference. (See *Prior Analytics*, $50^a 29$–39.) One thing that might be meant by a proof by refutation is simply an argument with this form. This, however, is not what is going on. For a start, such an inference does not depend on anyone saying anything. A *reductio* argument in this sense may start by making an *assumption*, α, but no one has to assert this. Moreover, by the end of the argument the assumption has been discharged. Hence we end up with a categorical proof of $\neg\alpha$ which is just what, according to Aristotle, we cannot have. Another problem with interpreting the argument in this way is that the form of inference cannot be assumed to be valid if one supposes that there are true contradictions (at least, not without a lot of further argument). If α entails something true, nothing follows. Hence, Aristotle's arguments would beg the question.[21]

Another thing that is often meant by a *reductio* argument is getting an opponent to retract a view held, by showing them that it leads to an absurd consequence. The consequence may be a contradiction, but it may also be something else: some non-contradictions (e.g. that I am a frog) are more absurd than some contradictions (e.g. that the Liar sentence is both true and not true). All that is necessary is that the consequence be one that the person regards as absurd. Arguments of this kind are sometimes called *ad hominem*, and some kinds of *ad hominem* arguments are fallacies (notably those where a view is attacked by attacking the character of the person who holds it). There is nothing fallacious about this kind of argument, however. Provided the person's views really do have these conclusions (at least, according to the person in question), there is nothing illegitimate about this form of argument.

It is sometimes suggested that such a form of argument must be useless against someone who denies the LNC.[22] This is not true. If the *absurdum* to which the view leads is a contradiction then there is no *a priori* guarantee that it is one that the person will regard as absurd, and so no guarantee that it will work. But the person need not accept everything, certainly not every contradiction; hence, the argument may well be effective. This is nicely illustrated by Aristotle himself in a later chapter. At $10^a 32$–$^b 1$ Aristotle argues against Herakliteans as follows. If all contradictions (about the physical world) and no other things, were always true, then *nothing* changes. Assuming that moderate Herakliteans do not want to deny their major thesis (after

---

[21] As Łukasiewicz (1910), sect. 13, notes. There are, as a matter of fact, restricted versions of *reductio* that are valid even in a paraconsistent logic.

[22] See, e.g. McTaggart (1922), 8. Łukasiewicz (1910), sect. 20, makes a similar claim. Without it, he says, I could not establish that I was not at the scene of a crime by demonstrating that I was somewhere else. This is false; a contradiction does not have to be impossible for this argument to work: improbable will do just as well. See *In Contradiction*, 7.5.

all, the situation that this describes is not itself, presumably, in a state of change), this consequence is unacceptable.

The situation concerning an *ad hominem* argument is quite different if the opponent is a trivialist. For such a person accepts everything: there is therefore no consequence of their view that will have the slightest effect.[23] There is therefore no point in entering into discussion with them. Moreover, there is no point for them either, since anything they would like you to believe, they already believe you believe. Again, we are very close to one of Aristotle's arguments here. So I will pursue this issue further when we reach the appropriate point in the text.

Is Aristotle to be interpreted as giving an *ad hominem* argument, in the sense just explained, here, then? This is certainly what he means by the phrase 'demonstration by refutation (*elenchus*)' elsewhere (e.g. *Prior Analytics*, bk. 2, ch. 20). So this is a natural supposition.[24] It is, however, problematic. For this kind of argument to work, it is necessary that the opponent have the views targeted; it is not necessary that they express them. Yet, as we have seen, Aristotle insists that the opponent must say something for the process of refutation to work. Moreover, it will turn out that the person does not even have to *claim* anything: all they have to do is say something they take to be meaningful. Finally, such an argument cannot possibly work against a trivialist, and surely this must have been obvious to Aristotle. Yet the trivialist is one of the people on whom Aristotle explicitly sets his sights.

Another interpretation of what Aristotle is up to is as follows. As we have noted, Aristotle requires of a demonstration, properly so-called, that the premises are general principles that explain the thing deduced. But we might have a deductive argument whose premises are not like this, but which are undeniable. This would clearly give an argument of sorts for the LNC. Let us give the word 'demonstration' to Aristotle, and use instead the word 'reason'. Some commentators[25] have suggested that Aristotle is giving a reason for the LNC. Most obviously, one can take Aristotle to be arguing that if utterances are to make sense, as they do, the LNC is necessary. One might call this a transcendental argument for the LNC.[26]

This strikes me as the most plausible interpretation, but it is not without its problems. The argument starts, not from some undeniable truths, but from an opponent saying something meaningful. It might be suggested that this is just a device, and what Aristotle is doing is showing that the LNC follows from the fact that there is meaningful discourse. But the opponent seems to be much more integral to the plot than this. In the passage in question, Aristotle is very concerned that *they* say something; and a few sentences later he is concerned that he should not beg the question: it is therefore necessary for *the opponent* to say something meaningful. This all sounds very *ad hominem*.

In the light of problems of this kind, some commentators have suggested that what Aristotle is attempting in this chapter is not any kind of demonstration of the LNC at all; what he is attempting to establish is something *about* the Law, e.g. that it must be

---

[23] Unless they were so slow that they did not realize that their view entails that all is one, that the Pope is a cabbage, etc.   [24] It is the way that Dancy (1975), ch. 1, interprets Aristotle.
[25] Notably, Irwin (1977–8).   [26] See Kirwan (1993), 204.

believed, or that it is a necessary condition for thought.[27] As such, he is not attempting to convince a dialetheist or a trivialist, nor does an appeal to the LNC (or LNT) beg the question: consistency or non-triviality can be taken for granted. I will call this kind of interpretation of the argument *perinomic*.

As an interpretation of the text, a perinomic interpretation strikes me as an act of desperation. Not only does it go against what Aristotle explicitly says he is doing. But the conclusion of the major argument is exactly a statement of the LNC, not something about it. Moreover, if this *is* what he is up to, why bring in the opponent saying something at all; and why call it a refutation?

The exegetical situation is desperate, then.[28] It is made impossible when we bring in the other six arguments Aristotle deploys. These are a motley crew, but the most striking thing about them is that none of them starts from an opponent's saying anything. The interlocutor has disappeared entirely. So what does Aristotle think he is up to? I doubt that there is any single answer to this question, or even that Aristotle has any clearly thought-out aims. He is just shooting with everything he can think of. As we shall see, the other arguments are most naturally interpreted in various of the ways we have considered, sometimes with respect to the LNC; sometimes with respect to the LNT—for Aristotle often slides blithely between the two.

At any rate, we have four things that any one argument might be trying to do: argue by *reductio ad absurdum*, provide an *ad hominem* argument, give a reason, and provide a perinomic conclusion. These will provide us with a set of yardsticks against which to measure what Aristotle actually achieves in his seven arguments.

1.6 FIRST REFUTATION: PART I (6^a28–$^b34$)

We now come to the first of Aristotle's arguments. This is long, complex, and can be divided into two major parts. But before Aristotle states the first, he has a throwaway remark. (Kirwan treats this as a separate argument.) The opponent of the LNC is invited to say something meaningful. It will turn out that they say 'man'. Aristotle then says (6^a28–30):

First, then, it is plain that this at least is itself true, that the name {'man'} signifies to be or not to be this particular thing, so that it could not be that everything was so-and-so and not so-and-so.

Let us say that something is true *simpliciter* if it is true and not false. The argument is that if it is true that 'man' signifies *man* (the property of being a man, or what it is to be a man, as Aristotle puts it later), it is true *simpliciter*. The argument is simply a *non sequitur* for a simple dialetheist or a trivialist. Nor, for different reasons, need either dissent from the conclusion. It has more bite against a Heraklitean: for if the

本地报刊杂志阅览室

---

[27] E.g. Code (1986). For further discussion of Code's view see Cohen (1986) and Furth (1986).

[28] Driven by desperation, perhaps, one commentator, Halper (1984), has even argued that the conclusion of the argument is not about the LNC at all. Rather, the Law is assumed, and the point is to establish claims about substance!

situation were of the kind where 'man' both does and does not signify *man*, it would not be one where 'man' signified *man*.

We now get the first part of the main argument (6^a31–6^b34). In essence it is simple. If we do not rule out ambiguity, then it is clear that there can be apparent violations of the LNC. We might say that Hipparchia, for example, is a man (human) and not a man (a woman). Aristotle has already said that such "dialectical" violations of the LNC are not what is at issue. Hence we select one meaning of the word and fix on it. In the case at point, we fix 'man' to mean *human* (two-footed animal, as Aristotle puts it).

Aristotle then says that if an objector (6^b6–8):

were to assert that {the word} signified infinitely many things, it is obvious that there would be no statement. For not to signify one thing is to signify nothing, and if names do not signify, discussion is eliminated with others; and in truth, even with oneself . . .

[handwritten margin note: if name does not signify one thing, signifies nothing]

This is slightly odd. Even if the word means infinitely many things, we can still fix on one of them. I think that for what Aristotle has in mind here 'indefinite' is a better word than 'infinite'. The objector he has in mind is the extreme Heraklitean, like Cratylus, who thinks that meanings are in a state of flux; in which case, a word has no definite meaning. Any such person who attempts to engage in discussion with others—or even think—therefore refutes themself. One might take issue with this argument; as Derrida—a modern proponent of this view—I am sure, would.[29] But a defence of such views is not on the agenda here. So let us grant Aristotle this step, and move on.

Aristotle concludes this step of the argument as follows (6^b28–34):

It is accordingly necessary, if it is true of anything to say that it is a man, that it be a two-footed animal . . . and if that is necessary, it is not possible that the same thing should not be, at that time, a two-footed animal . . . Consequently it is not possible that it should be simultaneously true to say that the same thing is a man and not a man.

Following Dancy (1975), let us call this passage the 'clincher'. Just before this (and after the discussion of ambiguity), there is a strange paragraph that appears to interrupt the argument (6^b13–28). I will discuss this in the next section. Let us deal with the main argument first.

The structure of this is ambiguous, depending on the scope of the modal operator 'necessarily'. Let us write Mx for 'x is a man' (Aristotle says 'it is true to say of x that it is a man', but these mean the same for him), Tx for 'x has the property of being a two-footed animal', and let a be an arbitrary object. Then the argument is one of the following:

(1) $\Box(Ma \rightarrow Ta)$
(2) $\neg\Diamond(Ma \wedge \neg Ta)$
(3) $\neg\Diamond(Ma \wedge \neg Ma)$

---

[29] See Priest (1995*a*), ch. 14.

$(1')$ $Ma \rightarrow \Box Ta$
$(2')$ $Ma \rightarrow \neg\Diamond\neg Ta$
$(3')$ $\neg\Diamond(Ma \wedge \neg Ma)$

The first interpretation is simpler. (1) is straightforward because of what we have taken 'man' to mean. (2) follows, provided that $\alpha \rightarrow \beta$ entails $\neg(\alpha \wedge \neg\beta)$. This inference holds on many accounts of the conditional, though it fails in others. Notably, relevant logics like B that contain identity, $\alpha \rightarrow \alpha$, but no truth-functional tautologies, and in particular, $\neg(\alpha \wedge \neg\alpha)$. In virtue of this, it could well be argued that this inference begs the question in this context. (3) follows from (2) since Ma and Ta are necessarily equivalent, and so inter-substitutable in modal contexts.

I will call the second argument the primed version. If this is the correct interpretation it turns on a certain kind of essentialism. There will be a lot more to be said about this later. For the present, the following will suffice. According to Aristotle, some properties of objects are accidental (contingent) and some are essential (necessary). Properties like being a man are essential; properties like being white are not. (If Aristotle ceased to be a man, he would cease to be; if he turned green, he would still be the same old Aristotle we all love.) One might take issue with this picture, but if it is correct, then $(1')$ is true. $(2')$ follows simply from $(1')$. What about $(3')$? Given that Ma and Ta are inter-substitutable in modal contexts, this is equivalent to $\neg\Diamond(Ma \wedge \neg Ta)$. The question then is whether $\neg\Diamond(\alpha \wedge \neg\beta)$ follows from $\alpha \rightarrow \neg\Diamond\neg\beta$. It does, provided that the conditional is strict,[30] a point one might well contest: couldn't the matter of whether or not a property is itself essential change from world to world? In our world, being a man is an essential property, but in a fairy-tale world, where Aristotle turns into a frog (and is still Aristotle), it is not.

We have now looked at the two interpretations of the argument. Which of these Aristotle intends is a question that can be answered with plausibility either way.[31] The major argument for interpreting it in the second way is that it appears to relate better to part 2 of the argument. I will examine and reject this claim later. The major argument against interpreting it in the second way is that if this were correct, the argument would establish at most the LNC for sentences where the predicate (or at least its disambiguation) is an essential one, whereas Aristotle's aim—which is stated again at the end of part 2 (7^b18)—is to establish it quite generally.[32] Hence, I think that the first version is the more plausible.[33]

---

[30] And that the modal operators are at least as strong as those of the modal system $K_\rho(T)$.

[31] For example, Dancy (1975) interprets it the first way, as does Kirwan (1993), 98; Anscombe in Anscombe and Geach (1961), and Cresswell (1987) are more sympathetic to the second. We will look at Cresswell's interpretation of the whole passage in more detail later.

[32] Łukasiewicz (1910), sect. 15, claims that Aristotle does hold the LNC only for statements with essential predicates. Given the rest of the text, I find this implausible. This position is more like that of Plato at *Parmenides* 129 b, c.

[33] Wedin (1982) argues that the consistency of essential predication entails the consistency of predication in general, on the following grounds. According to him, to say that Socrates is white is to say that there is some accident, x (being white all over), such that x inheres in Socrates and x is white, where this latter predication is essential. Hence to say that Socrates is white and not white is to say that for some accident, x, x inheres in Socrates and x is and is not white, which violates consistency for essential predication. Whatever one thinks of this as an act of Aristotelian exegeses,

Let us now turn to the question of whether or not the argument succeeds in its aim. Suppose, first, that its aim is to give a reason for the LNC. We have seen that both versions of the argument have steps at which one might cavil. I think, however, that these are relatively minor problems. Let us grant that the conclusion follows.

The first major problem is that the argument does not establish the LNC in general, as Aristotle requires. This is obvious with the primed version, as I have already observed. But *both* versions establish it only for subject/predicate sentences. And even if Aristotle thought that all sentences were subject/predicate, we now know better. Actually, this problem may be repaired, at least given certain assumptions. The argument (on the first interpretation) clearly generalizes to all atomic sentences, and in certain paraconsistent logics (e.g. *LP*) one can show that if every atomic sentence behaves consistently, every sentence does. Alternatively, if we interpret the argument in the first way, we may generalize the argument in a natural way. Let α be any statement and let β be a disambiguation. Then $\Box(\alpha \to \beta)$. Now, as before $\neg\Diamond(\alpha \wedge \neg\beta)$. (This strategy is not open to us if we interpret the argument in the primed way: there is no reason to suppose that every α is equivalent to a necessitive, $\Box\beta$.)

Dancy (1975), 38 ff., who interprets the argument in the first way, objects to it as follows. First, it is necessary to find some non-trivial definition of 'man' for the argument to proceed. We cannot just use the same word, or we could be fairly accused of begging the question. Secondly, most words do not have definitions. So, as a general argument for the LNC, the argument fails. Now it is not clear to me why using the word 'man' itself would make the argument any more question-begging than the one that Aristotle actually gives. The reason for choosing a different phrase is simply disambiguation. Moreover, I do not think it necessary that one be able to find a definition. The important point is that, once disambiguated, 'man' has a fixed and determinate meaning. (It means 'one thing'.) It is not even necessary that we should have to be able to spell out what that is. We could just call it 'X', and then get on with the rest of the argument.

With certain provisos, then, the argument appears to work. The important—in fact, crucial—point, however, is that it establishes nothing that someone who violates the LNC need disagree with. This is obvious if the person is a trivialist. But it is equally true for a simple dialetheist. Though some logicians have suggested that a suitable paraconsistent logic should not validate the LNC in this form, many paraconsistent logics, e.g. *LP*, render it a logical truth (see In Contradiction, ch. 5). And their modal extensions render its necessitation a logical truth too. Of course, given any truth of the form $\alpha \wedge \neg\alpha$ the law will generate a "secondary contradiction" of the form $(\alpha \wedge \neg\alpha) \wedge \neg(\alpha \wedge \neg\alpha)$. But this is no more problematic than the original contradiction.

Whitaker ((1996), 199) considers this reply, but rejects it on the ground that if someone 'genuinely accepts the truth of the Principle of Contradiction, then they no longer believe that contradictions are possible ...'. But this reply is entirely

---

the argument seems to me to fail, since all that Socrates is white and not white (e.g. black) seems to require is that there are accidents x (white all over) and y (black all over) such that x and y inhere in Socrates, and x is white and y is not. This is, presumably, false because of the first conjunct, which does not involve essential predication.

question-begging. Why can they no longer believe this? Because it would be contradictory! I suspect that what Whitaker means by 'genuinely accepts the truth of the Principle' is 'refuses to accept contradictions'. But subscribing to $\neg\Diamond(\alpha \wedge \neg\alpha)$ does not force one to do this at all. Hence Aristotle's argument does not establish the LNC in this sense.

Could we not interpret it as establishing this? Let us use $\dashv$ as an operator for denial (see Chapter 6, especially 6.4). Suppose that we take the conclusion of the argument to be $\dashv \Diamond(Ma \wedge \neg Ma)$. Then, in either version, the argument starts off with an assertion and ends with a denial. No argument is like this: an argument is a sequence of appropriately related assertions. We could, of course, invent a new rule: given an assertion of $\neg\alpha$, deny α (from $\vdash \neg\alpha$ go to $\dashv \alpha$). In the present context, such a rule would obviously beg the question, though: dialetheists think that one *can* assert $\neg\alpha$ without denying α. As we will see in 6.2, the rule is fallacious, even from a non-dialetheic perspective.[34]

Interpreted in the only way that both makes sense and is legitimate, then, the argument is sound, but has no sting for a dialetheist or trivialist. (Whether it causes a problem for Herakliteans, I leave scholars to argue about.) The other obvious interpretation of the argument is as *ad hominem*. But similar comments apply here. Interpreted in this way, it shows that one who violates the LNC is committed to certain secondary contradictions. But this is not something that should faze them. A dialetheist who believes α and $\neg\alpha$ need not feel constrained to retract the claim that α, when they assert its negation; similarly, someone who endorses *LP* as the correct logic, and who asserts $\alpha \wedge \neg\alpha$, need not feel constrained to take this back when they assert $\neg(\alpha \wedge \neg\alpha)$.[35] There being no other natural interpretations of the argument, let us move on.

1.7 FIRST REFUTATION: INTERLUDE ($6^b 34$–$7^a 20$)

We are not finished with the first refutation yet. There is a major second part. But before Aristotle gives this, there is another apparent interpolation. This seems to relate to the passage just before the clincher that I mentioned in the previous section. So let me deal with these two passages together.

The passage just before the clincher starts as follows ($6^b 13$–28):

Then it is not possible that 'to be a man' should signify just what 'not to be a man' [signifies], if 'man' signifies not only about one thing but also one thing (for we do not want to count

---

[34] How, exactly, to best formulate the LNC is a nice question. (Grim (2004) lists over 200 possible formulations!) Just because any assertion of it could, in principle, be accepted by a dialetheist, a natural formulation of it is as a denial. (See Brady (2004).) In another way, the principle of Explosion can also be seen as a statement of the Law (see Restall (2004))—though obviously not one that rules out trivialism. As we have already noted (n. 16), Aristotle did not accept Explosion. Nor, in this context, would it have helped him; for Aristotle has his sights set on the trivialist just as much as—even more than—the dialetheist, as we will see, and the trivialist can accept Explosion.

[35] Again, it might be suggested that if someone asserts the negation of $\alpha \wedge \neg\alpha$ then they ought to withdraw their claim that $\alpha \wedge \neg\alpha$ because of the connection between negation and rejection. However, if there were such a relation, Aristotle's argument would be otiose: it would show independently that no contradiction ought to be endorsed. In any case, I will discuss and reject the existence of such a connection in Chapter 6.

as signifying one thing this, viz. signifying about one thing, since in this way 'artistic' and 'pale' and 'man' would signify one thing, so that all will be one, because synonymous). And it {a thing?} will not be to be and not be the same thing unless homonymously, as if others were to term not-man what we term man. But what is found perplexing is not whether it is possible that the same thing should simultaneously be and not be a man in name, but in actual fact.

The paragraph then goes on to say something about not being a man and being a not-man; its sense would appear to be that these two things are much the same in this context, but I find it difficult to make any sense of the details of this argument. In any case, Aristotle merely seems to be setting aside a possible source of complication.

Prima facie, the import of the above passage is to establish that 'to be a man' and 'not to be a man' mean something different; and the fact that the argument comes immediately before the clincher, which starts with 'accordingly', would seem to suggest that if 'man' and 'not man' meant the same thing then it might be false of something that was a man to say that it was a two-footed animal—or at least, that someone might suppose this. But it is not at all obvious why this might be so.[36]

My guess about what is going on in this bit of text is as follows. Aristotle envisages an objector who says something like this—I change 'two-footed animal' to 'rational animal' to make things a bit punchier: 'Look, Aristotle, it's quite clear that contradictions can be true. Just consider Hipparchia; she both is and isn't a man. So it's not necessarily true that if anything is a man it is a rational animal. Hipparchia is a woman, so she's not rational. You are probably going to say that "man" and "not man" have two different meanings here, so the objection doesn't count. But "man" and "not man" *do* have the same meaning here. They both mean *her*'.

Against this, Aristotle replies as follows—the paragraph of the text just scrambles it a bit: 'Hipparchia may be a man and not a man, but only in different senses of the word "man". And of course, if you are going to allow different meanings of the word, there is no problem about finding contradictory sentences. But that's not what we were talking about. Provided you stick to a single meaning of "man", i.e. human, then it *is* necessarily true that anything that is a man is a rational animal. And saying that "man" and "not man" mean the same because they both mean her is just confusing what something means with what it is true of.[37] "Man" and "not man" can't mean the same, or pretty much everything would mean the same, so everything would be truly predicable of an object, and all would be one (as I shall go on to argue in my second refutation).'

This, at any rate, is the best sense that I can make of the text. Anyway, if the point of the text is that 'man' and 'not man' mean something different, this seems clear enough for us not to make a fuss about it: they clearly have different extensions. And

---

[36] Dancy (1975), 50–1 suggests that if 'man' and 'not man' meant the same thing then we would have to admit that necessarily if something is not a man it is a two-footed animal, which would 'foul things up right royally'. (Noonan (1977), following Aquinas, takes a similar line.) I fail to see this. As long as Aristotle's opponent will concede that necessarily if something is a man it is a two-footed animal, he has what he needs, whatever else the opponent is committed to.

[37] Dancy (1975) christens Aristotle's opponent 'Antiphasis', and spends some time showing why, in the light of the intellectual climate of the time, Antiphasis might have confused these things.

even a trivialist must concede that they mean something different: they agree with everything.[38]

Let us turn now to the second passage (6^b34–7^a20). This comes immediately after the clincher, and starts by saying 'The same argument applies also in the case of not being a man.' And so one might expect to find the main argument repeated, with 'not man' replacing 'man'; but we do not. What we do find is a swift argument for the claim that 'man' and 'not man' mean something different: 'man' and 'pale' obviously mean something different; but 'not man' is much more "strongly opposed" to 'man' than 'pale' is.[39]

Aristotle then continues (7^a7–9): 'If this is not possible, what we have stated follows, if he [the objector] will answer the question asked'. From the next few lines we gather that the question asked was something like 'Is this a man?' or 'What is this?' (pointing to a man). Since no such question has been asked explicitly, presumably Aristotle is thinking that the original speech-act of his opponent was prompted by a question of this kind.

Aristotle goes on by imagining that in answering the question, the respondent says 'man', but insists on adding 'and not a man' too. Aristotle objects to this. Why should he do this? He originally asked for one significant utterance. Now he has two; and he has already said that the argument can be run just as well for the second. So, it would seem, he should welcome the addition. The answer, I think, is that he has Herakliteans in his sights at this point. Aristotle's aim is to get his opponent to concede that 'man' is meaningful by asking 'what is that?' (pointing to a man). A Heraklitean will volunteer only 'man and not man', and this is not sufficient to continue the argument. Even if (sufficiently disambiguated) this phrase refers to some property or other, all the argument will give is: it is not possible for something to be (a man and not a man) and not (a man and not a man), which is an instance of the LNC with very little generality. Hence Aristotle's argumentation now becomes intelligible.

Since I have no desire to defend Herkliteanism, or, at least, Aristotle's version of it, I will not discuss this part of the text further. A simple dialetheism has other ways out of Aristotle's net anyway, as we have seen.

1.8 ARISTOTLE ON SUBSTANCE

We now come to the second main part of the first refutation (7^a20–$^b18$), which introduces some major new considerations. Violators of the LNC are said to destroy

---

[38] Łukasiewicz (1910), sect. 12b, finds an independent argument in this passage of text, which he paraphrases as follows. 'With the word A I signify something which is in its essence B. Consequently, the object A, which is its essence B, cannot at the same time be not-B, for otherwise it would not be unified in its {have a single?} essence. Accordingly, A cannot simultaneously be and not be B.' Whether or not this argument is in the text, it would seem to be fallacious, even assuming Aristotle's theory of substance. If B is an essential property, there is no reason to assume that not-B is one; and, as Łukasiewicz says in section 13, even if it were, that it is different from B.

[39] If someone held that 'man' and 'not a man' mean the same thing, it would be possible for them to argue that since it is true that Socrates is a man, it is also true that he is not a man. Hence he is and is not a man. Aristotle could have such a person in mind, but I doubt it. In this chapter he is advancing arguments for the LNC, not attacking arguments against it.

the notion of substance. To try to sort out what is going on here we need to get a few facts about Aristotle's ontology straight.[40] According to him, the ultimate constituents of the world are objects, such as Hipparchia. These, Aristotle calls 'substances' ('primary substances', in the *Categories*). One important role they have is to be the bearers of properties. That there are such things is not, of course, uncontentious; but it is a recognizably modern view. What follows is not. Objects such as Hipparchia are, logically speaking, composites of matter and form. A typical form is: being a man. The form of an object gives it its identity. Consequently, one says what an object *is* (and not merely what properties is has) when one gives its form, as in: Hipparchia is a man. Just to confuse matters, Aristotle calls form 'substance' too ('secondary substance' in the *Categories*), in the sense of being the substance *of* something. For example, he might say, the substance of Hipparchia is manhood/being a man/what it is to be a man/to be a man, as it is often put—or translated.

Consequently, we must distinguish between two senses of a sentences of the kind '*a* is *b*' for Aristotle. In the first, *b* gives the form of *a*. And since *a* could not exist unless it had this form, such sentences, if true, are necessarily true (as is required in the primed version of the argument of part 1): *b* gives the essence of *a*. In the second kind, '*a* is *b*' is to be interpreted in such a way that *b* is merely giving one of the properties, or accidents, of *a*. The property *b* "coincides" with *a*, as Kirwan translates it. Such sentences, if true, are contingently true.

For Aristotle, the essence of each object defines its species. Thus the essence of Hipparchia is being a two-footed animal—*animal* being the genus, and *two-footed* the *differentia* of the species. Since things belong to a single species, it follows that objects have a single essence; it also follows that properties that are trans-generic, like not being a man, are not essential.

Modern philosophy has done away with Aristotle's analysis of substance. There is but one notion of predication, and about the best one can do to make Aristotle's distinction concerning predication is to mark off those properties an object has necessarily (its essential properties) from the others,[41] by the use of a modal operator, as I did in discussing part 1 of the argument. This distinction is not the same, however. It is no part of modern essentialism, e.g. of Kripke's kind, that objects have a single necessary property.

1.9 FIRST REFUTATION: PART II (7ª20–ᵇ18)

With these preliminary comments out of the way, let us return to the text. This continues (7ª20) as follows:

Those who say this entirely eliminate substance and what it is to be. For it is necessary for them to maintain that all things are coincidences and that there is no such thing as what to be a man or to be an animal [is].

[40] For further discussion, see, e.g. Dancy (1975), ch. 5.
[41] Though, conceivably, one might want to single out those that are connected with criteria of identity, or something similar, as special.

The claim is clearly that someone is destroying the notion of substance, in the sense of essence (substance *of*). It is less clear who this person is.

The text goes on to argue: (i) if 'man' refers to the substance of man, it refers to one thing; (ii) hence if 'man' and 'not man' meant the same thing 'man' would refer to the substance of 'not man'; (iii) but the substances (meanings) of 'man' and 'not man' are different (which was already argued for in the interpolation to part 1 of the first refutation, 6^b13–28); hence 'man' would refer to (at least) two things. Contradiction. Hence, 'man' does not refer to the substance of man, by *reductio*.

From this, it is clear that the person who is destroying substance is the person who claims that 'man' and 'not man' mean the same thing. It also seems to be clear that given that 'man' and 'not man' do mean something different, and given that we specified that 'man' should refer to just one thing, this argument works.[42] If 'man' and 'not man' mean the same, 'man' is not an essential property.

But we are not finished yet. It is easy enough for someone simply to reject the claim that being a man is an essential property. Many modern philosophers (such as Quine) have, after all, rejected essentialism, and so the existence of substance in Aristotle's sense. In the next paragraph Aristotle goes on to give an argument for the existence of his substances. The argument is to the effect that if there are any properties, even accidental ones, there must be substances for these to be properties *of*. One might take issue with some of Aristotle's arguments for this. One might even bite the bullet and accept an ontology of properties but no bearers. However, someone who does this is certainly flying in the face of common sense. So let us grant that this follows, and that it is unacceptable. Still the argument has an obvious failing. For even granting that there are substances *simpliciter* (bearers of properties), it does not follow that there are substances of (essences). Whether Aristotle attempts to make good this lacuna elsewhere in his work, or whether he is simply a victim of ambiguity, I leave Aristotelian scholars to argue about. The point is that rejecting essentialism does not necessarily entail rejecting a subject/property ontology.

It remains to discuss how part 2 of the argument relates to part 1, and hence evaluate its significance. Some commentators have interpreted part 2 as an entirely separate argument.[43] This would seem to be manifestly incorrect, since the passage in question finishes (7^b17–18):

Consequently, there will be something signifying substance even in this case {i.e. if all properties are accidental}. And if this is so, it has been shown that it is impossible to predicate contradictories simultaneously.

Hence we are still with the main argument. So, how does it fit in? There would seem to be two major possibilities. The first is that we interpret the main argument as the second (primed) version. This appeals to the existence of essential properties, which Aristotle is defending here.

This strikes me as the less plausible interpretation. For a start, it makes Aristotle's defence of the existence of substances (*simpliciter*) irrelevant—though if Aristotle is

---

[42] At least against someone who cannot accept that one is two.   [43] e.g. Furth (1986), 379.

confused about the two notions of substance this might carry little weight. More importantly, if this interpretation is right then, as I have already said, the whole argument establishes the LNC only for statements with essential predicates, and this would presumably have been obvious to Aristotle. And yet his conclusion reiterates the more general conclusion.

The other major possibility is that in part two of the argument Aristotle is providing yet another argument against the person who claims that 'man' and 'not man' mean the same. It is this, after all, that is said to entail the denial of substance. If this is what is going on, then the argument is vulnerable to anti-essentialist objections (though not ones I would make). More importantly, this possibility was introduced as part of a (rather implausible to the modern ear) way of avoiding the clincher. Hence what we have here is not a part of the main argument at all, but a reply to one objection that no one is now likely to make. As such, it is irrelevant to our evaluation of the main argument.

1.10 THE ANSCOMBE/CRESSWELL INTERPRETATION

We have now dealt with the first refutation; before we move on to the others it is worth discussing what some further modern commentators have made of the first refutation.

Following Anscombe,[44] Cresswell has given a rather different interpretation of the text.[45] According to this, it is important that Aristotle start by taking a substance (essential) predicate, man. In a true such predication, '*a* is *b*', '*b*' is said to signify *a*, where 'signify' here is a technical term for Aristotle, quite distinct from 'means' and 'is true of'. Its use, according to Cresswell, is in giving the truth conditions of essential predications. '*a* is *b*' is true just if '*a*' and '*b*' signify the same thing, just as the sentence 'George Elliot is Mary Ann Evans' is true just if the two names flanking the identity sign refer to the same thing.

Given this background, Cresswell spells out the core of Aristotle's argument thus:

1. If F and G are both substance predicates, then if x is F and x is G, F and G signify the same thing (viz. x).
2. F and not-F never signify the same thing.
3. Hence, no x is both F and not-F.

1 is not argued for in the text, but is, according to Cresswell, Aristotle's account of predication to be found elsewhere in his writings (though $6^a 32$–4 is supposed to be a cryptic explanation of the technical sense of 'signify'). The heart of the argument is in the passage just before what I have called the clincher. It first states 2 at $6^b 13$, and then defends it against possible objections and misunderstandings. The clincher merely 'states the conclusion in explicitly modal terms'. The rest of the text then 'draws

---

[44] Anscombe and Geach (1961), 39 ff.
[45] Cresswell (1987), and especially (2004). Direct quotations from Cresswell are taken from the latter. Kirwan (p. 100) also makes similar suggestions.

out the consequences of the proof'. In particular, running the argument in reverse, if something is both F and not F, then F cannot be an essential predication. Hence, "substance has been destroyed". Part two of the argument expostulates, and defends the notion of substance.

I find this interpretation of the text less plausible than the one I have given, for several reasons. First, if it is correct, then the argument establishes the LNC only for essential predications (as Cresswell agrees). This is at odds with Aristotle's explicit statement at the start (5^b19–21), repeated at the end of the first refutation (7^b17), and again at 11^b14, that the LNC holds in general. Secondly, this interpretation seems to make less sense of the text. The crucial premise 1 is not only not argued for in the text, but is not even stated. The clincher, though it appears to be the *coup de grâce* of the argument, is not. It certainly does more than state the conclusion in modal terms: it is clearly an argument. But since it depends on none of the considerations about signification that Cresswell adduces, it shoots off at a tangent. Third, since premise 1 depends on Aristotle's technical notion of signification, there is absolutely no reason why an opponent should accept it. Worse, and most tellingly of all, another premise is required to make the argument work (as Cresswell notes), that not-F (not-man) is an essential predicate. But for Aristotle, if F is an essential predicate, then not-F isn't. So the argument is not sound, even in Aristotle's own terms!

Anyway, even if this is the correct interpretation of the argument, it need not worry a simple dialetheist. First, it establishes only that some contradictions are not true, not all of them. Secondly, it depends on Aristotle's theory of substance (in fact, more than this, as we have just seen), and we have already noted that this may be rejected without problem. Third, it depends also on a technical notion of signification and the "identity theory" of predication, which is now defunct[46] (and no sensible person would suppose that 'man' and 'not-man' mean the same thing in the non-technical sense). And finally, it shares the same failing as the argument as I have interpreted it: the dialetheist and the trivialist may accept both the conclusion of the argument and its negation.

1.11   SOME MODERN VARIATIONS I: TALKING OF OBJECTS

Some other commentators have given what seem to me to be looser interpretations of the text. One is Irwin (1988), sect. 98. He summarizes the upshot of Aristotle's argument as follows (p. 183, italics original):

(1) To deny every instance of PNC {LNC}, O must say that it is possible for the *same* subject, man, to have the contradictory of each of its properties. (2) If O is speaking of the same subject, he must acknowledge that he signifies the essence, the property that makes the subject of the two predications the same subject. (3) Hence, since the subject man is essentially F {two-footed animal}, a subject that is not F is not the same subject as the one signified by the first occurrence of 'man'. (4) Hence when O says that man is not F, O is committed to denying that this subject

---

[46] For some critical comments, see Geach (1972), 1.1 and 10.1.

(the one that is not *F*) is the same subject that {*sic*} as the one that he said is *F*, since being *F* is the essential property of man.

As the first sentence shows, Irwin is actually confusing the LNT with the LNC, and defending the latter. At its core, his argument is simple. Let *a* be any man. Then since *F* is an essential property, $\Box Fa$, and so *Fa*. Now suppose that $\neg Fb$; then $a \neq b$. Thus, the same thing cannot have contradictory essential properties.

Note that the argument, as given, establishes something weaker than the LNT: the LNC for essential predicates (the same as the Anscombe/Cresswell interpretation). Note, further, that the fact that *F* is essential is playing no real role in the argument. Since $\Box Fa$ is used to infer *Fa*, *F* could, in fact, be any predicate. So we do have an argument for the LNC. Unfortunately, it is fallacious, or at least question begging. This is so for two reasons. There is no reason to challenge Leibniz' Law here: $a = b \vdash \neg(Fa \wedge \neg Fb)$. But in this context one cannot assume its contrapositive: $Fa \wedge \neg Fb \models a \neq b$. Substituting '*a*' for '*b*', this gives that any object with contradictory properties has the very particular contradictory property of being non-self-identical ($a = a$ being a logical truth). Now, it may make sense to suppose that an object is non-self-identical sometimes (e.g. in dialectical contexts involving change), but the mere fact that it has contradictory properties should not entail that it has that particular one. It is not, therefore, surprising that the contraposed form of inference fails in standard paraconsistent logics.[47] Secondly, even if it did not fail, if the LNC does, the fact that $a \neq b$ does not rule out the fact that $a = b$. So the same object *can* satisfy both *F* and $\neg F$. It just has the further property of being non-self-identical.

Another account of the argument is given by Lear (1988).[48] His summary of its import is as follows (p. 260):

If 'not-man' could be said of the very same thing of which 'man' is said, there could be no substance, for there would be nothing which was just what it was to be a man. In Aristotle's view this is tantamount to destroying the possibility of discourse, for there is no longer a subject about which to make any affirmation or denial . . .

This is a version of the Anscombe/Cresswell interpretation, which I have already discussed. However, again, it is clearly directed against trivialism rather than dialetheism: there is *no* substance only if '*a* is *P* and not *P*' is true for *every* essential predicate, *P*.

Lear continues (p. 263):

Aristotle argues that an opponent of the principle of non-contradiction must eliminate substance, that there is nothing that his statements are about. But that an opponent cannot say anything follows only if one assumes that the correct account of language-use is the one Aristotle gives: that to say anything is to affirm or deny something of a subject . . . Why could not a . . . sophisticated opponent completely reject this world-view and theory of language? Could he not hold that . . . Aristotle's argument shows only that we must give up the picture of the world as composed of substances and properties?

---

[47] See, e.g. Priest (1991*a*), 194 f.
[48] Similar ground is covered in Lear (1980), but (1988) is his preferred account. See (1988), 249 n. 64.

Lear is right that the argument (thus interpreted) presupposes Aristotle's theory of substance, so that its conclusion may be avoided by rejecting this. However, he also seems to think that if one does this, then one must give up the picture of the world as composed of subjects and their properties—and so the claim that one can express oneself by predicating things of objects. If he does think this, he is incorrect. We can give up a picture of the world as composed of properties and substances *in Aristotle's sense*, without giving up an ontology of objects and properties. The more damaging conclusion would follow only if the non-existence of substances *simpliciter*, i.e. bearers of properties, followed from the non-existence of substances *of*, i.e. essences. But not even an essentialist must hold this.

1.12 SOME MODERN VARIATIONS II: MEANING

Lear is not finished yet though. He thinks that even if one rejects a subject/property ontology one can still extract a damning argument from Aristotle, to the effect that violations of the LNC have unacceptable consequences. Before we turn to this, let us look first at a similar argument in McTaggart:[49]

... it is impossible ... to assert anything without involving the law of {non-}contradiction, for every positive assertion has meaning only in so far as it is defined, and therefore negative. If the statement 'All men are mortal', for example did not exclude the statement 'Some men are immortal' it would be meaningless. And it only excludes it by the law of {non-}contradiction.

McTaggart claims that a proposition has meaning only if it rules something out. It is not immediately clear whether this claim is made in defence of the LNC or of the LNT. If it is the LNC, then a dialetheist might attempt to reply that even if a contradiction does not rule out its negation, it still rules something out. A trivialist does not have this reply since they believe everything, and nothing is ruled out. But whether directed against dialetheist or trivialist, the argument fails: the claim that a meaningful proposition must rule something out is just plain false. Consider, for example, the claim that everything is true. This entails everything, and so "rules out" nothing. But it is obviously meaningful (or what is Aristotle arguing against a lot of the time?). Moreover, consider its negation 'something is not true'. This is obviously true (it is entailed by: 'snow is black' is not true), and so meaningful. How could a meaningful sentence have a meaningless negation?

Maybe, then, "ruled out" has to be construed differently. We might take it to mean that there are certain situations (or worlds) in which the statement fails. This, at least, makes 'everything is true' rule something out. Unfortunately, this account of meaning is equally obviously false. Consider any necessary truth, such as '$13^2 = 169$'. This rules nothing out: it is true in all possible worlds. Yet it is not meaningless: its truth can be a substantial discovery.[50]

[49] McTaggart (1922), 8.
[50] This might be denied by someone who subscribes to a Tractarian view of language. But on such a view, nearly every statement in mathematics and philosophy comes out to be meaningless

Now let us return to Lear. His argument goes as follows:[51]

... one might wonder why Aristotle did not formulate a more abstract argument, one which is independent of his particular theory of substance. Certainly he had an argument immediately to hand. For within the details of his proof by refutation a valid point is being made that transcends both his theory of substance and his philosophy of language. An assertion divides up the world: to assert that anything is the case one must exclude other possibilities. This exclusion is just what fails to occur in the absence of the principle of non-contradiction, even when it is construed in its most general form: *for any statement S, it is not the case that both S and not-S*.

The paragraph then continues, but let us first deal with this. A preliminary comment: I, at least, find it impossible to read this argument into Aristotle. However, since my main concern is with substantive arguments against violation of the LNC, this is not presently important.

As is clear, the argument just recycles McTaggart, and therefore fails for reasons that we have already seen. It also has further problems. It is claimed that if the LNC fails, a proposition ('proposition' seems to be the better word here; it does not have to be asserted) does not divide up worlds (or situations) into those where it holds and those where it fails. This does not follow at all. All that the violation of the LNC requires is that for some αs there be an overlap between the worlds where α holds, and those where $\neg\alpha$ holds. This is quite compatible with each proposition dividing worlds in the required way[52]—and even with each proposition failing at *some* world (something that does not happen classically, note).

I suspect that Lear is thinking as follows: the worlds at which $\neg\alpha$ holds are exactly those where α fails. This division provides the required partition. Maybe so. But if these truth conditions for negation are not the correct ones, it hardly follows that there is no partition.[53]

We are not finished with Lear yet, but what follows raises quite new considerations. Before we turn to these, let us consider some other commentators who relate the LNC to the possibility meaning. The view that violation of the LNC is quite compatible with the possibility of meaningful discourse is defended in Dancy (1975), 34 ff. Dancy then goes on (p. 37) to raise the question of what would happen to meaning if someone were prepared to endorse all contradictions. Suppose that one met a trivialist, who was prepared to assent to anything in any situation. One could not then use what they say and do to get any kind of fix on what they mean. If one adopted the methodology of radical translation, one might well conclude that their language had no meaning.[54] But this would be too fast (as Dancy notes). Suppose that I start to read Heraklitus, or Protagoras, or whatever; in a fit of madness I come to the conclusion that they were right: everything *is* true. In virtue of this I start to utter indiscriminately. Does this

---

(including the *Tractatus* itself). I think one might take heart from the fact that contradictions are in such good company.

[51] Lear (1988), 263 f., italics original.   [52] See, for example, *In Contradiction*, 7.2.

[53] That there is an overlap between the worlds where α holds and those where $\neg\alpha$ holds, does, of course, require a different account of negation, but one that is quite defensible. See *In Contradiction* and Chapter 4.

[54] Or maybe that everything uttered means the same thing: 'something is happening here, now'.

mean that I have ceased to speak English, that 'table' in my mouth has ceased to mean table? I don't think so. How could a change in my beliefs, a private phenomenon, affect meanings, a public phenomenon? When I point to a chair, and say 'this is and is not a table', I mean exactly what I say. This, after all, is what I have become persuaded of. Loony it may be; literally meaningless it is not.

It might well be asked why I should bother to say anything at all, once I had become persuaded that everything is true. This is a fair question, but a different one; and since it is precisely an issue that some of Aristotle's other arguments raise, let us defer consideration of it until it comes up there. Further, suppose that everyone became convinced of the truth of trivialism, more or less simultaneously—what would happen to meaning then? Again, I will defer a discussion of this to a later point.

Taking off from a discussion of Putnam,[55] Thompson (1981) also suggests that violation of the LNT results in a destruction of meaning. The relevant passage goes as follows (p. 459):

> We might say that the minimal principle of contradiction {LNT} is true because we find from experience that it is impossible to express ourselves in a language without accepting the rule that not every statement is true . . . Failure to conform to the principle results in our meaning nothing at all. Whatever we say we mean, we would have to say it is true that we do not mean it. The qualification that in a sense we mean it and in a sense we don't will not help. For any sense in which we say we mean something, we must say that it is true that we do not mean it in that sense. Meaning in a sense becomes impossible.

Now, note first that the argument is not to the effect that if the LNT were false then there would be no meaning. (This is trivially true: every conditional starting 'if everything were true . . .' is a necessary truth.) Rather, the point is that if someone believes everything to be true (fails to "conform" to the LNT) there would be no meaning. Now, this is not true, as we have just noted. The person who believes that all is true will say that any utterance both means and does not mean anything one likes (they will say everything, after all). But that does not imply that their utterances have no determinate meaning. One might wonder of such a person why they should bother to say anything at all: what *they* could mean by any utterance. But, as I have just said, that is another matter, which we will come to in due course.

Before we move on to a different topic, let me make one final observation. A number of the arguments in this section can be thought of as attempting to give a transcendental argument for the LNT. Specifically, non-triviality is argued to be a necessary condition for the meaningfulness of language. And since we do have meaningful language, we must have non-triviality. Leaving aside the fact that none of these arguments appears to work, there is a general and profound problem about any attempt to provide a transcendental justification for the LNT. It is not that such arguments are difficult to find; the problem, rather, is that they are far too easy. That everything is true entails everything; in particular, for any α, $\forall x Tx \rightarrow \neg\alpha$. Hence, by contraposition

---

[55] Putnam's own defence of the LNT (1976), is a rather curious one. After a long discussion of reasons which he does not endorse, his brief reason at the end of the paper (which explicitly invokes Aristotle as a predecessor), turns out to be a defence not of the LNT but of *modus ponens*.

$\alpha \rightarrow \neg\forall xTx$. In other words, the LNT is a necessary condition for *everything*. There would seem to be little to be gained from a conclusion that can be bought so cheaply.[56]

1.13 SOME MODERN VARIATIONS III: NEGATION AS CANCELLATION

Let us now return to Lear. The last passage of his that I quoted (attempting to give an argument for the LNC that is independent of Aristotle's view of substance) continues:[57]

One cannot assert S and then directly proceed to assert not-S: one does not succeed in making a second assertion, but only in cancelling the first assertion. This argument does not depend on any theory of substance or on any theory of the internal structure or semantics of statements. It is a completely general point about the affirmation and denial of statements.

Note that this argument is quite distinct from the one given in the first part of the paragraph. That one is about an arbitrary proposition: if the LNC fails, it rules nothing out, and so is not meaningful. The argument is specifically about contradictory propositions, and is to the effect that such a proposition has no content; *a fortiori*, it has no true content. The argument hinges on quite specific claims about the behaviour of negation. Let us return to it in a moment, after a few appropriate background comments.[58]

One may distinguish between three accounts of the relationship between negation, contradiction, and content. (1) A cancellation account. According to this, $\neg\alpha$ cancels the content of α. Hence, a contradiction has *no* content. In particular then, supposing that an inference is valid when the content of the premises contains that of the conclusion, a contradiction entails nothing—or nothing with any content; it may entail another contradiction. (2) A complementation account. According to this, $\neg\alpha$ has whatever content α does not have. Hence $\alpha \wedge \neg\alpha$ has *total* content, and entails everything. (3) An intermediate account, where the content of $\neg\alpha$ is a function of the content of α, but neither of the previous kinds. According to this account, $\alpha \wedge \neg\alpha$ has, in general, *partial* content, neither null nor total. Hence, contradictions entail some things but not others.

An account of kind (3) is given in relevant and paraconsistent logics. An account of kind (2) is packed into orthodox modern logics, such as "classical" and intuitionist logic. An account of kind (1) is clearly distinct from either of these. It appears to have been an influential account in Ancient and early Medieval logic. Arguably, Aristotle subscribed to something like it, since he appears to have rejected the claim that $\alpha \wedge \neg\alpha$

---

[56] It might be suggested that there is more to a transcendental argument than I have allowed. The state of affairs in question must be shown to be not just any old necessary condition, but some necessary condition of a special kind. This may be true, but I know of no way of spelling out the idea which helps. For example, suppose that one takes it that in a transcendental argument we must establish that the state of affairs is a necessary condition for the *possibility* of something. Since $\forall xTx \rightarrow \Box\neg\alpha, \Diamond\alpha \rightarrow \neg\forall xTx$, and we are no better off. These arguments do depend on contraposition, however. One might therefore try to avoid their conclusions by denying this.

[57] Lear (1988), 263 f.   [58] These draw heavily on Routley and Routley (1985).

entails α. (See 1.4. We will have further evidence of this later.) It appears in Boethius and Abelard. It is intimately connected with principles such as $\neg(\alpha \rightarrow \neg\alpha)$, which are built into modern connexive logics.[59]

Though the cancellation and complementation accounts are quite distinct, some modern writers have run them together. A notable example of this is Strawson. In his book, *Introduction to Logical Theory* (1952), he gives the orthodox truth-tabular account of negation, and orthodox account of validity, according to which contradictions entail everything. But in his informal account of contradiction we read (p. 2 f.):

> Suppose a man sets out to walk to a certain place; but when he gets half way there, he turns round and comes back again. This may not be pointless. But, from the point of view of change of position, it is as if he had never set out. And so a man who contradicts himself may have succeeded in exercising his vocal chords. But from the point of view of imparting information, or communicating facts (or falsehoods) it is as if he had never opened his mouth . . . The point is that the *standard* function of speech, the intention to communicate something, is frustrated by self-contradiction. Contradiction is like writing something down and erasing it, or putting a line through it. A contradiction cancels itself and leaves nothing.

This is a clear statement of a cancellation view of negation—and quite different from an orthodox account. On an orthodox account, someone who asserts a contradiction is much worse off than someone who has asserted nothing: they are committed to everything.

Now let us return to Lear's argument. It is clear that this invokes a cancellation account of negation, and stands or falls with it. (And if I am right about Lear's thinking in the first part of his argument, he, too has confused a cancellation account with a complementation account.) Before we evaluate that account, we need to get clearer as to what, exactly, it is. Though Lear does not explain it, I take it to be something like this. Speaker's assertions (and here, 'assertion' does seem the appropriate word) normally convey information. Normally, when they make a new assertion this adds to the stock of information conveyed. But when the stock contains the information α, an assertion of $\neg\alpha$ adds nothing, but merely removes α.

Even filled out like this, the account is obviously sketchy and unsatisfactory. What does an assertion of $\neg\alpha$ do if α is not in the information store? It must do something; negative statements do, after all, have content. So presumably that content is merely added to the store. So why doesn't it do this if α is already there? (Inconsistent data bases are not news.) And what happens if α and β are in the information store, and $\neg(\alpha \wedge \beta)$ is asserted? A natural suggestion is that we delete either α or β; but we have, in general, no way of knowing which. So presumably we can only add $\neg(\alpha \wedge \beta)$ to the store. But if we can have α, β and $\neg(\alpha \wedge \beta)$ in the store, why not α and $\neg\alpha$?

In any case, and for quite general reasons, the cancellation account of negation doesn't stand up to inspection. For a start, in a borderline situation of, e.g. rain, one might say that it both is and isn't raining. This is, perhaps, something of a special case; but it shows clearly that negation does not have to function as a cancellation operator.

For a discussion and references see Routley *et al.* (1982), 2.4.

Or consider another sort of situation. One can, in considering one's beliefs, come to assert contradictory statements, and in so doing discover that they are inconsistent. The assertion of $\neg\alpha$ in this context does not "cancel out" the assertion of α—whatever this might be supposed to mean. The assertion of $\neg\alpha$ is providing *more* information about what it is one believes, not less. And it is precisely the inconsistent nature of this information that gives one pause; if what one said had no content, it would have no unsatisfactory content, so it is difficult to see why one should bother to revise one's beliefs at all.

Moreover, even if one does try to resolve the contradiction in such a situation, until one succeeds, one may well continue to use parts of the inconsistent information. (Think of scientific theories that are known to be inconsistent.) It is certainly not "cancelled out". Consider an extreme case, the paradox of the preface. A person writes a book and thereby asserts the conjoined truth of all of the claims in it. Being aware of the overwhelming inductive evidence, they also assert that there are mistakes in the book, i.e. the denial of that conjunction. This does not cancel out the claims in the book. Indeed, in this case, it might even be argued that believing the inconsistent totality of information is the rational thing to do, something that would make no sense if bits of it cancelled out other bits.[60] The account of negation as cancellation therefore fails, as does the second part of Lear's argument.

In the last three sections of this chapter we have looked at a number of philosophers who have been inspired by Aristotle's first refutation. In the end, none are any more successful than was Aristotle himself. Let us now return to Aristotle's text, and to his other refutations.

1.14 SECOND REFUTATION: ELEATIC MONISM (7^b18–8^a2)

The second refutation (7^b18–8^a2) starts: 'if contradictories are all simultaneously true of the same thing, it is plain that everything will be one. For the same thing will be both a warship and a wall and a man.' And a bit later we have: 'we also get the doctrine of Anaxagoras, that "every article is mixed together"; so that nothing is truly one.'

The premise of the argument is that every contradiction holds of all objects. Aristotle's conclusion is not entirely clear, though. In the first argument, what he is entitled to is that every object has exactly the same properties. It follows that every object is the same, in this sense. And maybe this is what he intends. The stronger conclusion that there is but one object follows if we are allowed to use the Identity of Indiscernibles. In the second argument, what Aristotle is entitled to is that nothing is a single stuff, but equally all stuffs. But, again, using an appropriate identity principle, we can wring out a conclusion about identity. If a has every property, it has both P and $\neg P$ (for any P). But if Pb and $\neg Pc$ then $b \neq c$. Hence, $a \neq a$.

To what extent Aristotle subscribed to these identity principles, I leave scholars to argue about. It is clear that one might take issue with both. (We have already noted that the second arguably fails, in discussing Irwin's argument in 1.11.) But we can

---

[60] See Priest (1993*a*) and sect. 6.2.

get the conclusions about identity from a much weaker premise and unproblematic identity principles. Suppose that just *one* thing, *a*, has all properties. Then it has both the property of being identical with *b*, so $a = b$, and that of being different from *a*, so $a \neq a$. The view therefore entails that there is but one thing, that is both identical with and different from itself. Parmenidean monism with a Heraklitean twist!

The most natural way of interpreting this argument is as *ad hominem*. As such, the argument clearly fails against a simple dialetheist since the required premise is, at the very least, that some object have every property. Presumably, it would have more success against a Heraklitean, since such a person is unlikely to buy into Parmenidean monism. It will fail against a trivialist: all *ad hominem* arguments always fail against a trivialist, as we have noted.

Aristotle then goes on to argue (7^b26 ff.):

> These people {who hold that every contradiction is true} seem, therefore, to be stating something indefinite; and while they consider that they are stating that which is, their statement is actually concerning that which is not (for the indefinite is what *is* potentially and *not* in complete reality).

I am really not sure I understand this argument. The best spin I can put on it is this. Suppose that for every P, $Pa \wedge \neg Pa$ then (i) *a* is neither definitely P, as opposed to $\neg P$, nor definitely $\neg P$ as opposed to P. But (ii) what is indefinite in this way is only potential. And (iii) what is potential does not really exist. Hence, (iv) trivialists cannot be describing what they think they are, that which exists. If this is the argument, it would seem to be *ad hominem*. It must therefore fail, as all such argument must. (Of course the trivialist thinks that they are talking about what does not really exist: they think everything.)

We might, instead, take (iv) to be: what is inconsistent cannot exist; and hence interpret the argument as giving a reason for the LNT. But even this fails. The problem is with (ii). According to Aristotle, if something is not actualized, it may be only potentially P and potentially $\neg P$, and so indefinite in that sense. (See 9^a31–5.[61]) But it does not follow (even for Aristotle, I think) that if it is indefinite in the (different) sense of (i), it is merely potential. In any case, the step just begs the whole question. Someone who takes contradictions to be true, just is affirming that the actual, and not merely the potential, can be indefinite in that sense, that is, contradictory.

On Kirwan's translation, the text continues: 'On the other hand their statements, at least, must affirm or deny everything of everything' (and goes on to give a new—and apparently otiose in the context—argument for this). This might be taken to suggest that the argument in question is a simple *reductio*. The absurd consequence is the very possibility of talking about the non-existent, of saying anything true or false about it at all. I doubt that this is the correct interpretation, since Aristotle himself often talks about the potential. But in any case, even if it is, the argument fails, for it is certainly possible to talk about mere *possibilia*. We often talk about events that may

---

[61] Łukasiewicz (1910), sect. 15, interprets this passage as saying that Aristotle held that the LNC holds only of the actual, not the merely possible. This strikes me as an implausible interpretation; more plausible is to interpret the sentence 'it is possible for the same thing to be simultaneously contradictory things potentially' as $\Diamond \alpha \wedge \Diamond \neg \alpha$ and not $\Diamond (\alpha \wedge \neg \alpha)$.

never, in fact, happen: a planned holiday, the birth of a child, retirement. Moreover, and crucially, the whole argument still begs the question, exactly as before, at step (ii).

1.15 THIRD REFUTATION: THE LEM AND ASSERTION ($8^a 2$–7)

Aristotle's next, and third, refutation is at $8^a 2$–7. (Kirwan treats it as part of the previous argument.) It goes as follows:

another {consequence of every contradiction being true} is that it is not necessary either to assert or deny. For if it is true that he is a man and not a man, plainly he will be neither a man nor not a man . . .

This appears to be an argument to the effect that violators of the LNC are committed to a denial of the LEM, too. (Kirwan and Ross both interpret it in this way.) Simply, $\alpha \wedge \neg\alpha$ entails $\neg\neg\alpha \wedge \neg\alpha$ by double negation, which entails $\neg(\neg\alpha \vee \alpha)$ by De Morgan. This argument obviously need not trouble a trivialist. The entailment need not trouble a simple dialetheist either. The fact that $\neg(\neg\alpha \vee \alpha)$ does not rule out $\neg\alpha \vee \alpha$. Thus, occasional violations of the LNC do not prevent the LEM from being logically valid. (It is valid, for example, in the semantics of LP; see *In Contradiction*, ch. 5.)

There is another possible interpretation of the argument. If neither α nor $\neg\alpha$ is true, it is not necessary to say either of these things. If this is true for all α, it is not necessary to say anything. Hence, if a trivialist says something—and does not adopt the silence of Cratylus—we have an *ad hominem* argument against them. They cannot really believe what they say. In this form, the argument is not very persuasive. For they *do* believe what they say: they believe everything. In any case, people often do what is unnecessary.

There is a deeper worry here, though. If someone believed that everything is true, there would be no *point* in their asserting anything. The point of asserting something is to get one's hearers to believe (or believe that one believes) the thing in question. But if one believes everything, one already believes that they believe it (or that they believe that one believes it). This still does not give an *ad hominem* argument against a trivialist who asserts things. The trivialist may have no point in asserting; but people do engage in pointless activity, e.g. for amusement. The importance of the observation is rather different. For a trivialist, assertion, *as an act of communication,* is pointless. In fact, all communicative activity (commanding, questioning, etc.) is pointless. For the point of communicative activity is, in the first instance, to induce certain mental states in the hearer. But the trivialist already believes the hearer to be in that state. Similarly, there is no point in a trivialist even listening to the communicative attempts of another. For whatever information they might hope to gain from the communication, they are already in possession of it: whatever the beliefs, desires, etc., of the other, the trivialist already believes the other to have them.[62] A general rejection of trivialism

---

[62] Evans and McDowell (1976), pp. xix ff., argue that much communication is habitual, and that it is implausible to suppose that speakers must have the beliefs the above account attributes to them.

is therefore integral to the rationale of communication, and hence the possibility of social life.[63]

This does not, of course, show that the trivialism is false. Indeed, we could all come to believe it true and take the consequences. But it at least establishes something important *about* it. This argument therefore has an important and sound perinomic interpretation. It can be thought of as a transcendental argument, not for the LNT, but for the fact that trivialism is generally rejected.

1.16 FOURTH REFUTATION: AN ARGUMENT BY CASES (8ᵃ7–34)

This brings us to the fourth refutation (8ᵃ7–34), which starts by distinguishing between some contradictions being true and all being true. What follows is aimed at the latter. Aristotle then distinguishes between two cases: (i) anything may be asserted iff it may be denied; (ii) anything that is asserted may be denied, but not vice versa. There would seem to be another case, viz. (iii): everything denied may be asserted, but not vice versa; but Aristotle ignores this. (Why, I am not sure.[64]) In any case, what follows is aimed squarely at case (i). In such a case there are two further possibilities; for all α either: (a) neither α nor $\neg\alpha$ is true separately (Herakliteanism); or (b) both are true (trivialism).

To wrap up the first case, Aristotle continues (7ᵃ20–3):

If it is not true to state {the contradictories} separately, then not only does he {the Heraklitean} not state these things but nothing whatever is—and how can things-that-are-not walk and talk. Also, everything would be one, as we said before . . .

The first complaint is puzzling. How do we get from the fact that the conjuncts of a true contradiction are not themselves true to the claim that nothing exists? I see no plausible way of doing this. Maybe this is a version of the argument that we met in connection with the second refutation, to the effect that what actually exists cannot be inconsistent. If it is, I have already dealt with it. The second complaint is that if all contradictions, and nothing else, hold of any object then all objects are identical. This recycles a version of another argument we met and dealt with in connection with the second refutation.

Against the second case, Aristotle argues (8ᵃ27–30):

Equally, even if it is possible to have the truth in stating all things separately, the result we have stated {that all things are one} follows; and in addition it follows that everyone would have

---

They argue, rather, that what is essential is that speakers must *lack* certain negative beliefs. Since trivialists lack no beliefs, the upshot of this account for trivialism is the same.

[63] It might be objected that there *is* a point in the trivialist communicating, since they believe that the hearer is *not* in the required doxastic state (as well). I will answer this point when it arises in a more general context in connection with Aristotle's sixth refutation.

[64] In his commentary (p. 104), Kirwan points out that in the *Posterior Analytics* Aristotle claims that assertions are 'prior to and more certain than' denials. I don't know what this is supposed to mean.

the truth and everyone would be in error, and [the disputant] himself is in error by his own omission.

The new argument here is clearly another *ad hominem* argument (compare *Theaetetus* 171 a, b), and fails against a trivialist, as all such arguments must. But a version of it might be thought to work against a simple dialetheist. Such a person asserts both α and $\neg\alpha$. So they are in error by their own lights; and a person is likely to reject the claim that they are in error.

This argument is no better, though. Suppose that we take being in error to mean simply 'stating an untruth' (as Ross, (1924), 267, glosses it). Then, given dialetheism, there is a simple fallacy in moving from '$\neg\alpha$ is true' to 'α is not true'. But even ignoring this, the argument will not work since it begs the question. A dialetheist who believes that α is both true and not true need not accept that believing α is an error. They are, after all, believing what is true.[65] Believing α would be an error if there were no evidence for it, but that is a different matter.

Aristotle appears to complete the argument against this horn of the dilemma as follows (8^a30–$^b2$):

in response to this person there is nothing for an investigation to deal with; for he says nothing. For he says neither that it is so-and-so nor that it is not so-and-so, but that it is both so-and-so and not so-and-so; and again he also denies both of these, saying that it is neither so-and-so nor not so-and-so.

At first, it might appear that Aristotle is going to make the point that if someone believed that everything is true, they would not bother to investigate anything any more.[66] But reading on, it becomes clear that his point is that the violator in question has said nothing, and so may be ignored. *Prima facie*, this is obviously false. The violator has said two things (in fact, three, α, $\neg\alpha$ and $\alpha \wedge \neg\alpha$). Aristotle is presumably, therefore, thinking that the assertion of $\neg\alpha$ "cancels out" the assertion of α and vice versa, and so appealing to the cancellation view of negation.[67] (This still leaves the conjunction, but presumably the violator will assert the negation of this too.) I have already discussed and rejected this view of negation, in 1.13; so we need pursue the matter no further.

Actually, this passage would appear to be more at home arguing against the first horn of the dilemma (as Kirwan notes, p. 104), but the point is the same. Such a person *has* said something: $\alpha \wedge \neg\alpha$ (unless the person is an extreme Heraklitean; in which case, the complaint has some force). So the thought must be that an assertion of $\neg(\alpha \wedge \neg\alpha)$ cancels this out. Similar comments therefore apply.

---

[65] See *In Contradiction*, ch. 4 and (1993), sect. 3. But see sect. 6.5 of this book.

[66] Leibniz, in fact, makes a similar point ((1696), p. 14 of translation): '{The LNC is} primitive, since otherwise there would be no difference between truth and falsehood; and all investigation would cease at once, if to say yes or no were a matter of indifference.' The point about the difference between truth and falsehood vanishing is, of course, incorrect. It may follow from trivialism, but not dialetheism. The point about investigation is a special case of Aristotle's claim that all action is pointless for someone who believes everything to be true, which we will come to in due course.

[67] This is the further evidence that Aristotle subscribed to a cancellation view of negation that I referred to in a previous section.

1.17 FIFTH REFUTATION: THE TRUTH-CONDITIONS
OF NEGATION (8^a34–$^b2$)

The fifth refutation is a swift one, and can be dealt with equally swiftly (8^a34–$^b2$):

> if whenever an assertion is true its denial is false, there can be no such thing as simultaneously asserting and denying the same thing truly. However, they {violators of the LNC} would doubtless assert that this is the question originally posed.

Whoever this argument is aimed at, its conclusion is simply a *non-sequitur*.[68] In the semantics of many paraconsistent logics (such as *LP*), α is true iff $\neg\alpha$ is false (and vice versa). Yet things of the form $\alpha \wedge \neg\alpha$ *can* be true. If 'false' is taken to mean 'not true', the situation is slightly different. The argument is then: α is true iff $\neg\alpha$ is untrue. Hence, (by the truth conditions of conjunction) $\alpha \wedge \neg\alpha$ is untrue. The truth conditions of negation are now contentious, but this is unimportant in the end. If certain contradictions can be true, then there is no *a priori* reason why 'α is true and not true' cannot be true. Indeed, this is exactly what happens in the case of the Liar Paradox, 'this sentence is not true'. The argument does, therefore, beg the question, as Aristotle suggests, at least against the simple dialetheist. It does not beg the question against a trivialist; nothing does; but we have already seen that no *ad hominem* argument against a trivialist will work. Let us move on.

1.18 SIXTH REFUTATION: PART I,
THE VEGETABLE (8^b2–12)

What Ross (and Kirwan) call the sixth refutation has two quite distinct parts. The first (8^b2–12) goes as follows:

> Again, are we to say that he who believes that things are in a certain state or are not, is in error, while he who believes both has the truth? For if he has the truth, what can be meant by saying that the nature of things-that-are is of that kind? If he does not have the truth, but has more truth than one who believes the former way, then the things-that-are would already be in some state, and that would be true and not simultaneously also not true.

The exact argument is, again, opaque, but seems to be this. Suppose that a believes $\alpha \wedge \neg\alpha$, and that b believes just one conjunct, say α. What is a to say about b's beliefs? a may say that b is mistaken—and presumably will, if they are a Heraklitean. But then what could it be for things to be like that? Alternatively, a may say that what b believes is true, but that a has more truth. In this case, something, presumably α, would be 'true and not simultaneously also not true'.

Both horns or Aristotle's dilemma are unpersuasive. The rhetorical question of the first horn is lame. The Heraklitean will reply: 'What could it be like? In a state of flux; just like that, Aristotle'. The second horn employs the invalid inference from truth

---

[68] As Łukasiewicz (1910), sect. 18, notes.

to truth *simpliciter* that we met in the throw-away argument at the beginning of the first refutation.

Aristotle then goes on to complain about a person who asserts all contradictions (8^b7–12):

there will be nothing for such a person to speak or say; for he simultaneously says this and not this. And if a man believes nothing, but considers it equally so and not so, how would his state be different from a vegetable's?

At the start of this it looks as though Aristotle is going to make the point about communication ceasing, which we have already discussed on connection with the third refutation. But by the second clause it is clear that Aristotle is claiming that the person says nothing. This has some force against an extreme Heraklitean. But against anyone else, it is just false (unless one buys into the cancellation view of negation that we have already discussed and rejected). Someone who asserts that something both is and is not a table *says exactly that*. (Recall the discussion of Dancy in section 1.12.) Aristotle then goes on to make the corresponding (and similarly fallacious) point about belief. Then comes the *ad hominem* crunch. Whether this is licit or illicit, is of no importance here. For even if the rest of the argument were correct, the final step would fail. The fact that someone has no beliefs does not mean that they have no other mental states: they may still be thinking, desiring, having emotions, having experiences, etc. So such a person is hardly a vegetable.

There is another point that can be extracted from this passage, however. Maybe Aristotle means that there is no more point in discussing with such a person than there is with a vegetable. The vegetable will not agree with anything; the trivialist will agree with everything. This point is right: the rejection of trivialism is a precondition of discussion. This is a special case of the perinomic point that a rejection of trivialism is a precondition of communicative activity in general, that we met already in connection with the third refutation.

1.19 SIXTH REFUTATION: PART II, ACTION (8^b12–31)

The second part of the sixth refutation (8^b12–31) goes as follows:

From which it is quite obvious that nobody actually is in that condition, neither those who state the thesis nor anybody else. For why does anyone walk to Megara rather than stay where he is, when he considers that he should walk there? Why does he not proceed one morning straight into a well or over a precipice, if there is one about: instead of evidently taking care to avoid doing so, as one who does not consider that falling in is equally a good thing and not a good thing? It is plain that he believes that one thing is better and another not better. And if so, he must also believe that one thing is a man and another not a man, one thing sweet and another not sweet. For he neither seeks nor believes everything indifferently when, considering that it is better to drink water or see a man, he thereupon seeks to do so; and yet he ought to do so if the same thing were equally a man and not a man.

This is an important argument. Essentially, it is to the effect that we can tell that someone does not believe a contradiction by looking at their non-linguistic behaviour.

Hence, we have an *ad hominem* argument against someone who claims to believe a contradiction.

Suppose, first, that this is an argument against a simple dialetheist. An immediate problem for the argument is that there are lots of contradictions that one might believe that have no *practical* ramifications in any immediate sense; and where, therefore, it is difficult to argue from the inappropriateness of behaviour. A paradigm example is the Liar Paradox: the Liar sentence is both true and not true. This would appear to have no consequence for action.

But even with contradictions that have practical ramifications, the argument will not work. Suppose, for example, that I believe that Jesus is a man and not a man. (Not necessarily the Christian Jesus, but he is not excluded.) Nothing at all follows from this about how I should act. It is also necessary to know my desires. Suppose, then, that I desire to see a man (any man). If I believe that Jesus is a man and not a man, then I believe he is a man; and if he is the most convenient man available, I will take steps to see him. Equally, if I desire (at a different time) to see something that is not a man, I may take steps to see him. In this way I actually demonstrate my inconsistent beliefs. I may even desire (at the same time) both to see a man and to see something that is not a man. I may demonstrate my belief that Jesus is both a man and not a man by satisfying both desires in the one act. The argument is therefore a failure.[69]

The situation is different if it is trivialism that is in question (which is what, presumably, Aristotle has in mind). Trivialists believe that everything is a man and not a man, and both desire and do not desire to see a man (or at least, they believe that they do). There is therefore no reason to do anything, as opposed to anything else—at least as far as seeing a man goes, and for the trivialist the same holds true of everything else. Aristotle infers that if we see a person engaging in apparently purposeful activity, we can therefore infer that they are not a trivialist.

Naturally, if someone behaved apparently randomly, then we could not take them to demonstrate purposeful activity, and so the argument would get no grip on their beliefs. Still, such a person is not likely to last very long. But even if a person does appear to show purposeful activity, I think that it is impossible to deploy the argument. For such a person might say: since I believe everything, there is no purpose to my activity. But I am well trained: I do whatever comes naturally. At certain times of the day I seek out food or a bed. Not because of any beliefs, but simply because that is what I am moved to do. Such a person might even compose poetry or philosophy if that is what the spirit moves them to do.[70] Alternatively, the trivialist in question might simply be suffering from some cognitive defect such as bad memory (one does not, after all, always remember all of one's beliefs) or bad faith (actively repressing certain beliefs).

---

[69] On the above points, see *In Contradiction*, 121 f.

[70] It is worth noting that a similar objection may be made against a radical sceptic—since they have no belief that things are thus and so, as opposed to thus and so, why do anything?—and that a similar reply is made by the sceptic Sextus Empiricus, *Outlines of Pyrrhonism*, I. 11., 23–4.

But there *is* an important point to be learned here. On reflection, a trivialist can have no reason for doing any one thing, as opposed to any other. Suppose, for example, that they desire to be at the North Pole. Since they believe that they are not at the Pole, they have reason to move; but since they believe that they are at the Pole, they have reason to stand still. Hence, they have no reason to do either as opposed to the other.

It might be suggested that the tie in this situation could be broken by some other fact, e.g. another desire. Some have argued that desires just are certain kinds of beliefs.[71] If this is right, then trivialists have all desires, and hence there is no hope of appealing to a particular desire to break the tie. But even if desire is *sui generis*, such a suggestion would still seem to fall to the fact that the trivialist believes everything. Suppose, for example, that the trivialist has the desire to act on beliefs of a certain kind. This will not help; for since they believe everything, they believe every belief to be of this kind. Or suppose that they desire to act on *this* belief more than *that*. Then since they believe that *this* belief is *that* belief, they will desire to act on *that* belief more than *this*.

I will have more to say about this argument in Chapter 3. But this will suffice for the present. What we have seen is that rational, purposeful, activity requires a rejection of trivialism. Our prior conclusion that the rationale of communicative activity presupposes a rejection of trivialism is just a special case of this.[72] For communication is one species of purposeful activity. In particular, then, if trivialism were generally accepted, the institution of communication would, presumably, cease. This would be the case—to return to a question raised in section 1.12—if everyone, more or less simultaneously, became convinced of the truth of trivialism. Whether any words that people uttered under such circumstances retained their old meanings, took on new ones, or lost meaning all together, depends on how, exactly, meanings supervene on intention and action; and this is too big an issue to take on here.

We have, at any rate, a firm and general conclusion concerning trivialism. A belief in trivialism is incompatible with reflective, purposeful action; and, in particular, with communication. This does not show that trivialism *is* false, or that no one cannot suppose it to be true. But its rejection is a precondition of this central feature of what it is to be a person (and not a vegetable). We can therefore interpret Aristotle's argument as perinomic, establishing this important fact.

1.20 SEVENTH REFUTATION: TELEOLOGY (8^b31–9^a6)

The seventh, and final, refutation, which brings the chapter to a close, is a swift one (8^b31–9^a6). Even if everything is true, some things are truer than others. For example,

---

[71] e.g. Humberstone (1987).
[72] In particular, the objection that we set aside, to the effect that there *is* a point in a trivialist communicating, since they believe that the goal state is not (yet) achieved, has been answered. There is no way to break the tie, and hence no reason for speaking, as against being silent.

'2 is even' is truer than '3 is even'. But then:

> there must be something true which the more true view is nearer. And even if that is not so,
> at least there is something more firm or truthlike, and we are rid of the unadulterated thesis
> which would prevent us from having anything definite in our thinking.

Whatever Aristotle is trying to achieve here, it would seem to fail, since it contains a number of fallacious steps. For a start, there is no reason, as far as I can see, that a trivialist must agree that some things are truer than others. They might reject talk of degrees of truth as just nonsense, and they are not committed to believing nonsense statements as true.[73] Certainly, a dialetheist is not committed to the claim that 'snow is white' is truer than 'this sentence is not true'. Secondly, and in any case, the existence of degrees of Xness does not imply a maximum, such that the degree of Xness is defined by proximity to this. Think of tallness, for example. Finally, as we saw in section 1.13, provided that one eschews a cancellation account of negation, a contradiction, $\alpha \wedge \neg\alpha$, can have a definite, non-empty, content—and so, therefore, may thinking one. This argument, then, can simply be ignored.

1.21 CONCLUSION

We have now reviewed all of Aristotle's arguments, as well as various others inspired by them. Let us step back and see what, if anything, they succeed in achieving. They do not provide any kind of argument against dialetheism. Neither do they provide any kind of argument against a trivialist. As we noted, nothing can do this. Nor do they give any transcendental reason for the LNC, or the LNT (as we saw, there are problems concerning the latter enterprise in any case). They do show, however, that a rejection of triviality is a precondition for reflective purposive activity, and especially for the institution of communication. This is a lot less than Aristotle advertised, but it is still an interesting and important conclusion. We will come back to the matter in Chapter 3. It is now time to turn to truth itself.

[73] Though they would also agree that no statement is nonsense.

2

Theories of Truth

2.1 INTRODUCTION

Aristotle's arguments against dialetheism are, as we saw in the last chapter, a failure. Where might one look for successful arguments? A natural place is the nature of truth itself. Maybe there is something about this that rules out contradictions from being true.

Characterizing contradiction is relatively easy: contradictories are any things of the form α and $\neg\alpha$. This definition hides a difficulty, though. What sort of things are we talking about here: sentences, statements, propositions, beliefs? This is a thorny issue.[1] Fortunately, then, nothing much seems to turn on the niceties of the question for present purposes. I will simply assume that α and its ilk are truth-bearers, whatever those are required to be. I will use angle brackets to refer to such bearers. Thus, $\langle\alpha\rangle$ is the name of the truth bearer α. If we write T for 'is true', the question of the possibility of true contradictions is that of whether there can be an α such that $T\langle\alpha\rangle$ and $T\langle\neg\alpha\rangle$.

Characterizing truth is much harder. Indeed, this is an old philosophical chestnut. There are, of course, many theories of truth.[2] Each of them gives an account of the nature of the beast. What I will do in this chapter is look at a number of such theories to see whether there is anything in them inimical to dialetheism, that is, in favour of the "Law of Non-Contradiction". There are certainly arguments for the "Law" which appeal to other considerations, but these will not be our concern in this chapter.[3] The question on the agenda is whether there is anything about the nature of truth that rules out dialetheism; and if there is, this should follow from a theory that spells out that nature.

It would be impossible to look at all the theories of truth that have been given. I will therefore restrict myself to the major ones. The traditional accounts are the correspondence, coherence, and pragmatist theories of truth. More modern accounts include the deflationist, semantic, and teleological accounts. It is these six theories that I will discuss—starting with the newer ones. Naturally, each of these accounts comes in different versions, sometimes very different versions; but in each case, there

---

[1] See, e.g. Haack (1978), ch. 6.

[2] For surveys, see, e.g. Haack (1978), ch. 7, Kirkham (1992), Grayling (1997), chs. 5, 6.

[3] We will meet a number of such arguments elsewhere in the book. See also Priest (1998b).

is a main motivating idea, which different versions develop in different ways. Some of these ways may, in fact, build in the impossibility of true contradictions. But, I shall argue, in every case there is nothing about the *idée maîtresse* that requires this; and if there are particular versions that render dialetheias impossible, there are, equally, versions that do not. Finally, let me emphasize that I am not at all concerned here with evaluating any of these accounts of truth and determining which theory—if any—is correct.[4] My concern is solely with the bearing of each of these theories on dialetheism.

2.2 THE DEFLATIONIST THEORY OF TRUTH

Let us start with the deflationist theory. The first major proponent of this was Ramsey, and more modern versions have been endorsed by a number of people, notably, Horwich (1990). According to this account, to say that α is true is to say neither more nor less than α itself. That is, truth is simply that property (or predicate), T, which satisfies the T-schema:

$$T\langle\alpha\rangle \leftrightarrow \alpha$$

for every truth-bearer, α, and a suitable biconditional, $\leftrightarrow$.

Is there anything inimical to dialetheism in this account? Not at all. The account is entirely neutral as to *what* things are true. Such matters of substance are deferred elsewhere. In particular, we have:

$$(T\langle\alpha\rangle \wedge T\langle\neg\alpha\rangle) \leftrightarrow (\alpha \wedge \neg\alpha)$$

Hence, the contradictories, $\langle\alpha\rangle$ and $\langle\neg\alpha\rangle$, are true iff α and $\neg\alpha$. If we are looking for arguments against the possibility of this, we will have to look elsewhere.[5]

As a matter of fact, the deflationist account is not simply neutral on the issue of dialetheism: it actually has a tendency to favour it. This is because of the well-known fact that the T-schema itself seems to give rise to contradictions. Given self-reference of any number of different kinds, it is easy enough to construct a truth-bearer, β, of the form $\neg T\langle\beta\rangle$. The T-schema gives us:

$$T\langle\beta\rangle \leftrightarrow \beta$$

i.e.:

$$T\langle\beta\rangle \leftrightarrow \neg T\langle\beta\rangle$$

Whence, by the law of excluded middle or *consequentia mirabilis* ($\alpha \rightarrow \neg\alpha \vdash \neg\alpha$), we have $T\langle\beta\rangle$ and $\neg T\langle\beta\rangle$. Writing γ for $T\langle\beta\rangle$, the instances of the T-schema for γ and its negation, give us $T\langle\gamma\rangle$ and $T\langle\neg\gamma\rangle$.

---

[4] In *In Contradiction*, ch. 4, I endorse a teleological account of truth.
[5] An obvious place to look is to the nature of negation. We will turn to this in the next part of the book.

This is, of course, the Liar Paradox. Naturally, one may try to avoid it by rejecting the principles of logic employed.[6] Typically, however, contemporary deflationists have not taken this line. Here, for example, is Horwich (1990), 41:

Indeed—and for that reason [the Liar Paradox] we must conclude that permissible instantiations of the equivalence schema [sc. the T-schema] are restricted in some way to avoid paradoxical results.

Though this is, of course, a possible move, it is also clear that it goes completely against the spirit of deflationism, whose prime thought is, after all, that 'α' and '$\langle\alpha\rangle$ is true' just amount to the same thing. It is thus a quite *ad hoc* manoeuvre. *Honest* deflationism is not only compatible with dialetheism; it leads in its direction.[7]

2.3   THE SEMANTIC THEORY OF TRUTH

Let us turn now to the semantic account of truth. This is the account which derives from Tarski's famous work on truth. (See Tarski (1956).) Tarski showed how to give a theory of a truth predicate (for a given language), or, more generally, a satisfaction predicate (truth being a special case of satisfaction—when there are no free variables in the formula concerned). The theory is a recursive one, in the sense that the truth of any compound sentence is specified in terms of the truth of its parts. The T-schema—or rather its slight generalization: $T\langle\alpha\rangle \leftrightarrow \alpha'$, where α' is a suitable translation of α—is not one of the axioms of the theory itself, but follows from them in a natural way. The exact details of the Tarskian construction are well known, and need no rehearsal here. The question at hand is whether there is anything in it which precludes contradictions from being true.

One immediate thought to this effect is as follows. Given that the Tarskian theory delivers the T-schema, if there were an α such that $T\langle\alpha\rangle$ and $T\langle\neg\alpha\rangle$, then it would follow that α' and $\neg\alpha'$.[8] If an explosive logic is used (in which a contradiction entails everything), then truth would be reduced to triviality. Of course, a similar argument can be deployed concerning any theory that delivers the T-schema. The answer would be the same in every case: use a paraconsistent logic—one in which contradictions don't entail everything. After all, no other logic makes much sense if you are a dialetheist. This answer might be thought to be unsatisfactory in the case of a Tarskian theory of truth, though. For it is sometimes said that a Tarskian theory must be based on classical logic: this logic is required for the construction to be performed. Such a claim is just plain false. It can be carried out in intuitionist logic, paraconsistent logic, and, in fact, most logics. A version of the construction based on a paraconsistent logic

---

[6] Though how successful this is, is another matter. Such moves always seem to succumb to extended paradoxes. See *In Contradiction*, ch. 2.

[7] The connection between dialethism and deflationism is pursued further in Armour-Garb and Beall (2001), and Beall and Armour-Garb (2003).   [8] Assuming that $(\neg\alpha)'$ is $\neg(\alpha')$.

can be found in *In Contradiction*, chapter 9. In fact, very little propositional logic is required to implement the Tarskian construction: little more than the substitutivity of provable equivalents.[9]

It might be thought that truth conditions for negation of the form:

$$T\langle\neg\alpha\rangle \leftrightarrow \neg T\langle\alpha\rangle \tag{$*$}$$

would rule out the possibility of true contradictions in a Tarskian theory. But, for a start, such conditions are not mandatory in the construction. For example, it is possible to give *joint* recursive conditions for the predicates T and F ('is false')—or, strictly speaking, their counterparts for satisfaction—where the conditions for negation are the pair:

$$T\langle\neg\alpha\rangle \leftrightarrow F\langle\alpha\rangle$$
$$F\langle\neg\alpha\rangle \leftrightarrow T\langle\alpha\rangle$$

Moreover, even a dialetheist *may* employ ($*$) as the truth conditions for negation. Such conditions merely mean that any contradiction shown to be true, $T\langle\alpha\rangle \wedge T\langle\neg\alpha\rangle$, turns into an explicit contradiction of the form $T\langle\alpha\rangle \wedge \neg T\langle\alpha\rangle$. And whilst there may be arguments against the possibility or desirability of this,[10] there is nothing intrinsic to the Tarskian construction itself. (In *In Contradiction*, chapter 9, it is shown how to give a truth-theory in each of the above ways.)

There is nothing, then, in the semantic account of truth which, in itself, is inimical to the possibility of true contradictions. More: just as with the deflationist account, the semantic account actually leads in this direction. For truth-theories of a Tarskian kind deliver the T-schema, and this produces contradictions in a very simple way, as we have already seen.[11] Tarski blocked off this consequence by insisting that the truth predicate for a language not occur in that language, and hence that appropriate self-referential sentences cannot be formulated. But, first, this is not essential to the construction. It is quite possible to give a paraconsistent Tarskian truth-theory for a language which contains its own truth predicate. *In Contradiction*, chapter 9 does just that.[12] Worse, for a formal language that is supposed to behave anything like a natural language, Tarski's restriction seems an entirely implausible and *ad hoc* one, which it is difficult to defend successfully, as most would now agree.[13] Just as with the

---

[9] This does rule out certain paraconsistent logics, however; notably those of da Costa's C family.

[10] See, e.g. *In Contradiction*, 4.9.

[11] The fact that it may not be the truth-bearer, α, that occurs on the right hand side of the T-schema, but a translation, α', is of no significance. For since translation preserves meaning, we have $\alpha \leftrightarrow \alpha'$.

[12] Though this does mean that the theory of truth cannot be turned into an explicit *definition* of truth. But since the theory entails all instances of the T-schema, it nonetheless provides a characterization of truth that is "materially adequate".

[13] See, e.g. *In Contradiction*, ch. 1 for discussion and references.

deflationist theory, then, the semantic account of truth is not just compatible with dialetheism; it actually leads in its direction.

2.4 THE TELEOLOGICAL THEORY OF TRUTH

The last modern account of truth that I will discuss is less well known than either of the preceding accounts. It arises out of some comments of Dummett (1959), and is advocated as an account of truth in *In Contradiction*, chapter 4. This is the teleological theory of truth.

The account starts by noting that 'is true' is a predicate with a *point*. Even if one knew the entire extension of the predicate, one would not understand what it was for something to be true, unless one knew that it is the truth that one aims at, in a certain sense. In the same way, one could know the extension of 'is a winning position', without understanding what winning is. One could know that a winning position in chess is when the opponent's king cannot avoid being taken on the next move, a winning position in bridge is when one scores more points than one's opponents, etc.; but one would not know what winning is unless one understood that it is winning that is, generically, what one aims to do in playing games: it is the *telos* of game-playing. In a similar way, truth is the *telos* of certain cognitive activities, notably, assertion (and related things such as belief). When one asserts, one aims, generically, to speak truly. If, for example, everyone started to aim to speak falsely, and this became common knowledge, then what was false would become the truth. It would be as if every utterance were prefixed with a tacit 'it is not the case that'.[14]

There is nothing in this account which tells against dialetheism. It is, in fact, quite neutral as to what *is* true. For what it is that fixes the extension of 'is true' we must, as in deflationist accounts, look elsewhere. Moreover, it may well be that there is no uniform answer to this question.[15] One sort of answer (the physical world) may be appropriate in dealing with assertions of the natural sciences; another (the existence of certain proofs) may be appropriate in dealing with statements of pure mathematics; another (certain kinds of social fiat) may be appropriate in dealing with discourse about legal rights, etc. And some of these possibilities also lead in the direction of dialetheism. Consider, for example, the last of these cases. If a duly constituted legislature passes legislation which makes it illegal for a certain person to do something (under one description) and makes it permissible for them (under another), this determines a true contradiction.[16] That arbitrary rules may eventuate in inconsistency is not news.[17]

The teleological account of truth may well, then, be a friend of dialetheism; it is certainly no foe.

---

[14] A similar account of truth is given by Grayling (1997), 179 ff. According to the account given there, to call something true is to evaluate it positively in a certain way. What is the end of such an evaluation? Grayling lists a number of ends, but notes that assertability may be seen as fundamental to all the others cited (p. 182).   [15] As Grayling (1997), 180 f. notes.
[16] See *In Contradiction*, ch. 13, esp. p. 232.   [17] See *In Contradiction*, 13.5.

2.5   THE PRAGMATIST THEORY OF TRUTH

The first of the traditional theories that I will look at is the pragmatist theory of truth. Important advocates of versions of this theory were the founding fathers of US philosophy, Peirce, James, and Dewey. According to pragmatism, something is true if it "works". The variations in the theory arise because of the different ways one may interpret 'works'. A central idea has always been that something works if it is verified in practice, and specifically by our sensory observations. This is the way I will interpret the notion here.

The first thing to note about this conception of truth is as follows. Only a very limited number of truth-bearers can be verified, directly, by observation. Though the early logical positivists claimed that all meaningful statements were, or were reducible to, ones that are directly verifiable, this idea ended in failure. We have to admit that there are meaningful statements that are not directly verifiable. How are we to understand talk of verification in these cases? The now familiar answer to this question is that a statement is verified if it has consequences that are, in fact, observed, and falsified if it has observable consequences that are not. An immediate consequence of this is that it makes little sense to talk of individual truth-bearers as being verified. The consequences of any one belief depend on what other things one believes. Our beliefs face the tribunal of empirical inquiry collectively, as Quine most famously observed. Hence it is better to talk of the truth of *theories*: deductively closed collections of truth-bearers.

Can inconsistent theories, i.e. theories that contain contradictory truth-bearers, be verified? The simple answer to this is 'yes'. Many have been. Bohr's original theory of the atom was inconsistent; yet it had striking observational confirmations. Newtonian dynamics was, for a long time, based on an inconsistent theory of infinitesimals. All of this is well known (and we will return to discuss the matter further in Chapter 9). Of course, if a theory is inconsistent, its underlying logic had better not be explosive. For we certainly do not perceive that everything of an observable kind is the case. But provided that a paraconsistent logic is used, there is absolutely no reason why a theory should not contain inconsistent statements of a non-observable kind, yet have quite consistent observable consequences, verified in the standard fashion.

One might argue at this point that a theory is not a candidate for the truth unless all its observable consequences under standard, classical, logic are observed—which no inconsistent theory's could be. Whatever the force of this philosophical move, it is out of place here. For pragmatism has no criterion for the truth of a theory other than verification, i.e. confirmed observable consequences. How such consequences are determined is of no relevance. If the theory works in practice, then it's true.

One might also try to argue that no inconsistent theory can be a candidate for the *real* truth: its acceptance can only ever be a temporary expedient. Bohr's theory, for example, was later replaced by another theory, as was the inconsistent infinitesimal calculus. These theories certainly were replaced,[18] but it can hardly be claimed

---

[18] Though the consistency of the replacement for Bohr's theory of the atom, based as it is on modern quantum mechanics, is still somewhat moot!

in this context that the acceptance of an inconsistent theory *must* be a temporary expedient. According to this account of truth, expedience is truth! And whilst an inconsistent theory—and indeed, any theory—may eventually be replaced, the claim that an inconsistent theory that has been verified is not a candidate for the truth, makes no sense unless one has criteria for the truth *other* than verification, which the pragmatist does not have.

The upshot of this discussion is that a pragmatic account of truth is not only quite compatible with the possibility of inconsistent theories being true, it actually protects inconsistent theories from important attacks to the effect that they cannot be true.

The preceding discussion relied on the fact that an inconsistent theory can have quite consistent observational consequences, if its underlying logic is paraconsistent. Before we leave the pragmatist theory of truth, let us ask what one would say of a theory whose observational consequences were themselves inconsistent. Could such a theory be verified? The answer, in fact, is still 'yes', provided that the consequences are of an appropriate kind. For inconsistent states of affairs *are* observed sometimes. For example, in visual illusions of certain kinds we perceive contradictory situations. Think for example, of perceiving "impossible objects", like cubes whose struts assume impossible orientations.[19] Such perceptions are not veridical, which we can tell, for example, by shifting the angle of perception. But I see no reason why a theory might not predict that an object have inconsistent properties, which were verified by perception "from all angles". And if so, it too would be verified *ceteris paribus*, and, assuming the pragmatic account of truth, true.

2.6 THE COHERENCE THEORY OF TRUTH

Let us turn now to the coherence theory of truth. Versions of this were endorsed by idealists such as Blanshard, and by some of the positivists, such as Neurath.[20] According to this theory, a truth-bearer is true if it belongs to a coherent, or perhaps better, maximally coherent, set of bearers. Just as with the pragmatist theory of truth, it is therefore more appropriate to talk of truth as applied to sets of truth-bearers in the first instance.

Of all theories of truth, the coherence theory is perhaps the most difficult to deal with here; but this difficulty arises because the notion of coherence itself has never really been satisfactorily spelled out. It is usually taken that consistency is a necessary condition for coherence. I will return to this later. No one has taken it to be a sufficient condition also. The reason is obvious; it is far too weak: any consistent truth-bearer is a member of some (maximally) consistent set of sentences. Some kind of deductive

---

[19] I will have more to say about this topic in Chapter 3.

[20] Standardly, Bradley is also cited as a coherence theorist; but this is severely misleading, if not plain false. He is more plausibly seen as subscribing, together with the early Moore and Russell, to a quite different theory: the identity theory. This can be thought of as an extreme form of the correspondence theory, where the correspondence is constituted by the identity relation. See Candlish (1989) and Baldwin (1991).

relationship is usually also required for coherence; for example, that each truth-bearer be entailed by others in the set. This is also a very weak condition, satisfied by any deductively closed set of sentences (theory). For if α and β are in a theory, so is $\alpha \wedge \beta$—which entails each of them. There must, therefore, be stronger criteria than this.

To understand what they might be, one needs to look at the rationale for the coherence theory of truth. Typically, those who endorsed the theory have held that it makes no sense to define truth in terms of some objective reality, independent of our cognitive functioning: there is no such thing, or if there is, we have no access to it. If we are to have any meaningful notion of truth, this can be defined only in terms of what we are justified in believing (maybe in the ideal limit). The criteria of coherence are therefore the criteria of justification.

Now, an important part of justification of any overall theory is empirical adequacy, that is, consonance with observation. This does not mean that a coherent set must include a statement describing *every* observation we make. Observation, as all admit, is fallible. For example, we all see things that are not really there sometimes. Hence, individual observation statements need not be in a coherent set if they fit ill with other aspects of the theory. This notion of fitting ill requires yet other criteria. (Again, consistency is not enough, since consistency may be produced in many ways—as Quine has always emphasized—some ways including the obdurate observation statement, some not.) And here the floodgates open: simplicity, explanatory power, non-adhocness, unity—whatever these things amount to. The upshot of all this for the present concern is that coherence is to be determined by a number of features including those of the kind I have just listed, plus consistency (maybe) and empirical adequacy.

Now let us return to the question of whether consistency is a necessary condition for coherence. However one cashes out the above criteria, it is clear that they may not all issue in the same verdict. One theory may be consistent but complex and highly *ad hoc*; another may be inconsistent, but simple and unified. Which theory is the most coherent in this situation? The only plausible answer would seem to be that it is the theory that is *overall* most satisfactory. That is, the most coherent theory is that which comes out best on most of the criteria. This is vague, but sufficient for present purposes.[21] For it is clear that if this is the case, inconsistency may be trumped by other considerations. (This was exactly what happened in the case of the Bohr theory of the atom for example.) Hence, consistency is not a necessary condition for coherence, merely one of a number of desiderata that may be overridden by other factors.

One may even raise the question of why consistency ought to be on the list at all. Of course, other desiderata require certain amounts of consistency. A theory could hardly be empirically adequate if it contained everything. But this does not require consistency as a *separate* desideratum.

One might argue that consistency is required because an inconsistent theory entails everything, which would certainly violate empirical adequacy. But this is a poor reply. For a start, if inconsistency is ruled out because it would violate empirical adequacy, it is hardly required as a separate criterion. More importantly, there is no reason to

---

[21] We will return to the issue in Chapters 7 and 8.

suppose that the underlying logic of the theory must be explosive. If coherence is our only criterion of truth, the true logic is to be determined holistically with the rest of the package, and it may well be that a theory based on a paraconsistent logic is overall simplest, least *ad hoc*, etc. Similarly, trying to justify consistency by appealing to the law of non-contradiction will not work: there is no *a priori* reason why the most coherent theory must contain this law.[22]

We see, then, that the coherence theory of truth does not mandate that the true (= most coherent) theory be consistent. Consistency may not even be a desideratum at all, except for such aspects of it as are required to fulfil other desiderata of coherence.

2.7 THE CORRESPONDENCE THEORY OF TRUTH

The final theory we will look at is also the most traditional: the correspondence theory of truth. It has its roots in Ancient and Medieval philosophy, but it flowered in early twentieth-century British philosophy. According to the correspondence theory, a true truth-bearer is one that corresponds to reality. A central problem in its articulation has always been how to spell out this notion of correspondence.

I have saved this theory till the last because it is the one, I think, that puts up the stiffest psychological resistance to the idea that there might be true contradictions. For it entails that reality itself is inconsistent in a certain sense, and how could that be? Reality is all there together: how could parts of it possibly contradict other parts?

One should note, for a start, that if one supposes reality to be constituted solely by (non-propositional) objects, like tables and chairs, it makes no sense to suppose that reality is inconsistent *or* consistent. This is simply a category mistake. But the most natural understanding of the correspondence theory of truth requires that there be more to reality than such objects. 'Brisbane is in Australia' is true because it corresponds to Brisbane's actually being in Australia. There must therefore be, in some sense, things like Brisbane's being in Australia, call them *facts* or *states of affairs* or whatnot. A correspondence theory of truth requires an account of things of this kind. One of the most sophisticated account ever given is undoubtedly that of Wittgenstein's *Tractatus*. And certainly, according to this, there are no contradictory facts.

But other accounts are possible. Here is one. The constituents of reality include a set of properties and relations, R, a set of objects, D, and a set of polarities, $\pi = \{0, 1\}$. Each property $r \in R$ has an adicity, n. I will indicate this with a subscript, thus: r_n. A (potential) atomic fact is a tuple $\langle r_n, d_1, \ldots, d_n, i \rangle$, where $r_n \in R$; $d_1, \ldots, d_n \in D$; $i \in \pi$. Intuitively, one can think of the fact $\langle r_n, d_1, \ldots, d_n, 1 \rangle$ as the fact that $d_1, \ldots, d_n$ are related by r_n (in that order), and $\langle r_n, d_1, \ldots, d_n, 0 \rangle$ as the fact that $d_1, \ldots, d_n$ are not related by r_n (in that order). Reality itself, W (the world), is just a certain set of atomic facts, the actual ones.

Given this account, it is a simple matter to articulate a correspondence notion of truth. Let $\mathcal{L}$ be the language obtained by closing atomic predications under negation, conjunction and disjunction and let δ be an assignment of meanings to the predicates

---

[22] Again, we will return to this matter in Chapter 7.

and constants of $\mathcal{L}$. Specifically, for each n-place predicate, P_n, $\delta(P_n)$ is an n-place relation in R; and for every constant c, $\delta(c)$ is in D. We define what it is for a sentence, α, to be true in W ($W \Vdash_T \alpha$) and false in W ($W \Vdash_F \alpha$), by standard recursive clauses:

$$W \Vdash_T P_n a_1 \ldots a_n \text{ iff } \langle \delta(P_n), \delta(a_1), \ldots, \delta(a_n), 1 \rangle \in W$$
$$W \Vdash_F P_n a_1 \ldots a_n \text{ iff } \langle \delta(P_n), \delta(a_1), \ldots, \delta(a_n), 0 \rangle \in W$$

$$W \Vdash_T \neg\alpha \text{ iff } W \Vdash_F \alpha$$
$$W \Vdash_F \neg\alpha \text{ iff } W \Vdash_T \alpha$$

$$W \Vdash_T \alpha \vee \beta \text{ iff } W \Vdash_T \alpha \text{ or } W \Vdash_T \beta$$
$$W \Vdash_F \alpha \vee \beta \text{ iff } W \Vdash_F \alpha \text{ and } W \Vdash_F \beta$$

The truth and falsity conditions for $\wedge$ are the obvious dual ones. $\Vdash_T$ is a correspondence relation; it holds between just those sentences that are true and the world. Moreover, as should be clear, it is quite possible for contradictions to be true. Ultimately, this is because W may contain both a "positive" fact, $\langle r_n, d_1, \ldots, d_n, 1 \rangle$, and its corresponding "negative" fact, $\langle r_n, d_1, \ldots, d_n, 0 \rangle$.

The theory is, in fact, a very well known one. It is essentially a simple part of situation-semantics, where atomic facts are more usually called 'states of affairs' or 'situation types' and sets of facts are called 'situations'.[23] A pair, $\langle W, \delta \rangle$, is also, essentially, a Dunn four-valued interpretation for the relevant logic of First Degree Entailment.[24] Hence, defining validity in terms of truth preservation over all such pairs characterizes validity in this paraconsistent logic.

The theory can be extended to handle more complex grammatical constructions, such as quantifiers and intensional operators, but the details of this are irrelevant to our present purpose, which is simply to illustrate what a correspondence theory of truth which allows for the possibility of true contradictions might be like. It is not metaphysically unproblematic. For example, one obvious question is what makes an atomic fact, such as $\langle r_n, d_1, \ldots, d_n, 1 \rangle$, a single entity, and not a mere congeries. This is a question that Wittgenstein struggled with in the *Tractatus*,[25] and one may simply run the same line as he did. Indeed, as far as I can see, one could simply rewrite the *Tractatus* substituting the above theory of facts for the one given there. The result would be almost exactly the same, except that the logic of the world would be First Degree Entailment and not classical logic.[26]

[23] See, e.g. Barwise and Perry (1983), esp. ch. 3.

[24] See, e.g. Priest (2002*b*), sect. 6.4, though things are set up slightly differently there. To translate: the extension of a predicate, $E(P)$, is simply $\{\langle d_1, \ldots, d_n \rangle; \langle \delta(P), d_1, \ldots, d_n, 1 \rangle \in W\}$, and the anti-extension, $A(P)$, is $\{\langle d_1, \ldots, d_n \rangle; \langle \delta(P), d_1, \ldots, d_n, 0 \rangle \in W\}$. $1 \in \nu(\alpha)$ iff $W \Vdash_T \alpha$, and $0 \in \nu(\alpha)$ iff $W \Vdash_F \alpha$. If we add the constraint that for any P and $d_1, \ldots, d_n$, $\langle \delta(P), d_1, \ldots, d_n \rangle \in E(P) \cup A(P)$, we get the logic *LP*.

[25] Not very successfully, I think. See Priest (1995*a*), ch. 12.

[26] There are a few inessential differences. For example, the above account distinguishes between properties and objects, whilst Wittgenstein talks just of objects. For him, however, objects have possiblities of combination internal to them. These possibilities will not be the same for all objects. It is therefore quite possible that properties form a distinct subclass of Wittgensteinian objects.

Are there any reasons for supposing that the above theory is metaphysically incoherent—or at least metaphysically incoherent in the way that the *Tractatus* is not? A correspondence theory of truth needs to suppose that there are, in some sense, facts in the world; it does not, though, have to suppose that there are facts corresponding to all true sentences: disjunctive facts, general facts, etc. (though it may[27]). The truth of disjunctions, generalizations, etc., can simply be defined in terms of more basic facts. The account just given does not have disjunctive facts or conjunctive facts, but it does have negative facts of a certain kind (things of the form $\langle r_n, d_1, \ldots, d_n, 0 \rangle$). Now many have felt a great reluctance to admit the existence of negative facts. For example, in his lectures on Logical Atomism, Russell, who did, in fact, accept the existence of negative facts at the time, writes:

Are there negative facts? Are there such facts as you might call 'Socrates is not alive'? . . . One has a certain repugnance to negative facts, the same sort of feeling that makes you wish not to have a fact '*p* or *q*' going about the world. You have a feeling that there are only positive facts, and that negative propositions have somehow or other got to be expressions of positive facts.[28]

What is this repugnance? One source of it is, I suspect, the obvious truth that everything that exists *is*. Add to this the thought that negative facts are *not*, and it follows that no such facts exist. This is a confusion, however, as old as Parmenides: negative facts are *not*, in the sense that they ground truths of the form 'it is not the case that so an so', but they *are* in exactly the same way that all existent things are, viz. they are part of reality.

An explicit argument against the possibility of negative facts was given by one of the people who heard Russell's lectures. According to Demos (1917), 189, negative facts are not to be countenanced since they are 'nowhere to be met with in experience'. Now it is not clear that we meet *any* facts in experience. We meet with people, stars, chairs, and other objects, but not facts or states of affairs. And if this is so, and the objection is cogent, it tells against all correspondence theories of truth. But, it might be argued, we do see facts: we see, e.g. that the sun is shining; but we never see negative facts, e.g. that it is not shining. This is a dubious argument, though: one *can* see negative facts. I can see, for example, that there is no one in the room when I walk through the door. Moreover, to be translucent is not to be opaque, and vice versa; yet I can see that something is translucent, and see that something is opaque. Whichever, then, is the negative fact, it can be seen.[29] In any case, Demos' objection is flawed by its simple empiricism. Why should one suppose that the mere fact that one cannot perceive a kind of entity entail that it does not exist? No reason that I can see, especially if one is a metaphysical realist of a kind that the correspondence theory is likely to appeal to.

---

[27] In (1969) van Fraassen gives a fact-based semantics for First Degree Entailment that has facts corresponding to all true sentences.   [28] Pears (1972), 67.

[29] For further discussion, see Chapters 3 and 9. It may also be worth noting that one of the motivations for situation semantics was to give an account of the semantics of verbs such as 'sees that', and this explicilty allows for seeings to have negative contents. See, e.g. Barwise and Perry (1983), 182, 204.

Another objection to a theory with negative facts might focus on the polarity objects, 0 and 1. What strange beasts are these? Of course, the use of 0 and 1 themselves here is purely conventional. Nor does one have to think of these things as objects. They simply code the fact that there are two ways that r_n, say, may relate to $d_1, \ldots, d_n$: positively or negatively. It is certainly the case that this polarity is built into reality. But there are lots of polarities built into physical reality (think, for example, of being a left hand or a right hand, or of the spin of an atomic particle). I don't see why metaphysical polarities should be any worse than these.

A final objection to the theory is possible because there are *two* relations of correspondence, $\Vdash_T$ and $\Vdash_F$. Given the symmetry between these, what makes *one* of these the truth? A first answer is that $\Vdash_T$ is truth because of its relation to the positive polarity, 1. But this just defers the question. 1 and 0 are symmetric, too. What makes one of them the one relevant to truth? The only answer that a correspondence theorist can give, as far as I can see, is simply that it is a brute fact. But more importantly here, one should note that *exactly* the same problem besets a theory where there are only positive facts. There is still a symmetry between truth and falsity in this. What makes one of these the truth? A first answer is that one is truth because of its relation to *existent* facts; falsity relates to non-existent facts. But again, this just defers the question. Existence and non-existence are symmetric too. What makes existence relevant to truth? Again, the only answer that a correspondence theorist would appear to be able to give is simply that it is a brute fact.

Maybe there are other arguments against negative facts,[30] but as far as I can see, this notion is in no way more problematic that the notion of a fact in general.

Even given the legitimacy of the notion of negative facts, one might still object that the above account does not make true contradictions possible, simply because this requires the world, W, to contain a positive fact and its corresponding negative fact, which cannot happen. But why not? Notice that the theory of facts, itself, delivers a *prima facie* presumption that this is perfectly possible. All the atomic facts, whether positive or negative, are independent entities, and can be mixed and matched at will.[31] It is, of course, possible, that there are considerations that override this presumption (for example, considerations which motivate the law of non-contradiction for other reasons), but these are not arguments that derive from the theory of facts itself, or from the correspondence theory of truth, which, as we have seen, is quite compatible with the existence of true contradictions.

---

[30] There is only one part of the *Tractatus* I am aware of which may be interpreted as an *argument* to the effect that there are no negative facts. At 4.0621 Wittgenstein says: 'It is important that "p" and "$\sim p$" *can* say the same thing. For it shows that nothing in reality corresponds to the sign "$\sim$".' What, I take it, Wittgenstein is pointing to here is that p and $\sim p$ have the same content, in the sense that what one affirms the other denies. But this commonality of content is explained, on the present account, by the fact that $\langle r_n, a_1, \ldots, a_n, 1 \rangle$ and $\langle r_n, a_1, \ldots, a_n, 0 \rangle$ share everything but their polarity bit.

[31] As Wittgenstein puts it, *Tractatus*, 1.2, 1.21: 'The world divides into facts. Each item can be the case or not the case while everything else remains the same.'

2.8 CONCLUSION

We have now considered six accounts of truth. There are certainly others, but, at any rate, these exhaust the major views on the subject. As we have seen, none of them provides any reason for rejecting dialetheism; a number of them even point in its direction. If there are arguments against dialetheism, the friends of consistency will therefore have to look elsewhere to find them. Perhaps the obvious place to look is to the notion of negation. We will turn to this in the second part of the book. We have not finished with truth yet: there is more to be said about the view that everything is true—trivialism.

3

Trivialism

3.1 INTRODUCTION

Is everything true? The answer, presumably, is no—and there is not likely to be much disagreement about that. But how do you know? As we saw in Chapter 1, Aristotle gave a number of arguments against trivialism. But as we also saw there, his arguments are less than successful. This chapter concerns whether it is possible to do better. The question of how you know that not everything is true may seem a rather arcane one, but it is certainly a significant one for a dialetheist. The trivialist believes that *all* contradictions are true. (Indeed, assuming that one believes a conjunction iff one believes both conjuncts, this is an alternative characterization of the trivialist.) It is often said by way of objection to dialetheism that if one is a dialetheist, one might just as well be a trivialist. This is a silly objection, as are most slides from 'some' to 'all'. (Compare: you believe some things to be true; why don't you believe all things to be true?[1]) Nonetheless, even though this is not a good objection, the question of why one should not accept everything is one that an honest dialetheist will ask themself. The question is also significant for a non-dialetheist; I will explain why later in the chapter.

The question of how to justify the common-sense view concerning trivialism is, in fact, one that can be interpreted in different ways. For a start, we need to distinguish between the following interpretations:

Interpretation 1: We do, presumably, have good grounds for supposing that trivialism is unacceptable. What are they?
Interpretation 2: Suppose that you met someone who took everything to be true. How could you justify your position *vis à vis* theirs?

If the distinction is not clear, just reflect on the following analogy. I know that I have some money in my bank account. You have no reason to doubt my word for this. But you may still ask how I know. I can then give you the following sort of explanation: 'In my last bank statement there was a certain amount of money in the account.

---

[1] I often find myself being asked the following question: 'Since you believe some contradictions, but not all, you must have a criterion for deciding between those that are true and those that are not. What is it?' In reply I usually point out that the questioner believes that some things are true, but not all, and ask them what criterion they have for deciding between those things that are true and those that are not. The answer is, I think, the same in both cases. Nice as it would be to have a criterion of truth, to expect one would seem to be utopian. One has to treat each case on its merits, whether the proposition concerned is a contradiction or some other thing.

I haven't spent that much since then, and the bank virtually never makes accounting errors.' This is a perfectly acceptable answer. But suppose that I meet a sceptic, who is convinced that I do not know that I have money in my account; then considerations of the kind just adduced will not be at all acceptable. They will fall to the usual range of sceptical considerations. In the same way, **Interpretation 1** takes it for granted that not everything is true, and just asks for an explanation of how we know this. But in a confrontation with a trivialist, the situation is quite different. One cannot, in this case, take it for granted that not everything is true: that, after all, is exactly what is at issue. A much more robust justification is required. This is **Interpretation 2**, and is much harder. Given the fact that the trivialist will agree with everything that is said, it is not even clear how to conceptualize the issue adequately.

I return to **Interpretation 2** in the second part of this chapter. In the first half we will look at **Interpretation 1**.

3.2 SEEING CONTRADICTIONS

Concerning **Interpretation 1** of the request for justification, I will argue that we have good *a posteriori* grounds for supposing that trivialism is unacceptable. To make the case for this, however, we need to look carefully at the connection between perception and contradiction.

When it is suggested that contradictions might be true, many an analytic philosopher will screw up their face into a look of anguish, and say 'But I just don't *see* what it could be for a contradiction to be true'. They might mean many things by this. 'See' might simply mean 'understand', in which case they might be complaining that classical two-valued semantics leaves no room, as it were, for something to be both true and false. Such a lack of understanding can be rectified by explaining to them the semantics of a suitable paraconsistent logic, which does allow for this possibility. But often, I think, the angst (real or imagined) is of another kind. What such a philosopher is trying to do is *imagine* what it would be like for a situation to be contradictory. They are trying to visualize how an inconsistent situation might look—and they fail. But it can be done.

3.3 PERCEPTUAL ILLUSIONS

How can one visualize a contradictory state? To visualize a situation (literally) it must, of course, be one of a visible kind. The Liar sentence might be true and false; and indeed one might be able to construct some quasi-visual mental representation of this fact; but the state of affairs itself is not of a kind that we can see, or, therefore, literally visually depict. Other things that have been suggested as true contradictions look more promising as candidates for a visible contradiction. It can be argued that some instantaneous transition states are contradictory; that, for example, at the instant a person leaves the room, they are both in it and not in it.[2] Now, being in a room and not being in it *are* the kinds of things that can be seen. Do we, in this situation, then, perceive a contradiction? No. For the contradictory state in question here is an instantaneous one, and one can perceive states only if they persist for some minimal time. (Suppose, for example, that you are watching something red which turns green for exactly an instant before becoming red again. You would perceive the thing as continuously red. The greenness has no duration.) Hence, though a moving object may realize instantaneous contradictory states, these are not such as can be seen.

But we are looking in the wrong place, and missing the obvious. The strategy pursued so far was: find a true contradictory state of affairs and look at it. If we were to succeed in this enterprise, the content of our visual experience would, by definition, be veridical. But the contents of our visual experiences are not always so: we experience many kinds of visual illusions. These are not necessarily of contradictory situations. Many, in fact, most, optical illusions are of quite consistent situations: they are just not veridical. Consider, for example, the well-known Hermann grid, a white grid on a black background. (See Fig. 1[3]) When one looks at this, one sees dark patches at the interstices of the grid. The dark patches are not really there, but there is nothing contradictory about the way the figure appears. There are, however, visual illusions where what is perceived is not consistent.[4] I will give three here.

Fig. 1   Hermann grid

---

[2] See *In Contradiction*, ch. 11.   [3] This is taken from Gregory and Gombrich (1973), 23.
[4] Let me state the obvious: I am not using 'perceive' here as factive, but merely as a way of referring to a perceptual phenomenological content.

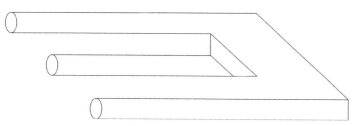

Fig. 2   Schuster figure

Example 1. The first kind of example concerns impossible figures: drawings of (or photographs which appear to be of) things which are physically impossible. These have become very familiar thanks to the art of Maurits Escher.[5] Not all impossible figures depict what we require, however. Consider, for example, the Schuster figure (Fig. 2). At the right end, the figure appears to have two protuberances; at the left, it appears to have three prongs. One can focus on either end of the figure and see that part coherently; but there is no way that one can focus on the whole and see it coherently. (This, at least, is my reaction.) One never, therefore, sees a contradictory situation. One can see parts of the situation, each of which is quite consistent.

But the situation is different with other impossible figures. Look, for example, at the Penroses' figure (Fig. 3). If one takes a corner, say the nearest one, one can see that, travelling continuously counter-clockwise, one can ascend to arrive back at the same place. The point, then, is higher than itself (but obviously, it is not higher than itself, as well). Moreover, one can take the whole figure in, visually parse it, all in one go. This *is* a case where we can see a contradictory situation.[6]

There is an intriguing auditory analogue of the continuously ascending staircase. It is possible to produce a collection of musical tones which appear to be continuously ascending in pitch whilst, at the same time, never getting any higher—again, a contradictory situation.[7]

---

[5] A general discussion of them can be found in Penrose and Penrose (1958); Robinson, J. O. (1972), 176; Gregory and Gombrich (1973), 86–8. Figs. 2 and 3 come from Robinson.

[6] The paper on which this part of the chapter is based drew flak from two referees at this point. One argued that we do not see that the corner is higher than itself, but we infer that it is. I think that this is a false dichotomy. *Seeing that* is always an interpretative process, and inference may well play some role in a rational reconstruction of how it proceeds. A trained eye might be able to see immediately that a person is suffering from jaundice, and no doubt it is the yellowness of the skin that informs this judgment. They see the jaundice nonetheless. Indeed, in the kind of pattern-matching that neural networks do, it is often hard to distinguish between perception and analogical inference. And whatever the facts of this matter, it remains the case that one can see that, by continuously ascending, one can return to where one started, a mathematical impossibility in a Euclidean space. A second referee objected that the illusion does not show what it would be like for the world to be inconsistent, because any normal object that appeared that way would not look contradictory from a different angle. Whether or not this is so, this is beside the point—which is that if the world were inconsistent (in a certain way), it would appear as does the illusion.

[7] See Shepard (1964) and (1983). An audio version of this is Tenney (1992).

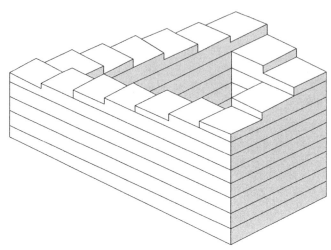

Fig. 3   Penrose figure

Example 2. The second kind of example concerns motion. It is often called the 'waterfall effect', and depends on a certain kind of visual afterimage.[8] If the visual field is conditioned by viewing continuous motion of a certain kind, say a rotating spiral, when the viewer then looks at a stationary scene, it appears to be moving in the opposite direction. But a point at the top of the visual field, say, does not appear to change place. As Blakemore puts it:

Any object viewed after looking at movement seems to be drifting in the opposite direction. And yet the apparently *moving* object does not appear to change its *position* relative to its surroundings.[9]

Yet to move is to change position. The situation is, therefore, contradictory.

An illusion of the same kind can be obtained with certain drugs. For example, if one consumes enough alcohol, then before one passes out, one's environment—the room—appears to "swim", that is, move—usually, spin. If one now focuses one's attention on a point in the room, it appears to be stationary. The rest of the visual field, however, appears to continue moving. But the internal spatial relations between the fixed part and the moving part do not appear to change. Again, we have a perception of stationary motion.

Example 3. The third example concerns colour. It is well known that the brain will "fill in" details of the optical field that are not there; for example, to fill in the fovea (blind spot). Now suppose a subject is shown a field, half of which is red and half of which is green, the two halves being separated by a black line. If the line is then

[8] It is disussed in Robinson, J. O. (1972), 227–33 and Gregory and Gombrich (1973), 30.
[9] Gregory and Gombrich (1973), 36. His italics.

removed, the brain fills in colours in the vacated space, and some observers report seeing that the boundary is now red and green.[10]

It may be possible to obtain a similar experience in a different way. It is easy to construct a pair of glasses that have a red filter on one lens and a green filter on the other. (It is possible to buy glasses of this kind for viewing old-fashioned 3-D films.) If I put such glasses on, and allow perception to stabilize, everything appears a uniform brownish hue. But for a short space of time,[11] until things stabilize, I have the very strange experience of seeing everything as red and as green, though the red and the green seem, somehow, to be at different depths in the visual field.

It might be said that being red and green is not a contradiction. But it is: red and green are complementary colours. It is, hence, a conceptual impossibility for something to be both colours. A feature of complementary colours is that they can't go together. There is no reddy-green, in the same way, for example, that there is a reddy-blue. Something that is red and green, is red and not red.

These examples show that it is quite possible to perceive a contradictory situation. What is it like to see something that is, at once, both higher than itself and no higher than itself? Consult the first example. What is it like to see something that is moving and not moving? Consult the second. What is it like to see something that is red all over and not red all over? Consult the third. Of course, the examples are not veridical; they are illusions; but they fulfil the required function nonetheless. They show that we may have perceptual experiences the contents of which are contradictory.[12]

3.4 THE NON-TRIVIALITY OF THE WORLD

After this prolegomenon, we may now return to trivialism. The cup in front of me sits on a table, and these are at rest with respect to each other. How do I know that they are not also not at rest, that is, in motion? I can see it. I know what it is like for things to be both at rest and in motion with respect to each other. That is exactly how things appear in example number two, and it is not like that. This, at any rate, is one contradiction I can see not to obtain. Similarly, the grass before me is green. How do I know that it is not also red? Again, I can see it. I know what it is like for something

---

[10] The experiment was done by Crane and Piantinada (1983). It is discussed in Hardin (1988), 124 ff. (I am grateful to Allen Hazen for drawing my attention to these.) It must be stressed that, unlike the first two examples, this is a relatively new result, and more work may need to be done to confirm it. It should also be stressed that not all observers report seeing the same thing. Some observers report seeing different kinds of "filling in".

[11] Maybe half a second, though I can hold it a bit longer sometimes. I should stress, also, that the experiences I report here are mine; I make no claim that everyone sees the same thing. It is not uncommon for different people to report different colour experiences under unusual conditions.

[12] I am indebted to Henry Flynt for making me see that phenomena of the kind described in this section are important—though we may disagree about what that importance is. Since the early 1970s, Flynt has been exploring the idea of taking illusions as the semantic content of inconsistent expressions; a number of his pieces of art relate to this idea. See, e.g. Flynt (1974; 1997).

to be both red and green. That is how things appear in example number three, and it is not like that. A similar argument can be based on example number one. I leave this as an exercise. We know, then, that the world is not trivial, since we can see that this is so.

One can put the point in an alternative way—I do so for the second example; it can be made the same way for the others. I see that the cup and table are at rest relative to each other. I do not see that they are in relative motion, which I would do if they were—even if they were at rest *and* in motion. There is something, then, about the world that fails to obtain.

These considerations, like all *a posteriori* considerations, are defeasible. Observation is as fallible matter, and what appears to be the case may not, in fact, be so. If it turned out, for example, that supposing grass in Australia to be red and green all over allowed us to explain and predict every fluctuation of the Australian dollar, but had no other untoward consequences, we would have strong evidence that our senses deceive us in this case, and that Australian grass is red and green. But there is no cogent evidence that our perception ever does deceive us by making an inconsistent situation appear consistent. Hence, the reasoning stands.

It is, in some sense, *a priori* possible that an inconsistent object appear in a consistent way. Indeed, a sceptic holds that our perceptions may always fail to reflect how things are. And a trivialist, who holds that everything is the case, will hold that all our consistent perceptions are misleading. Against such opponents, the above argument carries no weight—nor does any *a posteriori* argument. What to say about such a case we will turn to in the second half of the chapter.

3.5 THE CONSISTENCY OF THE EMPIRICAL WORLD

But before we look to this, let us pause to note one other fact. As I have argued, our perception tells us that not everything is true. We may establish something stronger and more interesting. Let us work our way up to it.

When we perceive, we can see that something *is* the case. Can we also perceive that something is *not* the case? Some have thought not.[13] We can perceive only that something *is* the case. For example, we cannot see that something is not green. We can see only that it is red. Any judgment to the effect that it is not green has to be added to what we see by inference. This, as we now see, is false. I can see directly that something is not green. Or consider another example: you enter a room; the whole room is visible from where you stand; there is no one there. You can see that Pierre is not in the room. No Pierre-shaped objects meet the eye.[14] Even the very distinction between seeing what is the case and what is not the case is a false one. Some seeings are both. With respect to actual physical objects, to be transparent is not to be opaque, and vice versa. But you can see that something is transparent and you can see that something is opaque.

---

[13] e.g., Vasil'év (1913).   [14] The example comes from Sartre (1943), ch. 1, sect. 2.

Next: if α and β are actual observable states of affairs, then so is their conjunction. We can see that something is a cat; we can see that the thing is black. Hence, we can see that it is a black cat. The principle needs appropriate qualification. If α and β record states of affairs that arise only at different times, or at places such that one cannot see both at once, then the principle is obviously not true. More importantly, it can be the case that one of the conjuncts occludes the others. Thus, suppose that α is 'the street sign is blue' and β is 'it is night'. Both of these states of affairs are observable, but if it is, indeed, night, then one cannot see that the street sign in question is blue. When we apply the principle, it must be with the appropriate qualifications.

To apply it: let α describe an observable state of affairs, that x is happening here and now. Then $\neg\alpha$ describes another observable state of affairs, that x is not happening here and now. But then the conjunction $\alpha \wedge \neg\alpha$ also describes an observable state of affairs. That is, if such a state of affairs were ever to be the case, it could be seen. Clearly, in applying the principle we do not need to worry about α and $\neg\alpha$ being at different places or at different times. But what of the possibility of occlusion? (This is raised by Beall (2000).[15]) Might it not be the case that our cognitive functioning makes it impossible for us to see inconsistent states of affairs? Maybe our perceptual mechanisms impose a "consistency filter" on what we see, so that we see only one of the conjuncts, which masks out the other? This is certainly an empirical possibility. But there is no empirical evidence that I know of to suppose that there is such a filter. Indeed, there is every reason to suppose that there is not. For as the examples of section 3.3 show, we *can* see both conjuncts of an inconsistent state of affairs. Beall raises the more general worry that we may just not know what contradictions look like.[16] If δ is an observable state of affairs, for example, what does $(\delta \wedge \neg\delta) \wedge \neg(\delta \wedge \neg\delta)$ look like? But we *do* know what contradictions look like. That, again, is what 3.3 showed us. In particular, $(\delta \wedge \neg\delta) \wedge \neg(\delta \wedge \neg\delta)$ is logically equivalent to $\delta \wedge \neg\delta$, and so would look like that. Still, it might be suggested, for all we know an inconsistent situation could appear quite consistent. But if one were to endorse a claim of this kind, we would collapse into total scepticism. Maybe, for all we know, people can appear like fried eggs; square things can appear round, etc. For such a worry to bite, there must be specific grounds for supposing things may not be as they appear to be. Are there such grounds? None that I am aware of.[17]

And now to the point. Consider the observable world, i.e. all that is observably the case. If there were inconsistencies in this, it would follow from the above that we would perceive them. But apart from the odd visual illusion, we do not: our perceptions of the world are entirely consistent. Hence, the observable world is consistent. Again, we can put the point in another way. If I look out of the window at the grass, I can

---

[15] Beall also has another objection, to the effect that though it may be true that one can see the contradiction, it does not follow that one would see it. I am not sure that I see the force of this objection. Would if what? If it can be seen then we will see it if we look in the right direction, have our eyes open, etc.   [16] As does Olin (2003), 31.

[17] But there certainly could be. Suppose it were to turn out that, according to the best theory of vagueness, statements about the borderline area of a sorites progression are true and false. Then one would have to accept that a contradiction might appear as how things appear in the borderline of an observable sorites (e.g. reddish-blue)—which would *seem* to be quite consistent.

see that it is green. How do I know that it is not also red, that is, not green? If it were red, I would see that it is—even if it were red and green—which I do not. Similarly for other observable situations.[18]

Here, again, it is possible to object. We do have perceptions with contradictory contents: the visual illusions themselves. Why, in this context, are we entitled to assume that they are illusions? The question is a good one, but there are simple answers. In the case of the first example, we are not actually perceiving a situation at all, simply a picture of one, which we interpret in a certain way. The second example is more complicated. How do I know that when I perceive the waterfall illusion, or am drunk, the room is not both moving and stationary? First, there is the testimony of my other senses. If I touch the spinning wall, it feels (consistently) stationary. Second, there is the testimony of others. Everyone else who perceives the room—or at least, everyone else who is capable of saying anything coherent to me—does not see it in the way that I do. Third, there are all sorts of other information. If the room were really spinning, the lamp would swing, things would fall off shelves, etc. Whilst all these facts could be explained away, the simplicity of the hypothesis that the apparent motion of the room is entirely subjective makes this overwhelming. The third example is very similar. How do I know that the room does not go red and green all over when I put on the glasses? Again, the facts that only I see it in this way, that the colouring comes and goes with the glasses, etc., clearly make the hypothesis that the colouring is subjective a superior one.

Could it be the case that, in the future, science will be able to conjure up actual situations that are inconsistent, perceivably so, and not illusions? Who knows?—science is a strange thing. But for the present, at least, there is good reason to suppose that the perceivable world is consistent.

Perhaps this is a major reason why a number of philosophers are not prepared to countenance dialetheism—unless that countenance be screwed up in anguish. Take the conclusion that the perceivable world is consistent, throw in a simple empiricism—what is so in the perceivable world is so everywhere—and the result follows. Given the state of modern science, the shortcomings of such empiricism, and so of this argument, require no further comment.

3.6 THE TRIVIALIST

Let us now turn to **Interpretation 2** of the request for justification, the harder issue of how one can justify one's position *vis à vis* trivialism against the trivialist themself.

---

[18] The conclusion here is, again, *a posteriori* and fallible. In particular, if it ever transpired that there were certain kinds of inconsistent situations that our perceptual apparatus could not take in, the conclusion would fold. Beall (2000) argues that although there is no reason to believe that we could see that $\alpha \wedge \neg\alpha$, were it true, nonetheless, when we see one of the conjuncts it is reasonable to believe that only it obtains, rather than the conjunction. He does this on the ground of simplicity—or better, a "principle of least action" in the same family as Occam's razor: don't accept more than is necessary to explain the situation. So, in the end, there is not much difference between us. We both take the inference from the statement of perception to a statement about the world to be a reasonable default inference.

Note that this problem of justification is just as hard for the classical logician as it is for the dialetheist. In reply to **Interpretation 1** of the question of justification, the classical logician can give a very simple answer. We know *a priori* that no contradictions are true. *A fortiori*, some things are not true. The dialetheist will, of course, contest the first claim: one cannot know *a priori* what is not true; they can, though, give an *a posteriori* justification as we have just seen (which is equally available to the classical logician).

But for **Interpretation 2**, the classical logician and the dialetheist are in exactly the same boat. No appeal to the properties of classical logic is going to help against the trivialist: the trivialist *agrees with* classical logic! Every principle of inference that a classical logician subscribes to, such as that a contradiction entails everything, the trivialist subscribes to too (indeed, this might be why they became a trivialist in the first place). Every semantic principle that the classical logician subscribes to, such as that nothing is both true and false, the trivialist subscribes to too. One cannot, therefore, simply appeal to classical logic when faced with the trivialist.

To get a feeling for the full difficulty of the problem, it will be helpful, for a start, to return to the analogy that I noted in section 3.1 between the trivialist and the sceptic. The trivialist will subscribe to everything;[19] the sceptic will subscribe to nothing. In this respect, they are dual figures. And both take such extreme positions that it is difficult for those who wish to hold the middle ground to know where to start the debate. It might be thought that, at least historically, scepticism and trivialism are not on a par. For there have certainly been sceptics, such as Sextus Empiricus; but there have been no trivialists. This is less than clear, though. As we saw in section 1.5, Aristotle takes Heraclitus and Protagoras to be trivialists—though whether this is fair to them may be a moot point. Perhaps more importantly, it is not at all clear that there have *really* been any sceptics. Sextus certainly claimed to be, but the fact that he navigated his way around his world may suggest that he did really believe some things to be true rather than others. At this point, we have already engaged in substantive philosophical issues; ones we will, in fact, return to later.[20]

In any case, whether there have really been any sceptics or trivialists is unimportant. It is the positions themselves that are important. Both of them are extreme and incredible, but it is exactly by taking such extreme views as foils that we come to understand better our own views, as the generations of debate related to scepticism have demonstrated in epistemology.

So how does one justify one's view *vis à vis* the trivialist's? Before we can engage the issue, there is a problem even about how to conceptualize it. It is easy enough to show that trivialism is not true—indeed, necessarily so. For it is either true or it is not. But

---

[19] In particular, the trivialist is not just someone who accepts 'Everything is true' (though they accept that too). The trivialist accepts *everything*. One who accepts that everything is true might yet not accept everything—if they do not accept universal instantiation, the *T*-schema, or *modus ponens*.

[20] Trivialism would seem to have a dual postion: that everything is false. Oddly, though, these two positions are one and the same. For if everything is true, 'everything is false' is true, so everything is false. And if everything is false, 'something is false' is false, and so everything is true. Now, there certainly have been philosophers who held that everything is false. For example, Bradley held that this was, strictly speaking, the case.

if it is true, it follows that it is not true (everything follows). Hence, in either case, it is not true. Does this settle the issue? Not at all: for the trivialist accepts that everything is not true! Quite generally, one cannot simply enter into debate with the trivialist as to whether or not everything is true. In fact, there is no point in engaging in debate with the trivialist about *anything*. We know that they are going to agree in advance! There is, as far as I can see, no way of getting the trivialist to change their position at all. Just because everything one says is something that they already believe, there is nothing one can say that will have the slightest purchase.

It makes more sense to ask how one would justify one's view to some independent third party, an arbitrator. The third party may be supposed to be neutral on the issue, at least initially. The job for each of the first two parties is to persuade them. The arbitrator will listen to arguments from each side, and, if convinced by either party, will judge in their favour.[21]

Convincing the arbitrator is still not as easy as it might at first appear, though. In particular, one must still not beg the question, or the arbitrator will rule 'foul'. For example, an obvious argument to use is that the trivialist's position is inconsistent, and so ought not to be believed. (Naturally, a dialetheist is not going to make this objection; but a classical logician might.) It is clear that this argument fails, though, since it begs the question. The trivialist affirms everything, including all contradictions. Simply to claim that these cannot be true is to take for granted part of what is at issue.

So what arguments can be used? There are a number of possible answers to this question, but I shall not attempt an exhaustive discussion here. What I will do is consider three answers that are interesting. The first two are less than completely successful, as I will argue; the third, I hope, is.[22]

3.7 ARGUMENT ONE: EVIDENCE

The first argument is as follows. The trivialist believes many strange things. They believe, for example, that you are a scrambled egg. This is objectionable since there is just no evidence to justify it. The rational person should not believe anything for which there is no reason. The arbitrator must agree. And if the trivialist argues that there is a reason, namely that it follows from trivialism, then it is they who now beg the question. The trivialist will also claim that there is independent evidence. (They will claim everything.) But claiming does not, of course, make it so. The evidence needs to be produced for the arbitrator.

---

[21] One might object here as follows. Since the arbitrator must agree with neither party initially, there must be something that they do not believe, viz. that any one of the parties is right. Hence, they cannot be a trivialist, and so are not neutral. But the fact that the arbitrator *does not* believe trivialism, does not entail that they *do* believe that trivialism is untrue. Hence, this does not threaten their impartiality.

[22] What is the modal status of the claim that everything is true? As we will note in sect. 8.4, there is indeed a world where everything is true; but the laws of logic there are not the same as those of the actual world (whatever one takes this to be)—every entailment is true there. Trivialism is, therefore, logically impossible. But it is quite possible to defend a logically impossible view in debate (e.g. any logical theory that is actually false).

Unfortunately, the trivialist is not out yet. There *is* evidence independent of trivialism that you are a scrambled egg. Consider a sequence of objects obtained, at each step, by replacing a micron of you with a micron of scrambled egg. I start with an object that is you, and if I have an object that is you, and replace a micron with a micron of scrambled egg, it is still you. Hence, the final stage of the sequence is still you. And the final stage is a scrambled egg. Hence, you are a scrambled egg. This argument depends in no way at all on trivialism.

Naturally, we will take it that there is something wrong with the argument. If it were patently invalid, say it proceeded by asserting the consequent, it would be easy enough to justify this. But the only form of inference that the argument uses (albeit 10^6 times) is *modus ponens*, and this is valid, at least *prima facie*. Moreover, its only premises (that you are you, and that something that is you is still you if a micron is exchanged) are also *prima facie* true. Hence the argument does appear to be sound. The trivialist has shifted the onus of proof.

If the argument were produced by a non-trivialist, we could say that since the conclusion is absurd—one can see, after all, that the conclusion fails—there must be *something* wrong with it. But against the trivialist, this move is of no avail, for it clearly begs the question. One might try a stronger argument. Let a be any physical object, and let F be any property, tolerant in its applicability with respect to small changes, possessed by some possible physical object, b. Then if soritical reasoning were sound, we could construct (at least in thought) a sequence of objects, each barely different from its predecessor, running between a and b, and hence establish that Fa.[23] In other words, if soritical reasoning were legitimate, we could show that every physical object has every tolerant physically possible property. Hence, soritical reasoning cannot be legitimate. Against an ordinary opponent, this argument is conclusive. But against the trivialist, the argument begs the question just as before. The trivialist holds that every physical object *does* have all such properties.

Let us take stock. Sorites reasoning of the kind we have been looking at does not establish trivialism in general. There is no way (as far as I can see) to use such reasoning to show that physical objects have all *sharp* properties (or to show anything much at all about non-physical objects—if there are any). It does not, therefore, constitute a complete reply to objection number one. But such reasoning does appear to show that every physical object has every tolerant physically possible property. Since this encompasses virtually every object and property we commonly deal with, this is as near trivialism as makes no difference for practical purposes. Let us call a person who takes all physical objects to have all such properties a *near-trivialist*. The sorites argument does provide a defence of near-trivialism against objection number one.[24]

---

[23] Most of the objects in question are, of course, hypothetical, rather than actual; but such is the case in most sorites arguments.

[24] It might be thought that standard solutions to the sorites paradoxes would be of some help here, but they are not. There are many proffered solutions, but each of them has some strongly unintuitive feature. Indeed, necessarily so. For the soritical reasoning is both simple and intuitively correct. This does not show that, as solutions to the sorites paradox, they are wrong. But it does show that they cannot shift the relevant onus of proof. In other words, in the present context, they are of no help.

3.8   ARGUMENT TWO: MEANING

For the next argument we return to Aristotle. As discussed in Chapter 1, in *Metaphysics* Γ 4, Aristotle gave a number of arguments in support of the Law of Non-Triviality, LNT (not everything is true)—which Aristotle tends to confuse with the Law of Non-Contradiction, LNC. As we also saw in section 1.12, Aristotle's major argument ($1006^{a}24$–$7^{b}18$) has sometimes been interpreted as showing that violations of the LNC or LNT would render language meaningless. I argued there that this inter-pretation is not very plausible, and in any case, does not succeed in establishing its conclusion. Here is another argument for the same conclusion.

To start with, let us consider the family of colour words. Let us suppose that the LNT failed for these. Thus, every (visible) object is green, and blue, and red, and all other colours. If such were the case, colour words would have no public meaning. For the public meanings of words have to be learned; and they are learned by contrasting situations where they do apply with situations where they do not. The lack of such a distinction would therefore undercut the possibility of public, transmissible, meaning. One might be tempted to reply that the meanings of such words could still be grasped since things at least *appear* different colours. But of course, if trivialism were true, everything would appear red, and appear blue, and appear green, and so on, too.

The argument generalizes. To convey the sense of any predicate, one depends on situations where it applies, and situations where it does not.[25] If there are no such situ-ations, public, communicable, sense is impossible. Hence, trivialism entails the mean-inglessness of public language. The arbitrator, as long as they are to be an arbitrator, clearly cannot accept this conclusion. Hence, they must find against the trivialist.

One might take issue with this argument. For example, it depends on a contrastive account of the communicability of meaning, which one might contest. But there are quite general reasons why this, or any, argument to the effect that violation of the LNT entails the meaninglessness of language must fail to do what is required in the present context. For the trivialist may simply take to heart the thought that public language is meaningless, and so cease to assert anything.[26]

It might be thought that this would take the trivialist out of the debate altogether. Since they say nothing, we are free to ignore them. Aristotle certainly thought this. This is too fast, however. They may not be able to assert anything, but that does not stop them uttering things. *They* may take themselves to be just "babbling"—to use a helpful phrase of Peter Unger. But *we* don't; and we still have to take into account the force of what they say, or at least, of what we take to be that force. The situation here is a very familiar one in the context of scepticism.[27] The sceptic claims that there is no ground for believing anything, as opposed to anything else. This means that they can assent to nothing. But they can still utter things; and we, who do assent to

---

[25] Non-Meinongians might make an exception for 'to be'; but being is always an odd thing.
[26] Note that one cannot run the same arguments against the meaningfulness of a private language—assuming such a thing to make sense—for the preceding argument depends on communicability.   [27] See, e.g. Priest (1995*a*), sect. 3.4.

some of the things uttered, cannot ignore their consequences. The sceptic, in a word, utters *ad hominem*. The trivialist does the same. If the trivialist is prepared to go in this direction, then any argument from meaninglessness fails.

3.9 ARGUMENT THREE: THE PHENOMENOLOGY OF CHOICE

As we saw in Chapter 1, the other arguments of *Metaphysics* Γ 4 against the LNT are pretty hopeless. For example, the arguments between 1007^b18 and 1008^a7 point out a number of apparently absurd consequences of everything being true; but such arguments simply beg the question against the trivialist, as I have already observed.

Aristotle's most interesting argument comes at 1008^b12–31, where he points out that if someone really believed everything to be true they would have no reason to act in any way, as opposed to any other. When they felt hungry they would have no reason to eat bread rather than broken glass, or for that matter, eat nothing at all, since they believe that each of these actions will satisfy their hunger. Such a person will, then, act erratically—and not for very long. Conversely, if we do see someone acting in a systematic and apparently purposeful fashion, we can infer that they do not really believe everything, whatever they say.

As we noted in 1.19, a similar argument can be urged against the sceptic who claims not to believe anything, as opposed to anything else. Indeed, Sextus considers just such an objection, and replies to it that, though the sceptic behaves systematically, they do not, in fact, behave on the basis of possessing reasons. They do what they do, simply because they are well trained. When they are hungry they reach for bread, not because they believe that it, rather than glass, will nourish them, but simply because they are conditioned to do so.[28] The same reply is available to the trivialist. They, too, may claim that when they reach for bread, it is not because they do not believe that glass would be just as good. It is simply because they have been trained to do so.

This does not get to the heart of the matter, though. Given some purpose, the trivialist can have no reason for behaving in one way rather than another to bring it about. But the situation is worse. The trivialist—at least whilst they remember that they are a trivialist—can have no purpose at all. One cannot intend to act in such a way as to bring about some state of affairs, s, if one believes s already to hold. Conversely, if one acts with the purpose of bringing s about, one cannot believe that s already obtains.[29] Hence, if one believes that everything is true, one cannot act purposefully. It might be retorted that if one believes that everything is the case, one believes that s

---

[28] *Outlines of Pyrrhonism*, ɪ. 11., 23–4.

[29] Kroon (2004), 247, points out, quite correctly, that believing that s will be the case is quite compatible with intending to act in such a way as to bring it about. One can believe that s will be the case *because* one believes that one will act in such a way to bring it about. But this is not the situation here. The trivialist not only believes that s *will be* the case; they believe that it *is* the case. Kroon goes on (p. 248) to suggests a problem for even a simple dialetheist here. Suppose that s is logically equivalent to $\neg s$. How, he asks, can they intend to act to bring about s knowing that what they do will bring about $\neg s$? The answer is easy: they know that they will bring about $s \land \neg s$. Whenever one acts one must acknowledge that, whatever one brings about, all of its logical consequences will also obtain.

is *not* the case, and so one *can* intend to bring it about. Normally, it is true, someone who believes ¬*s* does not believe that *s*; and so believing ¬*s* allows one to have the intention of bringing *s* about. But for the trivialist, ¬*s* does not rule out *s*; hence these considerations do not apply. The trivialist cannot aim to bring about *s*, because it is simply *part* of a situation that (they think) already obtains, viz. *s* ∧ ¬*s*.

But now: as long as a person is conscious, they make choices. They decide what to do, and what not to do. Even if they decide to "do nothing" they have still chosen a course of action. And the person who is running on Sextus' "autopilot" chooses to go along with it, and not override it. This observation that people must make choices may sound like an endorsement of free will. I do not intend it to be so. It may be that, at some level, our actions are determined by things that are quite beyond our consciousness, and so are unfree. I intend the observation purely as a phenomenological report of our consciousness. Having to choose is something phenomenologically unavoidable. The point was stressed, famously, by Sartre.[30]

But to choose how to act is to have a purpose: to (try to) bring about *this* rather than *that*. Not even to act on the toss of a coin is a counter-example to this. For to act on the toss of a coin is simply to let one's next purpose be determined by the result—and one has that purpose in tossing the coin, to boot. Choosing is an irredeemably goal-directed activity. And as we have seen, such action is incompatible with believing everything.[31] It follows that I cannot but reject trivialism. Phenomenologically, it is not an option for me. This does not show that trivialism is untrue. As far as the above considerations go, it is quite possible that everything is the case; but not for me—or for any other person.[32]

Notice that the argument is not vulnerable to the Ungerian trivialist of argument two. The meaning which they deny is a public phenomenon; I cannot guarantee that words are meaningful in this way simply by inspecting my own consciousness. But that I am (subjectively) a chooser, and cannot be otherwise, is something that is phenomenologically guaranteed. Notice, also, that this argument works just as much against the near-trivialist of argument one as it does against the trivialist. For one of the things about which we must choose is how to act in the physical world (at least, the phenomenological physical world). We cannot, therefore believe everything to be the case about this world.

As is clear, argument number three depends on an analysis of consciousness. Perhaps the best way to think of this is in Kantian terms. In the Transcendental Deduction of the *Critique of Pure Reason*, Kant tries to establish the applicability of the Categories from the nature of (the unity of) consciousness. Similarly, the argument I have

---

[30] e.g., in *Being and Nothingness*, though the point often comes out more forcibly in his stories.

[31] This can be seen in another way. One cannot choose between *this* and *that* if one believes that this and that are the same thing, which the trivialist does. Of course, the trivialist believes that this and that are distinct, too. But, as before, for the trivialist, two things being distinct does not rule out their being identical.

[32] Kroon (2004), 248, objects that this argument shows 'at best that the trivialist shouldn't believe her own position', and reminds us that act-utilitarians sometimes claim that it is 'best not to believe' act-utilitarianism, but that this is nonetheless true. Whatever one makes of the position in question, the matter is beside the point here. The force of the argument from choice is *precisely* that the trivialist cannot believe his or her own position. The only way that he or she can participate in the debate is, as it were, to disown it. This is a damning dialectical point.

deployed provides a transcendental deduction from certain features of consciousness to the impossibility of being a trivialist. In the context, this is the best kind of argument one can give. The arbitrator must rule in our favour if we can give them a transcendental proof that our opponent does not exist.

3.10 CONCLUSION

In this chapter, we have looked at two interpretations of the question: how do you know that not everything is true? In response to the first interpretation I gave an *a posteriori* answer: if everything really were true, we would see many contradictory states of affairs; but we do not. In reply to the second interpretation, I gave a transcendental argument against the possibility of any conscious being—at least, any being with a consciousness like mine—accepting trivialism. There are probably other ways in which one might interpret the request for justification of 3.1, and there is probably much more to said about the answers I have given. But enough for the present.

In the first part of the book we have looked at a number of issues concerned with truth and dialetheism. In the process, as the observant reader will have noted, a number of other topics of concern to the book have been broached. It is time to turn to the next of them: negation.

PART II
NEGATION

4

Contradiction

4.1 INTRODUCTION

Dialetheism is the view that some sentences of the form α and $\neg\alpha$ are both true, where $\neg$ is negation. As we saw in Chapter 2, there is nothing in the notion of truth that prevents dialetheism from being acceptable. The other obvious place to look for an argument for the same conclusion is in the nature of negation. Now there certainly are accounts of negation that rule out dialetheism; thus, any account, such as those provided by "classical" and intuitionist logics, according to which negation is explosive (that is, such that $\alpha, \neg\alpha \vdash \beta$, for an arbitrary β), rules out dialetheism—unless, of course, one is a trivialist. But such an account is by no means mandatory. Arguably, the correct account of negation both allows for the truth of some contradictions and is not explosive. To argue this is the point of the present chapter.[1]

Negation is one of a collection of notions central to logic. Nowadays, they are standardly called *logical constants*, though they have been called by different names at different times. For example, they were called *syncategoremata* by medieval logicians. Much of logic has therefore been devoted to an analysis of these notions. Thus, how to analyse conditionals and how to analyse what we would now call quantifier phrases have both been historically contentious issues. Consensus concerning the latter was achieved early in the twentieth century, due to the work of Frege and others. The debate concerning the former shows no similar sign of convergence.

Negation, too, has been the locus of very different views. Major theories of negation in the twentieth century included the "classical" (Frege/Russell) account and the intuitionist (Brouwer/Heyting) account. But rival accounts of negation have always existed. In section 1.13 I distinguished between three sorts of account of negation: those according to which contradictions entail:

1. nothing;
2. something (but not everything);
3. everything.

The classical and intuitionist accounts are accounts of kind 3; but later medieval accounts which endorsed both an extensional disjunction and the disjunctive syllogism also belong to this category. Connexivist accounts of the early Middle Ages, such as those endorsed by Boethius and Abelard (which we met in section 1.13) are of kind 1.

---

[1] Sainsbury (1994), 142, discerns a challenge for dialetheism: to provide an account of what understanding negation involves. This chapter goes a reasonable way towards meeting that challenge.

The accounts provided by contemporary paraconsistent and most relevant logics are of kind 2; but so was that provided by Aristotle.[2]

4.2   NEGATION OR NEGATIONS?

How, then, does negation behave?[3] There is a short way with this question. There is no such thing as negation; there are lots of different negations: Boolean negation, intuitionist negation, De Morgan negation. Each of these behaves according to a set of rules (proof-theoretic or semantic); each is perfectly legitimate; and we are free to use whichever notion we wish, as long as we are clear about what we are doing. If this is right, there is nothing left to say about the question, except what justifies us in categorizing a connective as in the negation family. And I doubt that there is anything very illuminating to be said about that. Virtually *every* negation-like property fails on some account of a connective that is recognizably negation-like: the law of excluded middle, the law of non-contradiction, double negation, De Morgan's laws, contraposition, and so on. All we are left with is a family resemblance whose fluid boundaries are largely historically determined.

I do not think that the answer is right, however. It makes a nonsense of too many important debates in the foundations of logic. Doubtless, philosophical debates do rest on confusion sometimes, but questions concerning the role of negation in discourses on infinity, self-reference, time, existence, etc., are not to be set aside so lightly.

At the root of this kind of answer is a simple confusion between a theory and what it is a theory of.[4] We have many well worked-out theories of negation, each with its own proof-theory, model-theory and so on. And if you call the theoretical object constituted by each theory a negation, then, so be it: there are many negations. But this does not mean that one can deploy each of these theoretical objects at will and come out with the correct answer. The theoretical object has to fit the real object; and how this behaves is not a matter of choice.

A comparison with geometry may be helpful here. There are, in a sense, many geometries. Each has its own well-defined structure; and, as an abstract mathematical structure, is worthy of investigation. But if we think of each geometry, not as an abstract mathematical structure, but, suitably interpreted, as a theory about the spatial (or spatio-temporal) structure of the cosmos, we are not free to choose at will. The theory must answer to the facts—or, if one is not a realist, at least cohere in the most satisfactory way with the rest of our theorizing.

---

[2] For a general discussion of historical theories of negation, see sect. 7.2 of Priest (2007).

[3] I will concern myself only with propositional negation, though this fits into a much broader family of negative constructions. See Sylvan (1999).

[4] See *In Contradiction*, ch. 14. The confusion is manifested by, e.g. Quine (1970), 81, when he complains that someone who denies *ex contradictione quodlibet* just doesn't know what they are talking about, since changing the laws is changing the subject. A similar confusion is apparent in those who argue that someone who suggests adopting a non-classical logic wants to revise logic, i.e. correct reasoning. Such a person need only be suggesting a revision of a theory of logic, *not* logic itself. One cannot simply *assume* that classical logic gets it right.

There is always an extreme conventionalist line to be run here. One might say, as Poincaré (n.d.) did, that we are free to choose our geometry at will, e.g. on the grounds of simplicity, and then fix everything else around it. Similarly, we might insist that we are free to employ a certain notion of negation and make everything else fit. But such a line is not only philosophically contentious, but foolhardy, at least in advance of a good deal of further investigation. The tail may end up wagging a dog of a considerable size. For example, as Prior (1960) pointed out a long time ago, we can determine to use a connective, $*$ (*tonk*), according to the rules of inference $\alpha \vdash \alpha * \beta$ and $\alpha * \beta \vdash \beta$. But the cost of this is accepting that if anything is true, everything is!

4.3 CONTRADICTORIES

I will return to the issue of the nature of logical theories in a more general context in Chapter 10. But enough for the present. We have seen that a simple voluntarism with respect to negation is unsatisfactory. If it is to be applied, an account of negation must be considered not just as an abstract structure, but as a theory *of* something, just as a geometry is a theory of physical space. And this will put substantial constraints on what an acceptable account is.

The next, and obvious, question is what, exactly, an account of negation is a theory of. It is natural to suggest that negation is a theory of the way that the English particle 'not', and similar particles in other natural languages, behaves. This, however, is incorrect. For a start, 'not' has functions in English which do not concern negation. For example, it may be used to reject connotations of what is said, though not its truth, as in, for example, 'I am not his wife: he is my husband'. (Some linguists call this 'metalinguistic negation',[5] though this is obviously not a happy appellation in the context of logic.)

More importantly, negation may not be expressed by simply inserting 'not'. For example the negation of 'Socrates was mortal' may be 'Socrates was not mortal'; but, as Aristotle pointed out (*De Interepretatione*, ch. 7), the negation of 'Some man is mortal' is not 'Some man is not mortal', but 'No man is mortal'.

These examples show that we have a grasp of negation that is independent of the way that 'not' functions, and can use this to determine when "notting" negates. But what is it, then, of which we have a grasp? We see that there appears to be a relationship of a certain kind between pairs such as 'Socrates is mortal' and 'Socrates in not mortal'; and 'Some man is mortal' and 'No man is mortal'. The traditional way of expressing the relationship is that the pairs are *contradictories*, and so we may say that the relationship is that of contradiction. Theories of negation are theories about this relation.

As usual in theorization, we may reach a state where we have to reassess the situation. For example, it may turn out that there are several distinct relationships here, which need to be distinguished. But at least this is the data to which theorization must (and historically did) answer, at least initially.

[5] e.g. Horn (1989), 370 ff.

Having got this far, the next obvious question is what the relationship of contra-diction is a relationship between: sentences, propositions, some other kind of entity? There are substantial issues here; but, as far as I can see, they do not affect the question of negation substantially. For any issue that arises given one reasonable answer to this question, an equivalent one arises for the others. So I shall simply call the sorts of thing in question, non-committally, statements, and leave it at that.

4.4 THE LAWS OF EXCLUDED MIDDLE AND NON-CONTRADICTION

So if α is any statement, let $\neg\alpha$ represent its contradictory. (Contradictories, unlike contraries and sub-contraries are unique—at least up to logical equivalence.) What relationships hold between these? Traditional logic and common sense are both very clear about the most important one: we must have at least one of the pair, but not both.[6] It is precisely this which distinguish contradictories from their near cousins, contraries and sub-contraries. If we have two contraries, e.g. 'Socrates was black' and 'Socrates was white', it is necessarily false that (Socrates was black $\wedge$ Socrates was white); but it is not necessarily true that (Socrates was black $\vee$ Socrates was white). Dually, if we have two sub-contraries, e.g. 'Socrates was under 2 m tall' and 'Socrates was over 1 m tall', it is necessarily true that (Socrates was under 2 m tall $\vee$ Socrates was over 1 m tall), but it may also be true that (Socrates was under 2 m tall $\wedge$ Socrates was over 1 m tall).

This fact about contradictories obviously gives immediately two of the traditional laws of negation, the law of excluded middle:

LEM $\Box(\alpha \vee \neg\alpha)$

and the law of non-contradiction:

LNC $\Box\neg(\alpha \wedge \neg\alpha)$, i.e. $\neg\Diamond(\alpha \wedge \neg\alpha)$

in each case, for all α. Note that one may formulate the law of non-contradiction in a number of very different, and non-equivalent, ways. As I have formulated it here, the truth of the principle is quite compatible with dialetheism, as we will have occasion to observe in a moment. The question of how to formulate the law in such a way that a dialetheist cannot accept it is, in fact, a very sensitive one.[7] At any rate, the LEM and

---

[6] Classically, these facts actually characterize contradictories up to logical equivalence. This, how-ever, is moot. If β satisfies the condition $\Box\neg(\alpha \wedge \beta)$ and $\Box(\alpha \vee \beta)$, and γ is any necessary truth, then so does $\beta \wedge \gamma$; but β does not entail $\beta \wedge \gamma$ unless one identifes entailment with strict implication.

[7] Let us write $\dashv$ as a force operator for denial (as we will do in 6.4). If someone thinks that α is a dialetheia then one utterance that they will not make is: $\dashv \alpha$. However, one cannot formulate the LNC as: for all α, $\Box \dashv (\alpha \wedge \neg\alpha)$; or even as: for all α, $\dashv \Diamond(\alpha \wedge \neg\alpha)$. Force operators make no sense embedded in a sentence. One can say: for all α one *ought to* deny $\alpha \wedge \neg\alpha$. But as we shall see in Chapter 6, this may not rule out having an obligation to assert $\alpha \wedge \neg\alpha$ for some αs, too. More to the point here, this is not the right way to formulate the LNC in the present context. The claim that two sentences are contradictories concerns their truth-relations: it has nothing, of itself, to do with rationality of obligation.

the LNC as formulated here are central aspects of the traditional characterization of contradictories. Maybe the traditional characterization—and consequently these two laws—is wrong; but it would certainly seem to be the default position. The onus of proof is therefore on those who would dispute it.

Disputation comes from at least two directions. The first is that of some (though not all) paraconsistent logicians. The argument here is that some contradictories are both true, i.e. for some βs we have $\beta \wedge \neg\beta$. We do not, therefore, have $\neg(\beta \wedge \neg\beta)$ (and so $\Box\neg(\beta \wedge \neg\beta)$). We will look more closely at the first part of this argument later. For the moment, just note that if it is correct, it undercuts the second part of the argument (at least without some further considerations). For if some contradictions are true, we may well have both $\beta \wedge \neg\beta$ and $\neg(\beta \wedge \neg\beta)$. Hence, the fact that some contradictions are true does not, of itself, refute the LNC (at least in the form in question here).

The second direction from which one might dispute the traditional characterization is that of those logicians who suppose there to be sentences that are neither true nor false. This includes intuitionist logicians (though they might not express their own position in this way). The argument here is that if α is neither true nor false, so is $\neg\alpha$. Hence, assuming that disjunction behaves normally, $\alpha \vee \neg\alpha$ does not hold.[8] The claim that certain statements are neither true nor false is clearly a substantial one. The claim that disjunction behaves normally is also challengeable. (If we give a supervaluationist account, $\alpha \vee \neg\alpha$ may be true even though each disjunct fails to be so.) However, we need discuss neither of these issues here. For from the present perspective there is an obvious objection. If $\neg$ behaves as suggested, it is not a contradictory-forming operator at all—merely a contrary-forming one. This would seem particularly clear if we consider the intuitionist account of negation. According to this, $\neg\alpha$ is true ($=$ assertible) just if there is a proof that there is no proof that α. This is obviously a *contrary* of α.[9]

A genuine contradictory-forming operator will be one that when applied to a sentence, α, covers *all* the cases in which α is not true. Thus, it is an operator, $\neg$, such that $\neg\alpha$ is true iff α is not true, i.e. is either false or neither true nor false. (In English, such an operator might be something like: *it is not the case that*.) For this notion, which is the real contradictory-forming operator, the LEM holds.

Those who believe in simple truth-value gaps (and, in particular, use a classical metalanguage) would seem to have little reply to this objection. The intuitionist does have a reply to hand, however. First, they can (though they need not) endorse the claim that $\neg\alpha$ is true iff α is not true, $T\langle\neg\alpha\rangle \leftrightarrow \neg T\langle\alpha\rangle$.[10] Given that $T\langle\alpha \vee \beta\rangle \leftrightarrow (T\langle\alpha\rangle \vee T\langle\beta\rangle)$, we can infer that $T\langle\alpha \vee \neg\alpha\rangle \leftrightarrow (T\langle\alpha\rangle \vee \neg T\langle\alpha\rangle)$, but provided that

---

[8] If conjunction behaves normally, the LNC may also fail for truth-valueless sentences.

[9] Most perspicuously, consider the embedding of intuitionist logic into $S4$ where the modal operator $\Box$ is considered as a provability operator. Then $\neg\alpha$ is translated into $\Box\neg\alpha^{+}$ (where α^{+} is the translation of α). In other words, $\neg\alpha$ is intuitionistically true iff the negation of α is *provable*.

[10] This does create a problem as to how, then, they express their attitude with respect to undecided sentences. If α is undecided, one can no longer say that $\alpha \vee \neg\alpha$ is not true, let alone false, since $\neg T\langle\alpha \vee \neg\alpha\rangle$ now entails $T\langle\neg\alpha \wedge \neg\neg\alpha\rangle$.

the logic of the truth-theory is intuitionistic we cannot infer the left-hand side of this, since we do not have the right. Thus, one can quite coherently give a homophonic intuitionist truth-theory for an intuitionist language.

Second, an intuitionist can argue that a contradictory-forming operator, conceived of as one that delivers the LEM, literally makes no sense. The argument is a familiar one from the writings, notably, of Dummett.[11] *In nuce*, it is as follows. If a notion is meaningful there must be something that it is to grasp its meaning. Whatever that is, this must be manifestable in behaviour (or, the argument sometimes continues, the notion would not be learnable). But there is no suitable behaviour for manifesting a grasp of a connective satisfying the conditions of a classical contradictory-forming operator. In particular, we cannot identify the behaviour as that of being prepared to assert $\neg\alpha$ when (and only when) α fails to be true. For this state of affairs may well obtain when there is no principled way for us to be able to recognize that it does. Meaning requires that a sentence, if true, can be recognized as such, in principle. This is often called the *Verification Constraint*.

There are subtle issues (and a substantial body of literature) here. And to deal with them satisfactorily would require taking up a disproportionate part of this chapter. But let me say at least something about the matter. For a start, I do not see why the grasp of a notion must be manifestable. There is no reason why, in general, certain notions should not be hard-wired in us. If, for example, there is a Fodor-style language of thought,[12] it is quite natural to suppose that single-bit toggling is a primitive operation. One might even tell an evolutionary story as to how the hard-wiring came about; for example, it is the simplest and most efficient mechanism for implementing dissent (which occurs in non-human animals as well as humans). In particular, then, a contradictory operator does not have to be learned; its use is merely triggered in us by certain linguistic contexts, in much the same way that the categories of universal grammar are, according to Chomsky.[13]

But even granting that the grasp of a notion must be manifestable, I do not see why it must be manifestable by anything as strong as the argument requires (which is, I agree, impossible). In particular, it can be manifested by being prepared to assert $\neg\alpha$ when in a position to recognize that α fails to be true, and refusing to assert it when in a position to recognize that α is true.[14] It could well be suggested that such a manifestation would not be adequate. There will be many cases where we are not in a position to recognize either. People could therefore manifest the same behaviour whilst disagreeing about how to handle new cases when these become recognizable, and so meaning different things. This is true. But if people not only behave as suggested, but also manifest a disposition to agree on new cases, this is sufficient to show (if not, perhaps, conclusively, then at least beyond reasonable doubt) that they are operating with the notion in the same way. In just this way, the fact that we are all prepared to

---

[11] See, e.g. Dummett (1975*a*), esp. pp. 224–5 of the reprint. A somewhat different argument is explained and dispatched in Read (1994*a*), 222–30.   [12] See Fodor (1975).
[13] See, e.g. Chomsky (1971).
[14] A different suggestion, though not one I would make, is that an understanding can be manifested by using classical logic. This raises quite different issues.

apply, or refrain from applying, the word 'green' to hitherto unseen objects when they come to light, shows that we all mean the same thing by the word. This is essentially what following an appropriate rule comes to, in Wittgensteinian terms.[15]

There is much more to be said here. But if the onus of proof is on an intuitionist, as it would seem to be in the case of a contradictory-forming operator, I know of no argument against the LEM that I find persuasive. (None of this contests the claim that one can tell a coherent epistemological/metaphysical intuitionist story. One may certainly contest this claim as well, however. In particular there is a well-known argument which can be seen as a *reductio* of the Verification Constraint. We do not need to go into this here, however.[16])

Before we leave the LEM it is worth noting that the fact that for every pair of contradictories one must be true (*simpliciter*) does not entail that for every world or situation one of each pair must be true at it. Thus, if $\Box(\alpha \vee \neg\alpha)$, one of α and $\neg\alpha$ holds at each possible world, but there may be impossible worlds where laws of logic such as the LEM break down, and so where neither α not $\neg\alpha$ obtains.[17]Alternatively, if one thinks of a situation as *part* of the world, then it may well be argued that neither of a pair of contradictories need be true of it. Thus, consider the situation concerning my bike. It may be the case that neither 'Ghent is in Belgium' nor 'Ghent is not in Belgium' is true of this situation.[18] The question of whether or not one needs to consider impossible worlds and partial situations is important in discussions of the semantics of conditionals, intentionality, and other areas; but we do not need to go into these matters here.

4.5 TRUTH AND FALSITY

So far, we have met two of the classical laws of negation, LEM and LNC. A third, the law of double negation (LDN) is simply derivable. The relationship of being contradictories is symmetric. That is, if β is the contradictory of α, then α is the contradictory of β. In particular, α is the contradictory of $\neg\alpha$. Hence, $\neg\neg\alpha$ just is α.

We are now in a position to look at another important feature of negation: its truth conditions. To do this we will need a definition of falsity. As already explained in the Introduction to the book, let us take 'α is false' to mean that $\neg\alpha$ is true. This is not the only plausible definition; one might also define it to mean that α is not true. It may turn out that these two definitions are equivalent, of course. However, to assume so here would be to beg too many important questions. And the present definition is one that all parties can agree upon, classical, intuitionist, paraconsistent, or otherwise.

The definition of falsity assures us that $\neg\alpha$ is true iff α is false. Dually, $\neg\alpha$ is false iff $\neg\neg\alpha$ is true (by the definition of falsity) iff α is true, by LDN. Hence, the

---

[15] See *Philosophical Investigations*, part i, esp. sect. 201–40.
[16] See, e.g. Hart and McGinn (1976) and Priest (2008).
[17] See Priest (2005a), sect. 1.6.   [18] See Restall (1999).

traditional understanding of the relationship between truth and falsity falls out of the understanding of negation as contradiction, and the definition of falsity.

Two more of the classical laws of negation, the Laws of De Morgan (LDM), can also be dealt with. These involve conjunction and disjunction essentially; and so we need to make some assumption about how they behave. Since this chapter is not about conjunction and disjunction, this is not the place to discuss the matter at great length. For present purposes, let us suppose that they behave as tradition says they do: a conjunction is true iff both conjuncts are true, and false iff at least one conjunct is false. The conditions for disjunction are the obvious dual ones.

One of De Morgan's Laws is the equivalence of $\neg(\alpha \wedge \beta)$ and $\neg\alpha \vee \neg\beta$. This can now be demonstrated thus: $\neg(\alpha \wedge \beta)$ is true iff $\alpha \wedge \beta$ is false iff α is false or β is false iff $\neg\alpha$ is true or $\neg\beta$ is true iff $\neg\alpha \vee \neg\beta$ is true. Dually, $\neg(\alpha \wedge \beta)$ is false iff $\alpha \wedge \beta$ is true (LDN) iff α and β are true iff $\neg\alpha$ and $\neg\beta$ are false (LDN) iff $\neg\alpha \vee \neg\beta$ is false. The other of De Morgan's Laws is an equivalence between $\neg(\alpha \vee \beta)$ and $\neg\alpha \wedge \neg\beta$, and can be verified by a similar argument.

The connection between negation and the conditional is more difficult to deal with, but this is because the conditional is itself more contentious. Indeed, the claim that there are different kinds of conditional (entailments, causal conditionals, indicative conditionals, subjunctive conditionals) is well known. If such distinctions are well-motivated, negation may well interact with different conditionals in different ways. A minimal condition for a conditional of any kind would seem to be that it preserve truth in an appropriate way from antecedent to consequent. Hence we have *modus ponens*, $\alpha, \alpha \rightarrow \beta \vdash \beta$. The most important question concerning a conditional in the present context is whether it preserves falsity in the reverse direction. For some conditionals, at least, this would seem to fail, as, e.g. Stalnaker and Lewis have argued.[19] And if $\alpha \rightarrow \beta$ fails to preserve falsity backwards, $\neg\beta \rightarrow \neg\alpha$ will fail to preserve truth forwards, and so will not be true. The law of contraposition (LC), $\alpha \rightarrow \beta \vdash \neg\beta \rightarrow \neg\alpha$ is not, therefore to be expected to hold for an arbitrary conditional. Of course, there may well be conditionals which do preserve falsity in the appropriate way; in fact one can always *define* one, $\Rightarrow$, in a simple fashion: $\alpha \Rightarrow \beta$ is just $(\alpha \rightarrow \beta) \wedge (\neg\beta \rightarrow \neg\alpha)$. For such a conditional contraposition will hold.

In this section, I have talked of truth. I have said nothing about truth-in-an-interpretation, as required, for example, for a model-theoretic account of validity. It is important to distinguish these two notions, for they are often confused. The first is a property (or at least a monadic predicate); the second is a (set-theoretic) relation. It is natural enough to suppose that truth is at least coextensive with truth-in-$\mathcal{I}$, where $\mathcal{I}$ is some one privileged interpretation (set).[20] And this may provide a constraint on the notion of truth-in-an-interpretation. But it, even together with an account of truth, is hardly sufficient to determine a theory of truth-in-an-interpretation. It does not even determine, for example, how to conceptualize an interpretation. So how are an

---

[19] e.g. Stalnaker (1968), Lewis (1973), and Priest (2001*a*), ch. 5. See also *In Contradiction*, sect. 6.5.

[20] Or, if worlds are involved, that truth at a world is relative to some privileged interpretation, and truth *simpliciter*, with truth at some privileged world of that privileged interpretation.

account of truth-in-an-interpretation, appropriate for the connectives we have been discussing, and a corresponding model-theoretic notion of validity, to be formulated? A model-theory for a relevant paraconsistent logic provides what is required.[21] But this takes us into areas of formal logic that I have forsworn in this book, so I shall not pursue the matter here.

4.6 TRUTH AND CONTRADICTION

Starting with a conception of negation as a contradictory-forming operator, we have now validated five standard laws of negation (LEM, LNC, LDN, and the two LDM), and a sixth (LC) in certain contexts. We have hardly settled all the central issues concerning negation, however. As we observed in 4.4, the fact that $\neg\Diamond(\alpha \wedge \neg\alpha)$ holds does not rule out $\alpha \wedge \neg\alpha$ holding too. This does not mean that $\neg$ is not a contradictory-forming operator. It just means that there is more to negation than one might have thought. Let us call this more, for want of a better phrase, its *surplus content*. The classical view is to the effect that negation does not have surplus content: any such content would turn into the total content of everything since $\alpha \wedge \neg\alpha \vdash \beta$. But the classical view has been called into question by dialetheists. The case for dialetheism is a long one, and, like the intuitionist case against classical negation, is too long to take up in detail here; but let me say a little.[22]

Many examples of dialetheias have been suggested, but perhaps the most impressive ones are those generated by the paradoxes of self-reference. Here we have a set of arguments that appear to be sound, and yet which end in contradiction. *Prima facie*, then, they establish that some contradictions are true. Some of these arguments are two and a half thousand years old. Yet despite intensive attempts to say what is wrong with them in a number of logical epochs, including our own, there are no adequate solutions. It is illuminating to compare these paradoxes with ones of equal antiquity: Zeno's. Zeno's paradoxes have also been the subject of intensive study over the years, and for these there *is* a well recognized and stable solution.[23] (Philosophers may still argue over some of the details, but then philosophers will argue over anything.) The fact that there is no similar thing in the case of the paradoxes of self-reference at least suggests that, in their case, trying to solve them is simply barking up the wrong tree: we should just accept them at face value, as showing that certain contradictions are true.

Because a major part of what is at issue in this chapter is the semantics of negation, the semantic paradoxes are particularly pertinent. Every consistent solution to these is generally acknowledged as wrong (except by the few who propound it). Moreover, there are general reasons why, it would seem, no consistent solution will be forthcoming. The reason is the following dilemma (actually, trilemma).[24]

The paradoxes arise, in the first place, as arguments couched in natural language. One who would solve the paradoxes must show that the semantic concepts involved

---

[21] See, e.g. Priest (2001*a*), chs. 9, 10.   [22] The case is made in *In Contradiction*.
[23] See, e.g. Sainsbury (1994), ch. 1.
[24] For versions of this argument, see *In Contradiction*, sect. 1.7, and Priest (1991*a*), sect. 1.

are not, despite appearances, inconsistent. And it is necessary to show this for all the concepts in the semantic family, for they are all deeply implicated in contradiction. Attempts to do this, given the resources of modern logic, all show how, given any language, L, in some class of languages, to construct a theory, T_L, of the semantic notions for L, according to which they behave consistently.

The first horn of the dilemma is posed by asking the question of whether the theory T_L is expressible in L. If the answer to this is 'yes' it always seems possible to use the resources of the theory to construct new semantic contradictions, often called extended or strengthened paradoxes. Nor is this an accident. For since T_L is expressible, and since, according to T_L, things are consistent, we should be able to prove the consistency of T_L in T_L. And provided T_L is strong enough in other ways (for example, if it contains the resources of arithmetic, as it must if L is to be a candidate for English), then we know that T_L is liable to be inconsistent by Gödel's second incompleteness theorem.

It would seem, then, that the answer to the original question must be 'no'. In that case we ask a second question: is English, or at least, the relevant part of it, E, one of the languages in the family being considered? If the answer to this is 'yes' then it follows that T_E is not expressible in English, which is self-refuting, since the theorist explained how to construct each T_L in English (assuming the theorist to speak English—and if they do not, just change the language in question). If, on the other hand, the answer is 'no' then the original problem of showing that the semantic concepts of English are consistent has not been solved.

Hence, all attempts to solve the paradoxes must swing uncomfortably between inconsistency, incompleteness and inexpressibility, a pattern that is clear from the literature.[25]

Let us take it, then, that truth and falsity overlap: for some αs we have both α and $\neg\alpha$. For such αs we have $\alpha \wedge \neg\alpha$, and so $\Diamond(\alpha \wedge \neg\alpha)$. We can now deal with another law of negation: Explosion: $\alpha, \neg\alpha \vdash \beta$. Unlike the other laws we have already met, this one has always been contentious historically. And its presentation to a class of students before they have been taught a logic course, is sure to draw pretty universal dissent. Given the present discussion, it can clearly be seen to fail. For we can simply take an α which is both true and false, and a β that is not true. This instance of the inference is not truth-preserving, and hence the inference is not valid (truth-preservation being at least a necessary condition for validity). For good measure, the equally contentious inference of Antecedent Falsity (AF), $\neg\alpha \vdash \alpha \rightarrow \beta$, must also be invalid, for exactly the same reason (*modus ponens* holding); as, again, and more contentiously, must be the disjunctive syllogism (DS): $\alpha, \neg\alpha \vee \beta \vdash \beta$.[26]

In the case of someone who endorses the idea that there are truth-value gaps, so that α and $\neg\alpha$ may both fail, one may object, as I did, that $\neg$ is not playing the role of a contradictory-forming operator. A genuine such operator is one given by the truth

[25] This is documented in Priest (1995*a*). See especially the last chapter.
[26] Against this, it might be argued that the DS must be valid, since we invoke it at many points in our reasoning. But the legitimacy of appealing to the DS—when it is legitimate—can be explained in ways perfectly accepable to a dialetheist. See *In Contradiction*, ch. 8, and Priest (1991*b*).

conditions:

$$T\langle\neg\alpha\rangle \text{ iff } \neg T\langle\alpha\rangle$$

It is therefore natural to suppose that a dual objection can be made if one takes it that α and $\neg\alpha$ may both be true. Dialetheic negation is merely a sub-contrary-forming operator. The displayed clause defines the genuine contrary-forming operator.[27]

The situation is *not* the same, however. Given the notion of negation employed with gaps, the LEM and LNC fail. Given the conception of negation I have just described, they do not; so the negation *is* a contradictory-forming operator. It may just have surplus content as well.

There is more to the matter than this, though. In fact, a dialetheist may say much of what the intuitionist is inclined to say about the matter. First, they can (though they need not) endorse the claim that $\neg\alpha$ is true iff α is not true. Given this clause, and that $T\langle\alpha \wedge \beta\rangle \leftrightarrow T\langle\alpha\rangle \wedge T\langle\beta\rangle$, we can infer $T\langle\alpha\rangle \wedge \neg T\langle\alpha\rangle$ from $T\langle\alpha \wedge \neg\alpha\rangle$. But provided that the logic of the truth-theory is dialetheic, so that Explosion fails, we cannot infer an arbitrary β from $T\langle\alpha \wedge \neg\alpha\rangle$. Thus, one can quite coherently give a homophonic dialetheic truth-theory for a dialetheic language.[28] Second, a dialetheist can argue that a contradictory-forming operator, conceived of as delivering Explosion, and so ruling out surplus content, literally makes no sense. In the next chapter, we will call negation, so conceived, Boolean negation, and I will argue just that. Before this chapter ends, however, there are a couple of other issues concerning negation which can be dealt with quickly.

4.7 ARROW *FALSUM*

Negation, as we have just seen, does not satisfy Explosion. But how can this be? There must be some sense of negation that satisfies it. For example, let $\bot$ (*falsum*) be a logical constant such that it is a logical truth that $\bot \to \alpha$, for every α. For example, if we have a truth predicate, T, satisfying the T-schema ($T\langle\alpha\rangle \leftrightarrow \alpha$, for some detachable conditional operator, $\to$, and every α), $\bot$ can be defined as $\forall x Tx$. We can then define $-\alpha$ simply as $\alpha \to \bot$ to obtain the appropriate Explosion. For we have $\alpha, -\alpha \vdash \bot$ and $\bot \vdash \beta$.[29] ($-\alpha$ is, of course, equivalent to $\neg\alpha$ in both classical and intuitionist logic.)

The point is well made. There is such a logical constant, and such a notion defined by employing it. But it is not negation. Its properties depend, of course, on the notion of conditionality employed. In particular, the LEM and LNC reduce to $\alpha \vee (\alpha \to \bot)$ and $(\alpha \wedge (\alpha \to \bot)) \to \bot$, respectively. There is no reason to accept the first of these. The only ground could be that the falsity of α suffices for the truth of $\alpha \to \bot$, i.e. AF; and we have already seen that this is to be rejected. The latter may

---

[27] Slater (1995), 453, makes this claim. He also claims that a genuine contradictory-forming operator rules out the possibility of surplus content, by definition. We will look at definitions of negation that might be thought to do this in the next chapter.
[28] See *In Contradiction*, ch. 9.   [29] See *In Contradiction*, sect. 8.5.

appear more plausible, but in fact fails in a number of accounts of the conditional, namely those that reject Contraction (Absorption): $\gamma \rightarrow (\gamma \rightarrow \delta) \vdash \gamma \rightarrow \delta$. (One should not confuse $\vdash (\alpha \wedge (\alpha \rightarrow \beta)) \rightarrow \beta$ with *modus ponens*, $\alpha, \alpha \rightarrow \beta \vdash \beta$.) The other laws also depend on properties of the conditional, often of a dubious nature.[30]

One might wonder whether a dialetheic solution to the semantic paradoxes can be sustained once the connective, $-$, is at our disposal, due to the reappearance of triviality-inducing extended paradoxes. It can. For example, the form of the Liar using, $-$, is just a sentence, β, such that $T\langle\beta\rangle \leftrightarrow (T\langle\beta\rangle \rightarrow \bot)$. If we could help ourselves to the principle of Contraction then we could infer $T\langle\beta\rangle \rightarrow \bot$, and so $T\langle\beta\rangle$, and so $\bot$. This is just, in fact, a Curry paradox. But contraction fails in numerous accounts of the conditional, and there are reasons to suppose that the conditional of the T-schema does not satisfy it.[31]

4.8   *REDUCTIO AD ABSURDUM*

Before we conclude, let me make one final comment on negation. This concerns *reductio ad absurdum* (RAA).[32] The purpose of a *reductio* argument is often to establish something of the form $\neg\alpha$ by deducing a contradiction from α. Dialetheism need not affect this enterprise. If the deduction establishes that $\alpha \rightarrow (\beta \wedge \neg\beta)$, and the $\rightarrow$ in question contraposes, then we have $(\beta \vee \neg\beta) \rightarrow \neg\alpha$ by contraposition LDM and LDN. $\neg\alpha$ follows by the LEM.

In a polemical context, the point of a *reductio* argument is not normally to establish something, but to try to force an opponent to give up a view. In a dialetheic context, establishing the negation of the view is not *logically* sufficient for this. However, whilst a contradiction may be logically possible,[33] it does not at all follow that it may be rational to believe it. That I will turn into a fried egg tomorrow is logically possible, but a belief in this is ground for certifiable insanity. (*A fortiori* that I both will and will not turn into a fried egg, since this entails it.) And an argument against an opponent who holds α to be true *is* rationally effective if it can be demonstrated that α entails something that ought, rationally, to be rejected, β. For it then follows that they ought to reject α. β may be a contradiction, or it may be the claim that I will turn in to a fried egg. Not all contradictions may work. For example, that the Liar sentence is both true and not true may be (in fact, is) perfectly rationally acceptable.

---

[30] If $\alpha \supset \beta$ is defined, as usual, as $\neg\alpha \vee \beta$ then it is not difficult to see that $\neg\alpha$ is equivalent to $\alpha \supset \bot$. But $\supset$ is not a conditional operator: *modus ponens* for it fails. (This is just the DS.)

[31] For arguments against Contraction, see *In Contradiction*, ch. 6, and Priest (1990), sect. 7. I will take up the issue again in the next chapter.

[32] The following material is covered at greater length in *In Contradiction*, sect. 7.5, and Priest (1989*b*).   [33] And impossible, of course.

4.9 CONCLUSION

The discussion of the previous section raised the question of when and why something *is* rationally acceptable. This question provides the topic of the third part of this book. But we are not finished with negation yet. For a start, the issue of Boolean Negation raised its head at the end of section 4.6. This is the topic to which we turn in the next chapter.

5

Boolean Negation

5.1 INTRODUCTION

In the last chapter I argued for a certain account of negation. The account, whilst respecting traditional features of the notion of negation, such as its being a contradictory-forming operator, nonetheless allowed for contradictions to be true without triviality—that is, as I put it there, for negation to have surplus content.

It might be argued, however, that, though the account may, in fact, be correct, this is in many ways beside the point. Grant that negation behaves as I say it does. It remains the case that there is a logical operation that has all the properties of classical negation. Classical logic is therefore perfectly correct provided that we understand its negation sign as meaning this. In particular, a dialetheic solution to the paradoxes of semantic self-reference—as advocated in 4.6—is ruled out, since we may formulate the Liar sentence employing this notion and apply the unrestricted T-schema to it, deriving a corresponding contradiction, and hence infer triviality.

The point may be reinforced by an appeal to the semantics of certain paraconsistent logics themselves. The negation of relevant logics, often called 'De Morgan negation', is of the kind that I described in the last chapter. However, Meyer and others have investigated relevant logics with two negations. One is the standard De Morgan negation. The other is a negation that behaves exactly as the classical account of negation says it does. This they called 'Boolean negation'.[1] Both negations are provided with a semantics and proof theory.

If one takes it that a dialetheic solution to the semantic paradoxes is correct, one must deny the coherence of Boolean negation. This I do, and the present chapter explains why (as promised at the end of section 4.6). As we will see, the coherence of an explosive notion of negation can be maintained, at best, only by question-begging.

5.2 INFORMATION AND AUGMENTATION

Let us write Boolean negation as $, and start with an argument to the effect that it is an incoherent logical connective.[2] The semantics of many logics, including relevant logics of the kind required for a plausible account of the conditional, involve the

---

[1] See, e.g. Meyer and Routley (1973; 1974).
[2] The argument is based on some observations of Restall (2000), 306 and ch. 16.

notion of worlds.[3] Suppose, for a moment, that these are to be thought of as states of information. States of information may well be incomplete. Thus, if w is a world then we may have neither Pa nor $\neg Pa$ holding in w, for some a and P. Clearly, it should be possible to add missing information about a sensibly. Thus, in the case at hand, it should be possible to add Pa to the state of information coherently. But if Boolean negation is a legitimate connective, then since $Pa \notin w$ and $\neg Pa \notin w$, $\$Pa \in w$ and $\$\neg Pa \in w$. Hence, the addition of either Pa or $\neg Pa$ to w will result in triviality. $\$$ can therefore have no sense; if it did, perfectly sensible pieces of information would be rendered impossible.

It might be suggested that when, say, Pa is added, $\$Pa$ ought to be removed. $\$$, it may be suggested, functions something like negation-as-failure in PROLOG.[4] When a PROLOG data-base is asked whether Pa, it searches for a proof of this. If it cannot find one, it reports that $\$Pa$. If Pa is added to the data base, it will then cease to report this. But this just shows that $\$Pa$ is not reporting a piece of information. It is simply reporting the *absence* of information. If it really did report information, then adding Pa and dropping $\$Pa$ would not be a case of augmenting incomplete information—some information would have been lost.

The point about the untoward consequences of $\$$ may be made, though perhaps less obviously, if we think of worlds, not as states of information, but ontologically. If the conditional $Qa \rightarrow (Pa \vee \neg Pa)$ is to fail, as it will do in any relevant logic, then there must be a world, w, where $Pa \vee \neg Pa$, and so Pa and $\neg Pa$, fail. w may not be a possible world. Indeed, if $Pa \vee \neg Pa$ is a necessary truth, it will not be: it will be an impossible world—but a world nonetheless. Now, there ought to be a perfectly sensible world which is just a little less incomplete, which is the same as w except that Pa holds as well. But as before, if Boolean negation makes sense, $\$Pa$ holds at w, and so a world that is the same as w, except that Pa also holds, collapses into triviality. If $\$$ were legitimate, it would render a perfectly sensible state of affairs incoherent. And again, if it be suggested that we should not expect $\$Pa$ to be preserved at this world, this just shows that $\$Pa$ is not something that holds *in w*, but merely something *about w*. In other words, $\$$ is not to be understood as an operator which acts on the content of Pa to give another content of the same kind. *A fortiori*, it is not a meaningful such operator.

The general situation, then, is this. Whatever worlds are, they may be incomplete with respect to a state of affairs/piece of information. If w is any such world, there must be a world that is essentially the same, except that this state/piece is added. Let us call this the *Augmentation Constraint*. Any connective which would produce worlds that violate the Augmentation Constraint generates violations of what makes sense; so it, itself, cannot make sense. Boolean negation—but not the standard connectives—fails this test. Compare the situation with intuitionism. An intuitionist subscribes to the Verification Constraint: any meaningful sentence is such that, if true, it can be recognized as such. As we noted in section 4.4, Boolean negation fails this test, too.

---

[3] For details, see Priest (2001*a*), chs. 9, 10.   [4] See, e.g. Clark (1978).

5.3 BOOLEAN NEGATION BY PROOF THEORY

The foregoing argument is not definitive. Someone might deny the Augmentation Constraint, just as a classical logician might deny the Verification Constraint. But it at least shows why the meaningfulness of Boolean negation is not necessarily to be taken for granted, and so why arguments that it is are centrally important. What might such arguments be?

Let us start by asking how Boolean negation is to be characterized. Some kind of definition is required. Clearly, an explicit definition, of the form '*dialetheia* means *true contradiction*', is not going to get us very far. Such definitions are eliminable without loss—or if they are not, they are creative, and so objectionable. We must appeal therefore to some notion of implicit definition. Two sorts of implicit definition (hopefully equivalent) recommend themselves here: proof-theoretic and model-theoretic. Let us consider the proof-theoretic characterization first.

This way of characterizing Boolean negation is to specify that it is governed by a set of rules which generate all (and only) those rules of inference that are valid according to the classical theory of negation. Unfortunately, proceeding in this way does not show that there is a coherent notion satisfying those conditions. If one is free to introduce a connective by stipulating that it satisfy a certain collection of rules, then there is any number of ways of getting into a mess with the T-schema. For example, we might just introduce a new zero-place connective, $*$, satisfying the rule $\alpha \leftrightarrow * \vdash \beta$. Triviality then follows from the instance of the T-schema $T \langle * \rangle \leftrightarrow *$.

The point is that stating that a connective be such as to satisfy a certain set of rules is no way to guarantee it a sense, that is, to ensure its intelligibility. The point is a familiar one thanks to Prior and *tonk*, as we saw in section 4.2. Thus, a dialetheist may simply deny the intelligibility of Boolean negation thus characterized.

It is worth noting a disanalogy at this point. Various consistent attempts to solve the Liar paradox run into trouble due to the fact that, though they may solve the pristine Liar, extended or strengthened versions are available which they do not solve. Thus, against someone who claims that the Liar sentence is a truth-value gap, one considers the sentence: this sentence is false or a truth-value gap. A contradiction is soon forthcoming. If someone is tempted by the thought that they can avoid the consequence by denying the intelligibility of the notion of a truth-value gap, they should not be tempted for very long. The coherence of this notion is required by the coherence of the very solution to the paradox: if the notion makes no sense, neither does the solution. Thus, a person who wishes to solve the Liar paradox by appealing to truth-value gaps, yet denies the coherence of that notion is open to a devastating *ad hominem* argument. By contrast, Boolean negation is nowhere needed by a dialetheist. In particular, dialetheic solutions to the Liar paradox do not make use of the notion at all. It is therefore impossible to mount an *ad hominem* argument for the coherence of Boolean negation.[5]

---

[5] Another argument to the effect that Boolean negation makes perfectly good sense is to the effect that it must be so, since we use the notion, at least, in reasoning about consistent situations. But in

5.4 CONSERVATIVE EXTENSION

So what other arguments might be given as to the intelligibility of Boolean negation characterized proof-theoretically? The obvious ones are those provided by the
standard replies to Prior on *tonk*. There are three of these, all of the form that some
constraint must be applied to a set of rules if it is to determine sense. The first (that
of Belnap[6]) and, I think, least satisfactory, is that the addition of the new connective
must produce a conservative extension. That is, the addition must not allow anything in the unaugmented language, that was unprovable before, to become provable.
Does Boolean negation do this? Obviously not: semantically closed theories with a
suitable underlying paraconsistent logic are known to be non-trivial.[7] The addition
of Boolean negation produces triviality. By this test, Boolean negation is, indeed,
senseless.

　　Things are a bit more complex than this, however. The notion of conservative extension is, of course, relative to a pre-existing notion of deducibility; and, in particular, to
the logical apparatus already present (as Belnap was at pains to note). It might, therefore, be replied that though Boolean negation produces a non-conservative extension
if added to a logic with an unrestricted truth predicate, it does not do so if there is
no such predicate. It is therefore the truth predicate the addition of which produces
triviality, and so lacks sense.

　　Now it is not always true that the addition of Boolean negation to a logic without
a truth predicate produces a conservative extension. The addition of the rules for
Boolean negation to classical positive logic is indeed conservative. But, as is well
known, the addition of Boolean negation to positive intuitionist logic is not con-
servative: it gives rise to "Peirce's law" ($\vdash ((\alpha \rightarrow \beta) \rightarrow \alpha) \rightarrow \alpha$), which is not
intuitionistically valid.[8] However, it is not intuitionistic logic that is at issue here,
but a paraconsistent logic, and the addition of Boolean negation to standard relevant
logics is conservative.[9] Unfortunately, it is equally true that adding an unrestricted
truth predicate to many such logics produces a conservative extension—even when
the machinery of self-reference is available.[10] Thus, it is the *joint* addition of Boolean
negation and an unrestricted truth predicate that is non-conservative. Where, then,

---

fact, we do not. De Morgan negation behaves in the same way as Boolean negation in consistent
situations. In reasoning about these, we are just, therefore, employing De Morgan negation.

　　[6] Belnap (1962).　　　[7] See, e.g. Priest (2002*b*), sects. 8.1, 8.2.
　　[8] See, e.g. Dummett (1991), 291–2.　　　[9] See Meyer and Routley (1972; 1973).
　　[10] For example, if $\nvdash_{LP} \alpha$ then there is a classical interpretation in which α does not hold. (See
In Contradiction, 98.) But given any classical interpretation it is possible to extend this to an *LP*
model of the *T*-schema in which all formulas without the truth predicate retain their classical value.
(See Dowden (1984) and Priest (2002*b*), sect. 8.1.) A similar result holds for certain relevant logics,
and can be extracted from Brady (1989). I indicate the proof. Let *L* be the set of logical truths of
any relevant logic of the kind that Brady considers, and let $\beta \notin L$. It is well known that, for most
relevant logics, *L* can be extended to prime theory, L^+, such that $\beta \notin L^+$. (See Routley *et al.* (1982),
sect. 5.6.) Using L^+ and Brady's fixed-point construction, we can define a model of the logic and the
T-schema in which all members of L^+ hold, but β does not. (See the proof of Theorem 0 in Priest
(1991*a*) or Priest (2002*b*), sect. 8.2.)

should the blame be laid? The conservative-extension test is silent on this issue, and we witness its limitation.

5.5 HARMONY

Given what we have seen, another shortcoming of the conservative-extension test is also clear. The mere fact that a notion does not produce a conservative extension of some pre-existent set of rules is absolutely no reason to suppose that the notion has no sense. The non-conservative nature of the extension may be attributed to the fact that the old set of rules was simply incomplete. This, for example, is what the classical logician will say about the addition of Boolean negation to positive intuitionist logic.

For the conservative-extension test to have any punch, the pre-existing rules must, in some sense, be complete. How is one to cash out the notion of completeness here? An obvious answer is that the rules should be complete with respect to an appropriate semantics. But let us set semantics aside for a little longer. Another way of trying to understand an appropriate notion of completeness is also proof-theoretic. The thought here is that the rules of proof say *everything* there is to be said about the meanings of the connectives employed. Thus, following Dummett and Prawitz,[11] suppose that our proof-theory is formulated in terms of some system of natural deduction or sequent calculus, and that each connective comes with an introduction and an elimination rule. The introduction rule can be arbitrary. It is exactly what characterizes the meaning of the connective. But if this is so, the elimination rule cannot be arbitrary. It can allow us to get out of a formula that is packed in by its meaning, but no more than this. In the jargon used, the introduction and elimination rules must be in *harmony*. How, exactly, to cash out the notion of harmony depends on the exact details of the kind of proof-theory employed. But a natural way is to require that consecutive applications of the introduction and elimination rules can be eliminated: they form a detour that takes us nowhere. To illustrate (and following Read (2000)), suppose that we formulate our proof theory in terms of a sequent calculus (sequents being of the form $\Gamma : \Delta$, where Γ and Δ are finite sets of formulas), and that the introduction and elimination rules for a connective operate on the right-hand side of sequents. Then if the appropriate introduction rule for conjunction is:

$$\frac{\Gamma : \alpha, \Delta \qquad \Gamma : \beta, \Delta}{\Gamma : \alpha \wedge \beta, \Delta}$$

the appropriate elimination rule is:

$$\frac{\Gamma : \alpha \wedge \beta, \Delta \quad \Gamma, \alpha, \beta : \Delta}{\Gamma : \Delta}$$

[11] For a discussion, see Sundholm (1986), 485 ff.

These are in harmony, for if the second rule is applied immediately after the first, we have:

$$\frac{\dfrac{\Gamma : \alpha, \Delta \quad \Gamma : \beta, \Delta}{\Gamma : \alpha \wedge \beta, \Delta} \qquad \Gamma, \alpha, \beta : \Delta}{\Gamma : \Delta}$$

The detour via conjunction may now be eliminated thus:

$$\frac{\Gamma : \beta, \Delta \qquad \dfrac{\Gamma : \alpha, \Delta \quad \Gamma, \alpha, \beta : \Delta}{\Gamma, \beta : \Delta}}{\Gamma : \Delta}$$

The cut rule:

$$\frac{\Sigma : \gamma, \Pi \quad \Sigma, \gamma : \Pi}{\Sigma : \Pi}$$

(which can be avoided if cut-elimination holds) is applied at each step.

Thus, it might be suggested that the conservative extension should be relative to a set of rules that are in harmony. In fact, once we have the notion of harmony to hand, an appeal to conservativeness becomes redundant. The rules for a coherent notion need to be in harmony; and this the rules for *tonk* fail to be—spectacularly. This is the second reply to Prior.[12] The introduction and elimination rules for *tonk* (∗) are:

$$\frac{\Gamma : \alpha, \Delta}{\Gamma : \alpha * \beta, \Delta} \qquad \frac{\Gamma : \alpha * \beta, \Delta \quad \Gamma, \beta : \Delta}{\Gamma : \Delta}$$

Successive applications gives:

$$\frac{\dfrac{\Gamma : \alpha, \Delta}{\Gamma : \alpha * \beta, \Delta} \quad \Gamma, \beta : \Delta}{\Gamma : \Delta}$$

But as is clear, there is no way that the *tonk*-introduction can be eliminated.

Now, what of the case for Boolean negation? Appropriate sequent calculi for relevant logics (which have De Morgan negations) are more complicated than those for classical and intuitionist logics. In particular, they require two distinct ways of grouping together antecedents and consequents: , (corresponding to extensional connectives) and ; (corresponding to intensional).[13] The extra complexities are largely irrelevant to the present situation, however. The appropriate introduction and elimination rules for Boolean negation are:

$$\frac{\Gamma, \alpha : \Delta}{\Gamma : \$\alpha, \Delta} \qquad \frac{\Gamma : \$\alpha, \Delta \quad \Gamma : \alpha, \Delta}{\Gamma : \Delta}$$

[12] It is given by Read (1988), 186–7, and (2000), 124.
[13] See Restall (2000), chs. 2, 3. Note that the standard structural rules, such as dilution, hold for , .

These are obviously in harmony, since successive applications give:

$$\frac{\Gamma, \alpha : \Delta}{\dfrac{\Gamma : \$\alpha, \Delta \quad \Gamma : \alpha, \Delta}{\Gamma : \Delta}}$$

From which $\$\alpha$ may be eliminated with a cut in the obvious way:

$$\frac{\Gamma, \alpha : \Delta \quad \Gamma : \alpha, \Delta}{\Gamma : \Delta}$$

So it looks as though Boolean negation passes the test. Unfortunately, exactly the same phenomenon arises as with conservative extensibility. The truth predicate has the following introduction and elimination rules:

$$\frac{\Gamma : \alpha, \Delta}{\Gamma : T\langle\alpha\rangle, \Delta} \qquad \frac{\Gamma : T\langle\alpha\rangle, \Delta \quad \Gamma, \alpha : \Delta}{\Gamma : \Delta}$$

These are obviously in harmony, since successive applications give:

$$\frac{\Gamma : \alpha, \Delta}{\dfrac{\Gamma : T\langle\alpha\rangle, \Delta \quad \Gamma, \alpha : \Delta}{\Gamma : \Delta}}$$

From which $T\langle\alpha\rangle$ may be eliminated with a cut in the obvious way:

$$\frac{\Gamma : \alpha, \Delta \quad \Gamma, \alpha : \Delta}{\Gamma : \Delta}$$

Thus, T also passes the harmony test. But if we have Boolean negation and the truth predicate (together with self-reference), triviality ensues. Here is the proof.[14] Suppose that we have a formula, λ, of the form $\$T\langle\lambda\rangle$. Then:

$$
\frac{
\dfrac{
\dfrac{
\dfrac{T\langle\lambda\rangle : T\langle\lambda\rangle}{: T\langle\lambda\rangle, \$T\langle\lambda\rangle}}{: T\langle\lambda\rangle, \lambda}}{: T\langle\lambda\rangle, T\langle\lambda\rangle}}{: T\langle\lambda\rangle}
\quad
T\langle\lambda\rangle : T\langle\lambda\rangle
\quad
\dfrac{
\dfrac{
\dfrac{
\dfrac{\$T\langle\lambda\rangle : \$T\langle\lambda\rangle \quad T\langle\lambda\rangle : T\langle\lambda\rangle}{\$T\langle\lambda\rangle, T\langle\lambda\rangle :}}{\lambda, T\langle\lambda\rangle :}}{T\langle\lambda\rangle, T\langle\lambda\rangle :}}{T\langle\lambda\rangle :}}{: \$T\langle\lambda\rangle}
}{\vdots}
$$

The harmony of the rules for each notion, does not, then, ensure coherence. In particular, though Boolean negation be harmonious, this is not enough. Of course, *tonk* does a lot more than violate conservativeness and harmony. It delivers triviality. This is what tells us that it is incoherent. The same, in the appropriate context, is true of Boolean negation.

---

[14] The idea is taken from Read (2000), 141 f. Read uses a logical constant (zero-place operator), •, instead of the truth predicate and self-reference.

5.6 BOOLEAN NEGATION BY MODEL THEORY

We are still in search of a constraint that may be imposed on a set of rules, and which is sufficient for coherence. Two proof-theoretic constraints have failed. The third possible constraint, and, I think, the most adequate one, is that the rules of inference in question must answer to some satisfactory semantic account of the connective, in the sense that the rules are demonstrably sound (and, if we are lucky, complete) with respect to the semantics.[15] This brings us to the second way of characterizing Boolean negation: in model-theoretic terms.

What is an adequate semantic characterization to which the rules of Boolean negation must answer? This raises the prior question of what an adequate semantics should be like anyway. The question is an important one. For if one is an intuitionist or constructivist of some other stripe, no semantics can be adequate unless it gives semantic conditions which we can effectively recognize as obtaining when they do. If this view is correct then Boolean negation is an immediate casualty. For, as intuitionists have stressed, classical negation does not have such semantics.[16]

However, the majority of people who have discussed Boolean negation in the present context are not intuitionists. And I have argued against the intuitionist critique of classical semantics in 4.4. So we may set this point aside. This only partly solves the problem of what a semantics for Boolean negation should be like, however; for even the defenders of Boolean negation have given different kinds of semantic account (four-valued ternary relational, two-valued ternary relational, algebraic, etc.). Fortunately, then, the differences between them are not relevant to the essential points that need to be made.

Suppose that we are giving a model theory in which connectives are given truth (and falsity) conditions.[17] Given an interpretation, $\mathcal{I}$, assume that the conditions for conjunction and disjunction in an interpretation are as usual.

$\alpha \wedge \beta$ is true in $\mathcal{I}$ iff α is true in $\mathcal{I}$ and β is true in $\mathcal{I}$
$\alpha \wedge \beta$ is false in $\mathcal{I}$ iff α is false in $\mathcal{I}$ or β is false in $\mathcal{I}$

$\alpha \vee \beta$ is true in $\mathcal{I}$ iff α is true in $\mathcal{I}$ or β is true in $\mathcal{I}$
$\alpha \vee \beta$ is false in $\mathcal{I}$ α is false in $\mathcal{I}$ and β is false in $\mathcal{I}$

---

[15] This was suggested by Stevenson (1961). '. . . we must show that, given a statement of the syntactic properties of a connective, the soundness of certain rules of inference can be demonstrated . . . we can state the syntactic [*sic*] properties of, say, a truth-functional binary sentence connective, "o", by stating in the meta-langauge, the way the truth-value of the well formed formula "$p \circ q$" is a function of (all possible combinations of) the truth-values of the components "p" and "q". We can then deduce from these statements, in a very rigorous way, a meta-theorem of the calculus (again stated in the meta-language) to the effect that such-and-such permissive rules are sound' (p. 126).

[16] See Dummett (1975*a*).

[17] See, e.g. *In Contradiction*, ch. 5. If interpretations have worlds, so that we must give truth-in-a-world (in an interpretation) conditions, this changes nothing essential. Merely insert the words 'at w' after 'true' and 'false' in the truth/falsity conditions, and follow through.

I will continue to use ¬ for (De Morgan) negation.[18] The model-theoretic generalization of the truth (*simpliciter*) conditions of 4.5 are:

¬α is true in $\mathcal{I}$ iff α is false in $\mathcal{I}$
¬α is false in $\mathcal{I}$ iff α is true in $\mathcal{I}$

Boolean negation can now be characterized semantically by:

\$$\alpha$ is true in $\mathcal{I}$ iff α is **not** true in $\mathcal{I}$
\$$\alpha$ is false in $\mathcal{I}$ iff α is true in $\mathcal{I}$

Note that the truth conditions for Boolean negation (unlike those for De Morgan
negation) actually *use* the notion of negation (boldfaced).[19]

One might contest the claim that these truth conditions provide an adequate specification of meaning.[20] However, let us grant them (at least for the sake of argument).
As can easily be checked, given that the negation employed in stating the truth conditions of \$ has the properties of De Morgan negation that we established in the last
chapter, we have the following. In every interpretation, $\mathcal{I}$:

1. α is true or \$$\alpha$ is true
2. it is not the case that α and \$$\alpha$ are both true

Hence, in every interpretation $\alpha \vee$ \$$\alpha$ and \$($\alpha \wedge$ \$$\alpha$) are true. To this extent, \$
behaves like ¬. The question is whether it satisfies the other principles of Boolean
negation—in particular, whether it satisfies Explosion, so ruling out the possibility of
surplus content.

5.7 EXPLOSION

In model-theoretic semantics, a valid inference is defined as one which is truth-
preserving in all interpretations. That is, $\alpha \models \beta$ iff for every interpretation $\mathcal{I}$:

3. **if** α is true in $\mathcal{I}$, β is true in $\mathcal{I}$

---

[18] One might note that the truth/falsity conditions for conjunction and disjunction are already
sufficient to show the equivalence of DS and Explosion, regardless of the truth conditions for negation.
For $\alpha \wedge (\neg\alpha \vee \beta)$ entails $(\alpha \wedge \neg\alpha) \vee \beta$, and this entail β if $\alpha \wedge \neg\alpha$ does. Conversely, if the DS
holds then so does Explosion, by the familiar argument. (See, e.g. Priest (2007), 4.9.2.) All these
inferences involve only conjunction and disjunction essentially and are validated by the semantics.

[19] In the semantics of relevant logics with the Routley *, the truth (in an interpretation) conditions
of negation are: ¬α is true at w iff α is not true at w^*. In this context, the ("Boolean") condition
that $w = w^*$ gives us: ¬α is true at w iff α is not true at w—and we are in the same situation.

[20] For example, consider the following *tonk*-like truth conditions (suggested by Steve Read):

$\alpha * \beta$ is true iff α is true
$\alpha * \beta$ is false iff β is false

Suppose that α is true; then $\alpha * \beta$ is true. This would seem to entail that $\alpha * \beta$, and so β, are not
false; which would seem to entail that β is true. Clearly, something has gone wrong here. If one takes
truth and falsity to be mutually exclusive and exhaustive the truth/falsity conditions obviously do
not meet these conditions. If one thinks that truth and falsity are not like this, the truth conditions
may be acceptable, but then one is going to reject the argument from the truth of α to the truth of
β, since the connections between truth and falsity appealed to may fail.

(Keep your eye on the boldfaced **if** here.) The validity of Explosion for $ now comes to this. For all $\mathcal{I}$:

   4. if $\alpha \wedge \$\alpha$ is true in $\mathcal{I}$, β is true in $\mathcal{I}$

What to say about the matter now depends on how we interpret **if**. Suppose, first, that we interpret it as a genuine possible conditional. A moment's thought suffices to show that the inference from 2 to 4 is a quantified version of the inference AF ($\neg\gamma \vdash \gamma \rightarrow \delta$). And this, as we saw in section 4.6, is fallacious. The argument to the effect that $ does not allow for surplus content therefore fails.[21]

Another possibility is that the **if** of 4 is taken to be the material conditional, $\supset$ (where $\alpha \supset \beta$ is $\neg\alpha \vee \beta$). Then the inference from 2 to 4 is a quantified version of the inference $\neg\alpha \vdash \neg\alpha \vee \beta$, which is perfectly valid. On this definition of validity, Explosion is indeed valid. But now we hit another problem. The validity of Explosion in this sense does not rule out surplus content, since it does not generally licence detachment! Though we certainly have:

   for all $\mathcal{I}$ (γ is true in $\mathcal{I} \supset \delta$ is true in $\mathcal{I}$) $\vdash$ (γ is true in $\mathcal{J} \supset \delta$ is true in $\mathcal{J}$)

we cannot, given the premise and the antecedent of the material conditional, detach to obtain the conclusion that δ is true in $\mathcal{J}$. For this is to deploy the Disjunctive Syllogism, which, as we saw in 4.6 does not support detachment in inconsistent contexts. In particular, then, suppose we can, through techniques of diagonalization (or whatever) come up with a "Boolean contradiction"—a sentence, α, such that $\alpha \wedge \$\alpha$ is true—and an interpretation, $\mathcal{J}$, which is in accord with the actual (in the sense that something is true in $\mathcal{J}$ iff it is true *simpliciter*). Then we are *obviously* in

---

[21] A complete account of the properties of $, characterized model-theoretically, will have to wait for a metatheory for the notion that is relevantly/paraconsistently acceptable. This is not on offer today. As a temporary measure, the following is a classical model of Boolean negation which shows, at least, that the truth conditions of Boolean negation do not deliver Explosion. (This draws on Priest (1980).) A propositional structure is a pair, $\langle \mathbf{L}, T \rangle$. $\mathbf{L}$ is itself a structure, $\langle L, \wedge, \vee, \neg, \rightarrow, \$ \rangle$. Intuitively, L is thought of as a set of propositions, or Fregean senses. The other components are operators on L of obvious arity. I use the same sign for the operator and the logical connective for which it is to be the interpretation. (Disambiguation will be provided by the style of variable it is used with.) $\langle L, \wedge, \vee, \neg \rangle$ is a De Morgan lattice, i.e. a distributive lattice, where $\neg$ is an involution of period two ($\neg\neg a = a$ and $a \leq b \Rightarrow \neg b \leq \neg a$). It is natural enough to suppose that propositions have the structure of such a lattice, with the lattice ordering capturing the idea of containment of sense, that is, entailment. T is a subset of L. Intuitively, it is thought of as the set of true propositions. This makes it natural for it to satisfy the following conditions. (1) T is a prime filter on the lattice (i.e. $a \wedge b \in T$ iff $a \in T$ and $b \in T$, and $a \vee b \in T$ iff $a \in T$ or $b \in T$; (2) $a \in T$ or $\neg a \in T$; (3) $a \rightarrow b \in T$ iff $a \leq b$; (4) $\$a \in T$ iff $a \notin T$. These last two conditions are exactly the ones one would expect for an entailment operator and Boolean negation. Now, an interpretation for the language is a pair, $\langle P, \nu \rangle$, where P is a propositional structure and ν is a map from the language into P, satisfying the natural homomorphism. We may read $\nu(\alpha) \in T$ as: α is true in the interpretation. A sentence, α, is a logical truth iff it is true in every interpretation. An inference with set of premises Σ and conclusion α is valid iff in every interpretation $\nu[\Sigma] \leq \nu(\alpha)$, where $\nu[\Sigma]$ is the meet of $\{\nu(\beta); \beta \in \Sigma\}$. Thus, a valid inference is one where the senses of the premises contain that of the conclusion. These are the semantics for a relevant logic with De Morgan negation. They therefore validate LEM, LNC, LDM, and LDN, and invalidate Explosion and DS. It is a simple exercise to show that they also validate $\alpha \vee \$\alpha$ and $\$(\alpha \wedge \$\alpha)$. They invalidate AF and Boolean Explosion. I leave the former as an exercise. To see the latter, just consider the propositional structure where L is the lattice of integers (positive and negative), $\neg a$ is $-a$, T comprises the non-negative integers, and $\$a$ is -3 if $a \in T$, and $+3$ if $a \notin T$. ($\rightarrow$ is irrelevant.) Map p to 6. Then the lattice value of $p \wedge \$p$ is -3. Now map q to -6 to give a counter-example to $p \wedge \$p \models q$.

an inconsistent context: we have $\alpha \wedge \$\alpha$ true in $\mathcal{J}$, even though it is not. There is therefore no way to conclude that β is true in $\mathcal{J}$, and so β, for an arbitrary β. The collapse of surplus content into total content does not eventuate.

At this point, it might be noted that the argument thus far has assumed that the negation in the truth conditions for Boolean negation, **not**, is De Morgan negation. If it is itself Boolean negation, then the crucial inferential moves that I have been discussing go through, as, therefore, does the argument to the effect that $\$$ has no surplus content. But now recall the dialectic. The point of the argument was precisely to establish the coherence of a notion satisfying the properties of classical negation. If the only way we can do this is by appealing to such a notion, and so presupposing its coherence, then the argument is clearly question-begging.

I have sometimes heard it argued that taking negation to be Boolean in the present context is perfectly acceptable, since that context is metatheoretic, and metatheory is (must be?) classical. This is a short-sighted argument. Any intuitionist or dialetheist takes themself to be giving an account of the correct behaviour of certain logical particles. Is it to be supposed that their account of this behaviour is to be given in a way that they take to be incorrect? Clearly not. The same logic must be used in both "object theory" and "metatheory".[22] Indeed, even this distinction is bogus for someone who espouses a dialetheic solution to the semantic paradoxes. The idea that the metatheory must be a distinct, more powerful, theory, is a response to the first horn of the dilemma of 4.6. It has nothing to recommend it once we give up trying to find a consistent solution to the semantic paradoxes. The distinction between a theory (say about numbers) and its metatheory makes perfectly good sense to a dialetheist. But there is no reason to insist that the metatheory must be stronger than, and therefore different from, the theory. Indeed, if the original theory deals with, say, numbers and truth, then the metatheory may be a *sub-theory* of the theory.

5.8 BOOLEAN NEGATION NEGATED

As we have now seen, the argument to the effect that there is an intelligible connective, $\$$, which rules out the possibility of surplus content may be rejected. If Boolean negation is characterized proof-theoretically, it is a connective like *tonk* that leads to triviality, and so has no coherent sense. And the classical truth conditions can be shown to deliver a connective having the properties of Boolean negation only by fallacious, or, at least, question-begging, arguments. The dialetheist is therefore at liberty to maintain that Boolean negation has no coherent sense.

It may come of a shock to some that the rules of classical negation characterize a connective that lacks sense. (We have been talking gibberish since Boole!) But one should not forget that whether or not something makes sense is *theory dependent*. And the dialetheist lines up with the intuitionist in this battle: the classical theorist has got it wrong. Nor has a classical logician any reason to feel smug about this. As we have

---

[22] Intuitionist metatheories for intuitionist logic are well known. See, e.g. Dummett (1977), esp. 214.

seen, if Boolean negation is meaningful, then a predicate satisfying the unrestricted *T*-schema cannot be—which seems no better.[23] Indeed, it is worse, since dialetheist accounts of negation are much simpler and more natural than any of the standard restricted accounts of truth.

It is always possible for someone to reply to all of this by agreeing that it is impossible to prove that $ behaves classically, but saying, nonetheless, that they intend to employ a connective, $, and let it be governed by the rules of classical negation, such as $\alpha \land \$\alpha \vdash \beta$. But this proves nothing. Someone can equally say: I am going to act according to the rule that people do not fall when they walk out of tenth-floor windows. All may, indeed, go well until a semantic paradox or a tenth-floor window is encountered. Both theorists must then prevaricate or take the consequences.

Though not, perhaps, strictly relevant, this is a good place to say a word about the history of relevant logic. Modal logic was born of a dissatisfaction with classical logic, and in particular with the material conditional. Lewis took himself to be offering a *rival* to classical logic. History has changed this perception of the situation. Modal logic is not a rival to classical logic, but an *extension*. A modal logic can be seen as classical logic extended by an intensional functor or two. History has a strange way of repeating itself. Relevant logic, too, was born of a dissatisfaction with the material conditional, and was proposed as a rival to classical logic (and modal logic to the extent that a strict conditional is supposed to give an adequate account of a genuine conditional). However, later there came voices, even those of erstwhile relevant logicians, according to whom it, too, should be seen as a mere extension of classical logic.[24] Classical logic is the logic of conjunction, disjunction, and negation—Boolean of course. Relevant logic merely adds to this two funny functors: De Morgan negation and an intentional $\rightarrow$. Whatever relevant logicians as such think about this proposal, it should be clear that from the perspective of dialetheism, this view is not only wrong, but highly misguided. De Morgan negation is not some funny add-on functor: it is the correct theoretical account of the negation that we commonly use and love. Boolean negation—to the extent that something can be characterized by this epithet—is either unintelligible, or else does not have the properties of classical negation. *It* is therefore the funny functor, if anything is. Dialetheic logic, unlike modal logic, does, therefore, provide a genuine rival theory to that provided by classical logic.

5.9 CURRY CONDITIONALS

To return from this digression: Perhaps the most fundamental lesson to be learned from the deliberations of section 5.7, and one that is already well known to most perceptive logic teachers, is that to show the validity of certain rules of inference, truth

---

[23] There is a third possibility here. Maintain the coherence of both Boolean negation and the truth predicate, but give up the coherence of self-reference of the appropriate kind. Given how natural such self-reference seems (in many forms), if one goes this way there is clearly no ground for smugness either.

[24] See Meyer (1985), though the seeds of this view can be found in Meyer (1974).

conditions alone are not enough. Inference must be made from those conditions; and those inferences *may* be just those whose validity one is trying to demonstrate.[25] (In fact, I suspect that one of the appeals of the view that the Boolean truth conditions are the correct ones for negation arises from the mistaken thought that these deliver the validity of the classical rules of proof for negation. As we have seen, they do not—at least on their own.)

A way of illustrating the same point is by considering another way in which a dialetheic semantics may be thought to fail in connection with the paradoxes of self-reference. It is not only Explosion that may cause triviality in a theory with an unrestricted truth predicate. As was demonstrated by Curry, amongst others, and is now well known, if the conditional employed in the T-schema (or the abstraction schema of naive set theory), $\rightarrow$, satisfies the rules of *modus ponens* and Contraction (or Absorption), $\alpha \rightarrow (\alpha \rightarrow \beta) \vdash \alpha \rightarrow \beta$, then triviality ensues.[26] *Modus ponens* is hard to get away from for any genuine conditional; so what this is naturally taken to mean is that Contraction must fail. Contraction must fail not just for $\rightarrow$, though. If there is any conditional, $\Rightarrow$, such that $\alpha \rightarrow \beta \vdash \alpha \Rightarrow \beta$, and which satisfies *modus ponens* and Contraction, triviality follows.[27] Call any connective that satisfies these conditions a *Curry conditional*. Someone who subscribes to a dialetheic solution to the paradoxes of self-reference must hold that no connective, including $\rightarrow$, is a Curry conditional.[28]

In fact, it is not difficult to give an account of a conditional appropriate for the T-schema that is not a Curry conditional: any contraction-free relevant logic will provide one.[29] But it might, again, be suggested that there are other perfectly intelligible Curry conditionals. Making the case for this is prone to fail for exactly the same reasons that the corresponding case for Boolean negation fails, however. If such a connective is characterized proof-theoretically, then its intelligibility may simply be denied: it clearly fails to give a non-trivial extension. Rules for a contracting conditional, if they are harmonious, still give triviality when combined with the harmonious rules for the truth predicate (given self-reference). We merely reproduce Curry's paradox in this context.

Establishing that the rules for the conditional pass the semantic test is the same task as demonstrating that an appropriate semantics for the conditional shows it to validate Contraction and *modus ponens*. The details of the argument will depend on the form that one thinks the semantics of conditionals ought to take. However, essentially the same sort of situation will arise whatever this is. So let me illustrate with a simple

---

[25] For two essays on this theme, see Dummett (1975*b*) and Haack (1976).

[26] See, e.g. Meyer, Dunn, and Routley (1979), and *In Contradiction*, ch. 6.

[27] Merely consider the instance of the T-schema for the self-referential sentence, α, such that $T\langle\alpha\rangle \leftrightarrow (\alpha \Rightarrow \bot)$. Since $\rightarrow$ is stronger than $\Rightarrow$, it follows that $T\langle\alpha\rangle \Leftrightarrow (\alpha \Rightarrow \bot)$. Now run the argument in the usual way.

[28] Boolean negation and Curry conditionals are not the only connectives that give rise to triviality in the context of the unrestricted T-schema. Another is given by Denyer (1989). But invariably the situation with respect to the argument for the coherence of such notions is exactly the same. With repect to Denyer, this is pointed out in Priest (1989*c*).

[29] See also *In Contradiction*, ch. 6.

case. We suppose the semantics of conditionals simply requires us to give truth (in-an-interpretation) conditions. (As before, adding the machinery of possible worlds, does nothing to change the situation essentially.)

Then to give the truth conditions for a conditional, $\Rightarrow$, one might use clearly extensional connectives, such as disjunction and negation, as in:

$\alpha \Rightarrow \beta$ is true in $\mathcal{I}$ iff α is not true in $\mathcal{I}$ or β is true in $\mathcal{I}$

or else one might use a conditional itself:

$\alpha \Rightarrow \beta$ is true in $\mathcal{I}$ iff **if** α is true in $\mathcal{I}$, β is true in $\mathcal{I}$

The notion, defined in either of these ways, is quite intelligible. But the first reduces *modus ponens* for $\Rightarrow$ to the DS, whence it is not semantically valid.

What happens in the second case depends, of course, on what properties the conditional used in stating the truth conditions, **if**, is taken to have. As is easy to see, $\Rightarrow$ inherits its properties from **if**. In particular, assuming that **if** satisfies *modus ponens*, so does $\Rightarrow$. And the only way that $\Rightarrow$ can be shown to satisfy Contraction is to assume Contraction for **if**. But this is to assume, in effect, that there is an intelligible Curry conditional, which was just what was to be shown. The argument is therefore viciously circular.[30]

5.10 CONCLUSION

To establish the validity of various inferences one needs more than truth conditions; one needs various inferences. And the inferences may be the ones whose validity we are trying to establish. In other words, the process requires a certain amount of bootstrapping. But this by no means implies that we must fall back on classical logic willy-nilly. Many logical theories can provide the relevant bootstrapping. Decision between them has to be made on other grounds. The grounds include the many criteria familiar from the philosophy of science: theoretical integrity (e.g. paucity of *ad hoc* hypotheses), adequacy to the data (explaining the data of inference—all inferences, not just those drawn from consistent domains!), and so on. This is a topic to which we will turn in the next part of the book. All that this chapter has attempted to demonstrate is that the dialetheist can legitimately reject that claim that there is a coherent connective satisfying the conditions of classical negation. And thus, in particular, a dialetheic solution to the paradoxes of self-reference is not impugned.

---

[30] To illustrate how the same problem may arise in a more complex case, consider the supposedly contracting conditional proposed by Everett (1994). He works within the context of a modal logic, and calls a world, w, reflexive just if wRw. Now, define a conditional, $\Rightarrow$, by the following truth conditions: $v_w(\alpha \Rightarrow \beta) = 1$ iff for all reflexive w' such that wRw', if $v_{w'}(\alpha) = 1$, $v_{w'}(\beta) = 1$. Now suppose that $v_w(\alpha \Rightarrow (\alpha \Rightarrow \beta)) = 1$. Then for all reflexive w' such that wRw', if $v_{w'}(\alpha) = 1$ then (for all reflexive w'' such that $w'Rw''$, if $v_{w''}(\alpha) = 1$ then $v_{w''}(\beta) = 1$). Hence, for all reflexive w' such that wRw', if $v_{w'}(\alpha) = 1$, then, if $v_{w'}(\alpha) = 1$ then $v_{w'}(\beta) = 1$. To get to the truth of $\alpha \Rightarrow \beta$, we next need to contract the conditional 'if $v_{w'}(\alpha) = 1$, then, if $v_{w'}(\alpha) = 1$ then $v_{w'}(\beta) = 1$'. The problem is pointed out and further discussed in Priest (1996*b*).

We are still not finished with negation, however. This chapter and the last have been concerned largely with the semantics of the notion. But there is usually thought to be an intimate connection between negation and pragmatic notions—particularly the notions of denial and rejection. It is often claimed that this connection provides trouble for the dialetheist. To this subject we turn in the next chapter.[31]

---

[31] Parts of this chapter were given at a seminar at the Free University of Brussels (May 2004) and at a meeting of the Australasian Association of Logic (July 2004). I am grateful to those present for their thoughtful comments, and in particular to Jean Paul van Bendegem, Ross Brady, Kit Fine, Chris Mortensen, and Greg Restall.

6

Denial and Rejection

6.1 INTRODUCTION

The core topic of this chapter is rejection, of the propositional kind. The linguistic expression of rejection is denial, an act that has often been thought to be intimately connected with negation. In the first part of the chapter, we will investigate the connection and some of its consequences—or otherwise—for dialetheism.

Rejection is also connected with the core concept of Part I of the book: truth, or more precisely, untruth. The second part of this chapter explores the connection. This will raise the issue of rational dilemmas of certain kinds; and in the last part of the chapter we will look at that topic.

Let us start by getting some of these basic notions straight, starting with rejection and its correlative notion, acceptance. Acceptance and rejection (as I shall use the terms—of course they can be used in other ways) are cognitive states. To accept something is simply to believe it, to have it in one's "belief box", as it were.[1] To reject something is to refuse to believe it: if it is in one's belief box one takes it out, but whether or not it was in there before, one resolves to keep it out. Accepting something and rejecting it would certainly seem to be exclusive; but they are not exhaustive. One might not believe something because one has never considered it, or because one has considered it but found no evidence, or found insufficient evidence. In such cases one is agnostic about the claim in question; the jury is still, as it were, out; and in such cases, one neither accepts nor rejects it. Rejecting something is a lot stronger than agnosticism of this kind: it is putting a bar on accepting it (although, of course, one can change one's mind about this in the light of new evidence, etc.). When justified, it is so because there is evidence against the claim: positive grounds for keeping it out of one's beliefs—rather than the mere absence of grounds for having it in.[2]

Assertion and denial, unlike acceptance and rejection, are not cognitive states but kinds of linguistic acts. Equivalently, one may think of them as illocutory forces with which utterances may be made. They are not the only such forces: questioning and commanding are others. Thus, consider an utterance of the sentence 'The window is open'. Given the appropriate context, this could be an assertion, a question, or a

---

[1] Or maybe to believe it to a high enough degree, depending on what one takes to be the connection between degress of belief and belief *simpliciter*.

[2] See, further, the discussion in *In Contradiction*, sect. 7.3.

command (to shut it). It could even be a denial (consider an utterance heavily laden with irony).

Assertion and denial are closely connected with cognitive states, however. Crudely, they are the linguistic expression of acceptance and rejection, respectively. Less crudely, the typical aim of assertion is to indicate that the utterer accepts the thing asserted, and, it may well be added, has appropriate grounds for doing so. (Derivatively, then, it often aims at getting the listener to accept it too). The typical aim of denial is to indicate that the utterer rejects the thing denied, and, again, one may add, has appropriate grounds for doing so. (Derivatively, then, it often aims at getting the listener to reject it too.)[3]

6.2 NEGATION AND DENIAL

So far, things are reasonably straightforward. Henceforth it is more contentious. Although assertion and denial are distinct linguistic acts, Frege argued[4] (and many now accept[5]) that denial is not a *sui generis* linguistic act. Specifically:

to deny α is simply to assert $\neg\alpha$

If negation is understood in the way that I suggested in Chapter 4, this identity is not at all plausible. If I assert a sentence that is the contradictory of α, I certainly do not, in general, expect a hearer to reject α or to believe that I do. The sentence may well be a complex one; and the fact that it expresses the contradictory of α may not be obvious—or even known—by either of us. The identity is more plausible if one takes $\neg\alpha$ to be something like α prefixed by 'it is not the case that'. Even that is not quite right though. A sentence of this form can be used to make a "metalinguistic negation" (see sect. 4.3): just consider 'It's not the case that Hitler was a bad man—he was downright evil.' Still, it might be thought, once negation is purged of idiosyncrasies of this kind, Frege was right enough.

He was not. For a start, there are many ways of denying something that do not involve the assertion of anything. Thus, I can shake my head, say 'no', or even stomp off in a rage. Perhaps more importantly, consider someone who supposes that some sentences are neither true nor false. Let α be a sentence that they take to be of this kind. They will then deny α; but their denial is certainly not to be taken as an assertion of $\neg\alpha$. They take this to be neither true nor false as well, and so will not assert it. And it makes no difference if you think that there are no truth-value gaps. The point is

[3] I am not claiming that 'deny' is always used in this way in the vernacular: 'negation' and 'denial' are often, in fact, used interchangably. However, it is important to distinguish clearly between propositional content and linguistic act. For this reason I will stick to using these two words as explained. There is, in fact, a tradition in philosophy, going back to Aristotle himself, for using 'denial' and 'assertion' for the propositional contents of negated and unnegated sentences (respectively). In the case of 'assertion', this invited a confusion that bedeviled logic until Frege cleared it up. (See Frege (1919).) I suspect that the confusion in the case of 'denial' is still taking its toll. See, e.g. the discussion of Lear in sect. 1.13.   [4] See Frege (1919).

[5] See, e.g. Smiley (1993).

that you understand someone who thinks that there are. You understand their denial, and do not understand them as asserting the negated sentence.

Conversely, a dialetheist who has ground for believing that α and $\neg\alpha$ are both true may assert $\neg\alpha$ without thereby denying α. Thus, for example, I will assert both 'The Liar sentence is true' and 'The Liar sentence is not true'. In asserting the latter I most certainly do not intend you to come to believe that I reject the former: I don't. Nor does it matter if you are not a dialetheist yourself. You understand me perfectly well.

Even without taking dialetheism into account one can see that asserting a negation (in the Fregean sense) is not necessarily a denial. In explaining their views, people often assert contradictions unwittingly. In this way, they discover—or someone else points out to them—that their views are inconsistent. In virtue of this, they may wish to revise their views. In asserting $\neg\alpha$ in this context, they are not expressing a refusal to accept α and so denying it. It is precisely the fact that they accept *both* α and $\neg\alpha$ that tends to promote belief revision. But it may even be rational sometimes (completely independently of any consideration of dialetheism) to hang on to both beliefs and continue to assert them. Consider, for example, the Paradox of the Preface. In this, one has evidence (as good as you like) for the joint truth of a certain number of claims, say those in a book, $\alpha_1, \ldots, \alpha_n$, and so their conjunction—call this α; but we also have very strong inductive evidence that at least one of these claims is false: $\neg\alpha$. In such a situation, the rational thing to do is to accept both contradictories (whilst, possibly, noting that the situation is anomalous). If this is right—and philosophers as orthodox as Arthur Prior have thought so[6]—someone who asserts $\neg\alpha$ does not reject α, and rationally so. And even if Prior were wrong, this does not matter. If to assert $\neg\alpha$ were *ipso facto* to deny α, Prior's suggestion could not even make any sense—which it does.

Denying is not, therefore, the same thing as asserting something starting 'it is not the case that'. Yet acts of denial *can* be performed by asserting negations. If, for example, I am in a discussion with someone who claims that the truth is consistent, it is natural for me to mark my rejection of the view by uttering 'it is not', thereby denying it.

This raises the question of when the uttering of a negated sentence is to be interpreted as an assertion, and when as a denial. There is, in general, no neat answer to this question. One has to assess the intentions of the utterer. The information provided by tone of voice, context, etc. will provide relevant clues here. Nor is there anything novel in this kind of situation. The utterance of the sentence 'would you close the door' can constitute linguistic acts with quite different illocutory forces (e.g. commanding, requesting). One often needs to be a very fluent speaker of a language (including having a knowledge of the social practices and relations in which the language is embedded), and have detailed knowledge of the context, to be able to determine which kind of linguistic act is, in fact, being performed.

In most contexts, an assertion of $-\alpha$, that is, $\alpha \rightarrow \perp$ (see section 4.7), would constitute an act of denial. Assuming that the person is normal, they will reject $\perp$,

---

[6] See Prior (1971), 85. Rescher and Brandom (1980), 47, draw the same conclusion.

and so, by implication, α. The qualifier 'in most contexts' is there because if one were ever to come across a trivialist who accepts $\bot$, this would not be the case. For such a person, an assertion of $-\alpha$ would not constitute a denial: nothing would.

6.3 EXPRESSIBILITY

With this understanding in place, we can now confront a common objection to dialetheism. It is often charged that dialetheists cannot express their own views.[7] A dialetheist cannot say anything which rules something out, and so which expresses disagreement. For example, if you say α, I do not express disagreement when I say $\neg\alpha$. For it is logically possible that both are true. More generally, whatever I say, there are models of both it and α (if only the trivial one, where everything is true).[8] As a special case of this, it is claimed, a dialetheist cannot even express the claim that a sentence is true but not false. They can, of course, use these words; but the fact that a sentence is not false does not rule out its being false as well; it may *still* be both true and false.

One particular reason why this charge is significant—though the objection is a quite general one—is that a standard objection to someone who espouses a truth-value gap solution to the semantic paradoxes is precisely that they cannot express their own theory—or the notions involved would engender extended paradoxes. (See section 7.5.) The dialetheist, it would seem, is no better off.

Note, first, however, that with respect to the paradoxes of self-reference, the problems for the gap theorist and the dialetheist are not the same. The gap theorist *does* have the words to express their views. Those words just turn out to be untrue—if consistency is to be maintained—and so we have a case of self-refutation. Thus, a gap theorist wants to say that the sentence 'This sentence is untrue', is neither true nor false. But in that case, it is untrue—and hence true. So they cannot say that (truly). The dialetheist also has the words to express their views: to say that something is true and not false, they can use those very words. There is nothing—even in the paradoxical case, that prevents them from being true. The words may turn out to be false as well sometimes too; but that's the nature of the beast. Thus, the dialetheist *can* express their views truly.

What the dialetheist cannot do, whether the topic is paradox or anything else, is ensure that views expressed are consistent. The problem, then, for a dialetheist—if it is a problem—is that they can say nothing that *forces* consistency. But once the matter is put this way, it is clear that a classical logician cannot do this either. Maybe they would like to; but that does not mean they succeed. Maybe they intend to; but intentions are not guaranteed fulfilment. Indeed, it may be logically impossible to fulfil them, as, for

---

[7] See, e.g. Parsons (1990), Batens (1990). The following material draws on Priest (1995*b*).

[8] It is sometimes argued, further, that if a statement cannot rule anything out it must be meaningless: any meaningful statement rules out *something*. But as we saw in sect. 1.12, this last claim is just not true. The statement 'everything is true' entails everything, including its own negation, and so rules nothing out; yet it is quite meaningful. See, further, *In Contradiction*, sect. 7.2.

example, when I intend to square the circle. Even if dialetheism were unacceptable and Boolean negation, contra the argument of the last chapter, made sense, asserting $\$\alpha$ does not rule out α, at least in this sense: someone who asserts $\$\alpha$ may *still* assert α: the cost is that this occasions a collapse into triviality. But there is no *logical* guarantee against a person being a trivialist. Moreover, a dialetheist can assert something with exactly the same effect. Asserting $\neg\alpha$ will not do, but, as we noted in section 4.7, asserting $-\alpha$, that is, $\alpha \to \bot$, will.

It may be replied that asserting $-\alpha$ still does not express disagreement. After all, this would be asserted by someone who thinks that everything is true, and so who agrees with α. If we are searching for a mode of expressing disagreement that even a trivialist can use, then there is, indeed, nothing that can be asserted that will do the trick. But in the previous sections of this chapter, we have seen exactly how someone, be they a dialetheist or otherwise, can show that they reject something, and so express disagreement. They simply deny it (which is not the same as asserting any negation). The objection against dialetheism therefore lapses. A dialetheist can express disagreement.[9]

I end this section with the following observation. In this part of the book we have met (at least) three distinct notions: negation, denial, and arrow *falsum* ($-$). We have seen that all of these notions make perfectly good sense from a dialetheic perspective. They are just not the same thing. The orthodox classical account of negation fuses them together. But this fusion is a confusion: they need to be kept distinct. It is common enough in the development of science for us to come to realize that we had run together different concepts (e.g. rest mass and inertial mass). The case at hand is another such. And in this case, an antipathy towards dialetheism may well be a product of this confusion.[10]

6.4 DENIAL AND PARADOX

Now that we have clearly distinguished denial from negation, it might be wondered, in the context of paradoxes such as the Liar, whether this allows us to formulate damaging versions of the liar paradox in terms of denial. Let us see.

Let us write $\dashv$ as a force-operator for denial. Thus, $\dashv \alpha$ represents an utterance of the sentence α with the force of a denial. In a similar way, one might write $\vdash \alpha, ?\alpha$, and $!\alpha$, for utterances of the sentence α with the forces of assertion, question, and command, respectively.

It is natural to suppose that one may formulate a version of the Liar as an utterance u, of the form:

$\dashv u$ is true

---

[9] In particular, then—in case one was wondering—when I said in sect. 6.1 that one cannot accept and reject something, I was denying the claim that one can do this.

[10] A more extended discussion of expressability can be found in sect. 20.4 of the second edition of *In Contradiction*.

This utterance does not even make sense, however. It is not utterances that are true or false, but their propositional contents (the αs inside the force-operators). Hence, the supposed Liar has to be an utterance, v, of the form:

⊣ the content of v is true

But what is the content of v? It is 'the content of v is true'. Thus, the content of v is a standard truth-teller sentence. v is therefore simply a denial of the truth-teller. What to make of this, we might argue about. If one takes the truth-teller to be a truth-value gap, this is exactly what one should do to it. If, on the other hand, one takes it to be a truth-value glut (as in *In Contradiction*, section 4.7), and so true, then one should not deny it. But whatever one says about this matter, it is clear that there is nothing problematic about denying or asserting the truth-teller.

Similar comments apply to an utterance, w, of the form:

⊣ the content of w is false

except that this time the content of w is that the content of w is false; so the content is a standard Liar sentence. If one takes this to be neither true nor false, then one should deny it; if one takes it to be both true or false, one should not: one should assert it. But again, there is no problem in either case.

What these examples illustrate is the fact that attempts to formulate distinctive Liar paradoxes in terms of denial fail, since ⊣, being a force-operator, has no interaction with the content of what is uttered.

It might be thought that there should be an operator on content that, in some sense, mimics force-operators. But there would appear to be no such thing. It is true that, for example, in English one can transform 'The door is open' into 'Is the door open'. An utterance of the former would normally be an assertion, and an utterance of the latter would normally be a question. But as a little thought will certify, in the right context an utterance of either could be either—or other things as well, such as a command.

About the best one can do in this regard is employ prefixes such as 'I am denying that', 'I am asking whether', etc. So what should one say about someone who utters:

I am denying that this sentence is true

If this is uttered with the force of assertion, this is clearly false (and so should not have been uttered). If it is uttered with the force of denial, then what it appears to be denying is α, where α is 'I am denying that α [is true]', which is true, so it should not have been denied. Alternatively if the demonstrative refers differently, the utterance could be interpreted as a denial of 'I am denying that β', where β is 'β is true.' This is simply false: what one is denying is that one is denying β. It is therefore correctly denied.

We see, then, formulating Liar sentences in terms of denial produces nothing much of interest.[11]

[11] For further discussion on this matter, see Parsons (1984), sect. 3. Parsons also argues against identifying denial with the assertion of negation.

6.5 TRUTH AND REJECTION

Having explored the connection (or lack thereof) between rejection and negation, let us now explore the connection between rejection and truth—or untruth.

It is natural enough to claim that one ought to believe what is true. Put in this way, though, the claim is false. There is no onus to believe something simply because it is true. There is, however, if there is good evidence that it is true. Thus:

Accept. One ought to accept something if there is good evidence for its truth.

The 'ought' here, note, has nothing to do with what morality or prudence require: it might well be the case that one ought not to believe things that are evidentially grounded, in those senses. (Having true beliefs can well get you into trouble!) The 'ought' here is one of rationality. It is rational to believe what is evidentially grounded (and irrational to believe what is not). This raises the question of what evidential grounding is, but we do not need to pursue that matter here; we will return to it in the next part of the book.

What we will pursue now is the possibility of a claim about rejection dual to **Accept**. Anyone who believes that there are truth-value gluts or gaps must distinguish between falsity (that is, truth of negation) and untruth—that is, between $T\langle\neg\alpha\rangle$ and $\neg T\langle\alpha\rangle$. If there are truth-value gaps, something can be untrue without being false. And if there are truth-value gluts, then, at least *prima facie*, something can be false without being untrue.[12]

A natural dual to **Accept** is:

Reject(F). One ought to reject something if there is good evidence for its falsity.

There is nothing in the existence of truth-value gaps that threatens this principle, but it is unlikely to recommend itself to a dialetheist. Consider something taken to be both true and false, such as 'this sentence is false'. Call this λ. Half of the paradox argument for this provides good evidence for $\neg\lambda$, but one would not, on this count, want to reject λ. For the other half of the paradox argument provides evidence for λ. **Accept** itself, therefore, counsels its acceptance.[13]

---

[12] Though as I noted in section 4.6, a dialetheist *can* accept that falsity and untruth are the same, at the cost of spreading contradiction.

[13] The principle **Accept** (and the principle **Reject(F)**) makes use of the notion of good evidence. Appropriately understood—with 'good' meaning 'good enough'—this serves to make the principle little more than a truism. What is not a truism is how much evidence is good enough. Clearly, whatever one means by this, evidence may not always be good enough. But, in the present context, it is natural to ask what of those situations where we have evidence for α and evidence for $\neg\alpha$. Can the evidence for α be good enough? Certainly: the evidence for α may simply overwhelm that for $\neg\alpha$—for example, when all my senses except vision tell me that the room is stationary (see sect. 3.5). But suppose that the two evidences are equally balanced? The case is underdetermined. Maybe the appropriate thing to do in this case is to suspend judgment. One might do this if one is told α by a reliable friend and $\neg\alpha$ by another, equally reliable, friend. In the absence the other testimony, each would be sufficient to carry the day. But with both, one may simply suspend judgment. On the other hand, information may make it appropriate to accept both α and $\neg\alpha$. Thus, in the case of the

The lack of symmetry between **Accept** and **Reject(F)** might be felt to be uncomfortable. Why the one, but not the other? But one should recall that falsity is nothing other than truth of negation. So the correct principle concerning falsity is that delivered by **Accept**:

One ought to accept ¬α if there is good evidence for the falsity of α.

The dual of **Accept** looks more plausible if we formulate it in terms of untruth, not falsity. After all, if it is the truth that one is after, it is the untruth that one wishes to avoid. Thus we have:

Reject(U). One ought to reject something if there is good evidence for its untruth.

Even this dual may be resisted, however. Take the liar paradox in the form 'this sentence is not true'. The standard argument establishes that it is both true and untrue. Should one reject it on this count? Not obviously. The principle concerning rejection might be something like: one ought to reject something if there is good evidence for its untruth, unless there is also good evidence for its truth. Thus, **Reject(U)** may be understood as an acceptable default rule, but not as an indefeasible one.[14]

The failure of symmetry in this case is might be thought to be more troubling, however. Falsity is not the opposite of truth: it is a sub-species of it. Untruth, by definition, is. So does the acceptance of **Reject(U)** damage dialetheism? The answer is 'no'. It is quite open to a dialetheist to accept both **Accept** and **Reject(U)**. Suppose that we have some α for which there is good evidence that it is both true and untrue. Then, by these two principles, one ought to accept α and one ought to reject α. We have a dilemma, since we cannot do both.[15] (It should be noted that this is not the situation which we are in with respect to most paradoxes of self-reference. In these we have arguments for things of the form α and ¬α; but, in general, α is not of the

Paradox of the Preface (see sect. 6.2), there can be independent evidence—as strong as one likes—for each contradictory, and neither would seem to undercut the other. In other cases, the evidence may support the conjunction α ∧ ¬α, and so both contradictories together. This is the case with the Liar Paradox. The fact that no one has been able to explain in satisfactory terms what, if anything, is wrong with this evidence in over 2,000 years makes it pretty damn good.

[14] Whichever way one goes on the matter, this provides an answer to Olin (2003), 32, who asks what epistemic reasons could lead us to justifiably reject a claim to the effect that α is a true contradiction. (She puts this in terms of accepting that α is not true and false, but it is really rejection that she needs.) She also asks (p. 33) why, given evidence for both α and ¬α, we do not simply suspend belief. On this, see the previous footnote.

[15] Even if a dialetheist does not subscribe to **Reject(U)**, if they take it to be the case that there are indefeasible grounds for rejecting something they must, in some sense, contemplate the possibility of rational dilemmas. For they will then have things of the form:

if Ground *A* then one ought to accept α
if Ground *B* then one ought to reject α

A dialetheist cannot rule out *a priori* the co-occurrence of Ground *A* and Ground *B*, and so of the dilemma generated.

form: β is true. It can be in special cases, such as the Liar Paradox in the form 'this sentence is not true'—but not in the form 'this sentence is false'.[16])

6.6 RATIONAL DILEMMAS

A dilemma is not a contradiction. Let us use the operator O, 'It is obligatory that', from standard deontic logic. Paradigm dilemmas are of the form: $O\alpha$ and $O\neg\alpha$, where α is a statement to the effect that something be done.[17] More generally, in a dilemma there are two such statements α, β, such that $\Box\neg(\alpha \wedge \beta)$, yet $O\alpha$ and $O\beta$.

Now, arguably, the existence of dilemmas is simply a fact of life. The thought that there are irresolvable moral dilemmas is commonplace.[18] And in *In Contradiction*, chapter 13, I argued for similar legal dilemmas. The obligations in these cases are not the obligations of rationality. But if one sort of system of norms can produce dilemmas, why not other sorts? It might be thought that there is something special about rationality, though. Could people really be rationally required to do the impossible? How could rationality be so stupid? Well, arguably, it is. One can formulate apparent rational dilemmas that have nothing to do with **Reject(U)**.

Consider a claim of the form, 'It is irrational to believe this claim', i.e. something of the form:

It is irrational to believe ρ

where it, itself, is ρ. Supposes that you believe ρ. Then you believe something, and at the same time believe that it is irrational to believe it. This, presumably, is irrational. Hence, you ought not to believe ρ: $O\neg B\rho$. But we have just shown that ρ is true! Hence, you ought to believe ρ, $OB\rho$ (by **Accept**). This is a version of the Irrationalist's Paradox.[19] The argument may be formalized as follows. Let I be 'It is irrational (to bring it about) that'. Let B be 'you believe that' and let ρ be of the form $IB\rho$. There is one principle about rationality appealed to, namely: for any α, $IB(\alpha \wedge IB\alpha)$. From this, it follows that $IB(\rho \wedge \rho)$, and so $IB\rho$, that is ρ. Given that $IB\alpha \vdash O\neg B\alpha$, and that if $\vdash \alpha$ then $\vdash OB\alpha$. The dilemma follows.[20]

It is, note, just as much a paradox for the non-dialetheist as for the dialetheist. In fact, it is worse for the classical logician. The Irrationalist's Paradox deploys the

---

[16] Of course, if one subscribes to the Exclusion principle $T\langle\neg\alpha\rangle \rightarrow \neg T\langle\alpha\rangle$, then any contradiction is going to give rise to a dilemma of the kind in question. But there are good reasons to reject this principle. (See *In Contradiction*, sect. 4.9.)

[17] A dilemma will generate a contradiction if one accepts the commonly invoked deontic principle $O\neg\alpha \rightarrow \neg O\alpha$; but this is not plausible in contexts of dilemma. See *In Contradiction*, sect. 13.4.

[18] For discussion, see the Introduction to Gowans (1987), and the papers in that collection, especially those by Williams, Lemmon, and Barcan Marcus.

[19] Due to Littman (1992). A variant of it is the sentence: you ought (rationally) to reject this sentence.

[20] I revert, here, to using '$\vdash$' in its more usual logical sense. Similar problems arise with the sentence σ: 'I do not believe σ' (see Kroon (1993)). Suppose that one decides to believe σ; then one will be believing something one knows to be untrue. One ought, then, not to believe it. But if one decides not believe σ, one knows it to be true. So one ought to believe it. Given that one cannot do both, we have a dilemma.

principle that if one believes that (α and to believe that α is irrational), then one's belief is irrational ($IB(\alpha \wedge IB\alpha)$). A dialetheist might contest this: it is not irrational if one *also* believes that to believe α *is* rational. The supposition that believing that α may be both rational and irrational is unlikely to appeal to a classical logician, however.

Actually, the situation is even worse for a classical logician, since not just dilemma but contradiction lurks in the wings. Let R be 'It is rational (to bring it about) that.' It would seem just as plausible a fact about rationality that, for any α, $\neg RB(\alpha \wedge \neg RB\alpha)$. Now let ρ be $\neg RB\rho$. Then, as before, we can show that $\neg RB\rho$, that is, ρ. And assuming that if $\vdash \alpha$ then $\vdash RB\alpha$, we have a flat contradiction. Note that since this paradox makes no use of semantic or set-theoretic notions, none of the standard solutions to paradoxes of self-reference gets a grip on it.

6.7 GAME-THEORETIC DILEMMAS

The Irrationalist's Paradox does not depend on **Reject(U)**, but it still depends on **Accept**, and it also employs self-reference. It might therefore be wondered whether there are rational dilemmas that are independent of anything connected with dialetheism. There certainly appear to be, and in the last part of this chapter I will explain some of them. These are rational dilemmas that arise in connection with well-known situations in game theory.[21] Standardly, commentators accept one or other horn of the dilemma and try to dispose of the other. I want to set things up in such a way that if you accept one, you should accept both.[22]

I will give two arguments of this kind. Both depend on a certain principle of rationality, which is as follows. Suppose that a person has to choose between two alternatives, and they know that if they choose one alternative, the benefit derived will be a certain amount; and if they choose the other alternative the benefit derived will be a lesser amount. Then they ought to choose the first alternative. Call this principle *Rat*. We may formalize it thus:

$$C(\gamma, \delta)$$
$$M\gamma \rightarrow Gc_\gamma$$
$$M\delta \rightarrow Gc_\delta$$
$$\frac{c_\gamma > c_\delta}{OM\gamma}$$

The premises are above the line; the conclusion is below. $C(\gamma, \delta)$ means that you have a choice between making γ true and making δ true; $M\gamma$ means that you make γ true; Gx means that you gain x. $\rightarrow$ denotes the indicative conditional. Strictly speaking,

---

[21] See, for example, Sainsbury (1995), ch. 3, or the papers in Campbell and Sowden (1985).

[22] One possible reaction is to accept neither. For example, one may simply reject the principle of rational choice about to be enunciated. However, this is so central to most of game theory that its derogation is not an enticing one.

the premises should be within the scope of an epistemic operator, K (it is known that), but in what follows this will go without saying.

Now to the first dilemma: Newcome's Paradox. This comes in different versions; let me spell out the one that I have in mind. There are two boxes, a and b, and you are to choose between taking either the contents of both boxes, or the contents of just one box, box a (the aim being to maximize your financial gain). b is transparent, and you can see a \$10 note inside. You do not know what is in box a, but you do know that money has been put inside by someone who knows exactly what you are going to do, a perfect predictor, p. That is, if you are going to choose one box, p knew this; and if you are going to choose both boxes, p knew this too. If p predicted that you would choose one box, \$100 was put inside a; if p predicted that you would choose two boxes, nothing was put inside a. Should you choose one box or two?[23]

We may now show that you ought to choose one box, and that you ought to choose both boxes. Let α be 'you choose just box a' and β be 'you choose both boxes'. Then we have $C(\alpha, \beta)$ and $\neg(M\alpha \wedge M\beta)$. The two horns of the dilemma proceed as follows.

Horn 1: Let c be an abbreviation for the description 'whatever is now in box a', where this is to be understood as a rigid designator. If you make α true, then you get c: $M\alpha \rightarrow Gc$. If you make β true, you will get c plus the extra \$10: $M\beta \rightarrow G(10+c)$. But $10 + c > c$. By principle *Rat*, it follows that $OM\beta$.

Horn 2: If you make β true, then p knew that you were going to choose both boxes. Hence, there is \$10 in a, and nothing in b; so you get \$10. That is: $M\beta \rightarrow G10$. On the other hand, if you make α true, then p knew that you were going to choose one box. Hence, there is \$100 in a, which is what you get. That is: $M\alpha \rightarrow G100$. But clearly, $100 > 10$. By principle *Rat*, it follows that $OM\alpha$.[24]

A second example of a rational dilemma is provided by a suitably symmetrized version of the prisoners' dilemma. The following will do. You are in a room with two buttons, and you have to choose between pressing them. If you press button a, you will receive \$10. If you press button b you will receive nothing (by your own efforts), but the person next door will receive \$100. That person is in exactly the symmetric situation. Moreover, you have known the person in the other room for a long time, and you know that they are just like you: in choice situations you always both choose the same thing. Which button should you press?

---

[23] It does not make much difference if p is not a perfect predictor, but merely a very good one. For then the conditionals in the argument take the form: if you do so and so, *it is very likely that* such and such. But much the same argument goes through with these.

[24] Yi (2003) objects that there must be something wrong with these arguments. They make no mention of whether or not one *knows* what is in box a. But suppose that box a is itself transparent. Then, the argument goes, it is clear that the conclusion that one should take box a is misplaced. I do not think so. Even if you can see that there is \$0 in box a, both arguments of the dilemma still hold. In particular, you still *ought to* take box a. If, *per impossibile* given that there is \$0 in the box, you do choose box a, there *will be* \$100 in there. (The information entails this.) Of course you know, in the context, that you won't, even though you ought to.

Let α be 'you press button a'; let β be 'you press button b'. Then we have $C(\alpha, \beta)$, and $\neg(M\alpha \wedge M\beta)$. The dilemmatic argument proceeds as follows.

Horn 1: Let c be an abbreviation for the description 'whatever is obtained as a result of the action of the other person', where this is to be understood as a rigid designator. If you make α true, then you get $10 + c$: $M\alpha \rightarrow G(10 + c)$. If you make β true, you will get just c: $M\beta \rightarrow Gc$. But $10 + c > c$. By principle *Rat*, it follows that $OM\alpha$.

Horn 2: If you make α true, then so will the person in the other room. Hence, you will get 10 plus nothing else: $M\alpha \rightarrow G10$. If you make β true, then so will the person in the other room. Hence, you will get 100: $M\beta \rightarrow G100$. Since $100 > 10$, by principle *Rat*, $OM\beta$.

6.8 OBJECTIONS

The most plausible line of objection to the preceding arguments, it seems to me, concerns the nature of the conditionals employed. In particular, one may argue that the first horn of each dilemma is invalid as follows. I give the argument for the Newcome problem; the argument in the prisoners' dilemma example is similar.

Let us suppose that, as a matter of fact, you do choose the one box, a, and consequently that $c = 100$. Consider the conditional $M\beta \rightarrow G(10 + c)$. If you *were* to make β true then you would *not* get $10 + c$, i.e. 110, but 10, since there would be 0 in box a. (Recall that c is a rigid designator, and so does not change its value in different hypothetical situations.) Hence this conditional is false. Similarly, let us suppose that you do, as a matter of fact, choose both boxes, and consequently that $c = 0$. Consider the conditional $M\alpha \rightarrow Gc$. If you *were* to make α true, you would *not* get c, i.e. 0, but 100, since that is what would be in box a. Consequently one or other of these conditionals is false.

Assuming the standard distinction between indicative and subjunctive conditionals, this objection fails since what it establishes is that certain subjunctive conditionals are false (note the 'were's). But the conditionals employed in the arguments are, in every case, indicative, not subjunctive. (Go back and check them!)

At this point, it might be argued that a correct formulation of the principle *Rat requires* the use of subjunctive conditionals. But why should one suppose this? After all: the reasoning, including the formulation of principle *Rat*, seems quite in order as it is.

Here are two bad reasons why the conditionals in *Rat* must be subjunctives. The first: we are reasoning about cases at least one of which will not arise. Hence, the conditionals are counterfactuals, and reasoning about counterfactual situations requires subjunctive conditionals. Not so. Counterfactuals are often expressed by indicative conditionals, not subjunctives. The bus is due. I tell you: *if we don't leave now, we'll miss the bus*; and so we leave, and catch the bus, which is on time. The conditional I uttered was a true indicative conditional, though it is also a counterfactual. Even in cases where the antecedent is not just false, but its truth would require the past to be different from what it was, we can still use indicative conditionals. Let us suppose that you do not know who won the Grand Final yesterday. You do know that *if you read in a reputable paper today that the Broncos won the Final, then they won it yesterday*. This is a perfectly legitimate indicative conditional, even though the Broncos did not, in fact, win yesterday.

The second, and more sophisticated, argument to the effect that condition *Rat* requires subjunctive conditionals goes as follows.[25] Again, I use the Newcome example to illustrate. Suppose that, as a matter of fact, you make β true; then you do not make α true, $\neg M \alpha$. Then by the properties of the material conditional, $M \alpha \rightarrow G100$. So if you know that you will make β true then you know that $M \alpha \rightarrow G100$. You ought, therefore, to make α true, since you know that $100 > 10$. And quite generally, whenever you have decided what to do, so that you know what you are going to do, you ought to do the opposite! So the principle, formulated with indicative conditionals, is incoherent.

The flaw in the argument is in identifying the indicative conditional with the material conditional (so that we can reason $\neg \gamma \vdash \gamma \rightarrow \delta$). Standard indicative conditionals are *not* material conditionals. There are just too many clear counter-examples to the identity for it to be credible. Of the many that could be given, here is just one.[26]

There is an electrical circuit with two switches in series, both off. If both switches are on (and only if both switches are on) a light in the circuit will go on. Let α be 'switch 1 is turned on'; let β be 'switch 2 is turned on'; let γ be 'the light goes on'. Then we have: if α and β then γ. If this conditional were material, $\supset$, and since $(\alpha \wedge \beta) \supset \gamma \vdash ((\alpha \wedge \neg \beta) \supset \gamma) \vee ((\beta \wedge \neg \alpha) \supset \gamma)$, it would follow that one or other of the following is true: 'if only switch 1 is turned on, the light will go on', 'if only switch 2 is turned on, the light will go on'. Both are clearly false.

6.9 CONCLUSION

The view that there are rational dilemmas is, as we have now seen, a plausible one—even dilemmas that have nothing to do with dialetheism. If there are such things, the next obvious question is what one should do if one finds oneself in one. What one *should* do, is, of course, the impossible. But one can't do that. Rationally, one way or other, one is damned. *C'est la vie*.

We have now completed our tour of issues concerned with negation, and covered much ground in the process. The last issue to raise its head was rationality. But as far as that goes, we have only just scratched the surface. The next part of the book brings rationality to centre stage.

---

[25] The argument is a variation of a point sometimes made in discussions of backwards induction. See Priest (2000), n. 31.

[26] For others, see Priest (2001*a*), ch. 1, where the claim that the indicative conditional is not material is defended in more detail.

PART III

RATIONALITY

7

Rational Belief

7.1 INTRODUCTION

When we describe someone as being inconsistent, we may mean many different things. If someone is fickle, changing their views or emotions from day to day, we call them inconsistent. If someone, such as a judge, fails to treat like cases alike, we call them inconsistent. When someone refuses to accept an obvious logical consequence of something they believe, we call them inconsistent. And of course, when someone believes things of the form α and $\neg\alpha$ we call them inconsistent. In all such cases, calling a person inconsistent would normally be some form of criticism. The first three cases will not concern us in this chapter; only the last.

The sense of belief that I have in mind here is explicit, unqualified, belief. Sometimes one might describe a person as having inconsistent beliefs if their views, unbeknownst to them, entail a contradiction. This is not the sort of belief at issue here. Or, as we noted in section 6.2, situations of the kind involved in the preface paradox appear to make it rational for a person to believe a contradiction explicitly. But in such cases, the person would be inclined to admit that their beliefs have gone wrong somewhere, though they knows not where.[1] This is not the sort of belief I have in mind either. The beliefs in question are ones that a person will knowingly endorse without any reservation—other than, perhaps, one of general fallibility. The topic of this chapter is precisely whether criticism of a person with inconsistent beliefs of this kind, on the ground of the inconsistency, is perforce justified. I shall argue that it is not. In the process, I will give an account of rational belief.

7.2 THE HISTORY OF THE BELIEF IN CONSISTENCY

Let us start with the history of the view that criticism on the ground of inconsistency (in the appropriate sense) is justified. This is a curious one, not to say a little puzzling. There were certainly Presocratic philosophers who, presumably, thought it was perfectly legitimate to believe contradictions, since they did so. Heraclitus, for example, held that 'We step and do not step into the same rivers; we are and we are not.'[2] Even

---

[1] Thus, some philosophers (e.g. van Fraassen (1980), 12) distinguish between believing something and merely accepting it. The case at hand might be one of mere acceptance.
[2] Fragment 49a; translation from Robinson (1987), 35.

Plato seems to have been prepared to countenance the possibility that ordinary things might have contradictory properties—though not the forms:

Even if all things come to partake of both [the form of like and the form of unlike], and by having a share of both are both like and unlike one another, what is there surprising in that? . . . when things have a share in both or are shown to have both characteristics, I see nothing strange in that, Zeno, nor yet in a proof that all things are one by having a share in unity and at the same time many by sharing in plurality. But if anyone can prove that what is simple unity itself is many or that plurality itself is one, then shall I begin to be surprised.[3]

Of course, interpreting texts such as these, especially the Presocratices, may be a contentious matter. But at least Aristotle interpreted his Presocratic precursors in this way. For as we saw in Chapter 1, in book 4 of the *Metaphysics*, he launched a sustained attack on them. He argued that nothing is more obvious or certain than that a contradiction cannot be true (the LNC)—so much so, he says, that one cannot give a proof of this fact.[4] This is odd for two reasons. The first is this: if the LNC is so obvious, how come it wasn't obvious to the people he was attacking? The second is that straightaway he goes on to give seven arguments for the LNC. He says that these are elenchic arguments, not proofs; but what, exactly, this comes to, and whether all the arguments are of this kind is not at all clear.

But let that pass. Reading the arguments makes it clear that they do not succeed in rendering obvious the LNC. The first, and longest, argument is so opaque, it is entirely unclear what it is. I defy any sensible person to read it and claim that it makes its conclusion obvious. (It is not, of course, irrational to believe something merely because it happens to be untrue. It is the evidential status that is important.) The other arguments are even less successful: for their conclusion is patently that it is not the case that *all* contradictions are true (or the even weaker: it is impossible for someone to believe that all contradictions are true). Even if this is true, and were manifestly so, nothing at all follows about the possibility that *some* contradictions are true. Again, we saw all this in Chapter 1.

It is true that, at various times since Aristotle, various thinkers have wittingly endorsed contradictions. This is particularly true of thinkers in the Neoplatonist tradition.[5] Plotinus himself, for example, denies that anything positive can be said of the One (*Enneads*. v. 6); but also describes it as a simplex, something which is beyond being, the source and generator of all else. Cusanus goes even further, saying that (*Of Learned Ignorance*. i. 3):

---

[3] *Parm.* 129 b, c. Translation from Hamilton and Cairns (1961). Indeed, in the *Republic*, he even seems to endorse the contradictory nature of the material world: 'If being is the object of knowledge, and not-being of ignorance, and these are extremes, opinion must lie between them, and may be called darker than the one and brighter than the other. The intermediate or contingent matter is and is not at the same time, and partakes both of existence and non-existence.' *Rep.*, 478. Translation from Jowett (1931).

[4] Note the suppressed premise here: if something is obviously not true it is irrational to believe it. As we saw in sect. 6.5, one might well take issue with this: it is not irrational to believe it if is mainfiestly true too.

[5] I include Hegel in this number. For the influence of Neoplatonism on Hegel, see Kolakowski (1978), ch. 1.

in no way do they [distinctions] exist in the absolute maximum [*sc.* God]. The absolute maximum ... is all things, and whilst being all, is none of them ...

But it is fair to say that, at least since the Middle Ages, Aristotle's views concerning contradiction have been orthodoxy. (This is so obvious, that it is hardly worth documenting.) They are taken for granted so much that, as far as I know, there is no sustained defence of the LNC in Western philosophy other than Aristotle's. Why? I really don't know. It is certainly not because of the rational persuasiveness of Aristotle's arguments. I suspect (unhappily) that the view was accepted simply on the basis of the magisterial authority of Aristotle's texts in the Middle Ages. In general, that authority disappeared long ago, of course. In logic it hung on till the twentieth century; most of it there has been swept out since then, but the views about contradiction have hung on doggedly.

Before we leave the history of philosophy, and to emphasize the parochial nature of Western philosophy on this issue, let us consider briefly the situation in Indian philosophy. The LNC certainly had its defenders here. Logicians of the Nyaya school, for example, adhered to it. But the classical orthodoxy in this case was exactly opposite from that in the West. The standard view in classical Indian logic, going back to about the same time as Aristotle, was that on any issue there are always four possibilities to be considered: that a view is true (and true only), that it is false (and false only), that it is both, and that it is neither. This is the *catushkoti* ("four corners").[6] The difference in the two traditions could not be more acute.

So far, then, we may conclude that if figures in the history of Western philosophy held that it was irrational to believe a contradiction, this view was itself irrationally held. The LNC is not at all obvious. And wise people, as Hume put it,[7] proportion their beliefs according to the evidence. Those who subscribed to the orthodox view, were not, then, wise.

A caveat: no one is an expert in many areas, and we all have to accept things on the say-so of experts in some areas. If someone believes that it is irrational to believe contradictions on the basis of experts in logic and philosophy, their belief is not irrational. The charge of irrationality is levelled against people who ought to have known better.

7.3 IS CONSISTENCY MANDATORY?

Is the situation essentially any different in contemporary philosophy? Not as far as I can see. The knee-jerk reaction of most modern philosophers will be that it is patent that no contradiction can be true, since, if it were, everything would be true, which it is patently not—everything follows from a contradiction. This is so in standard logic, of course; but it is so because of the fact that in the semantics of this logic, truth, and falsity are taken to be exclusive—something that may fail in a paraconsistent logic,

---

[6] For a fuller discussion, see Priest (2007), sect. 3.3.
[7] *Enquiry Concerning Human Understanding*, sect. 10, part i, Selby-Bigge (1902), 110.

where contradictions do not entail everything. The assumption that truth and falsity are exclusive is simply packed into nearly all presentations of standard logic without comment. In other words, it has the same dogmatic status as the LNC itself. This does not provide a justification.

It might be thought that the exclusivity of truth and falsity holds by definition. Falsity just is the lack of truth. It does not. The relevant sense of falsity here is truth of negation; and the claim that $\neg\alpha$ is true when α fails to be true is not a definition. As we saw in Chapter 4, it is a substantial theory about the way that negation works. It is denied in modern logic by logicians who subscribe to truth-value gaps or gluts. How negation behaves is, in fact, a highly contentious view historically. At least until the later Middle Ages, a common view of negation, with which Aristotle had some sympathies, was that $\neg\alpha$ simply cancels out α. (See section 4.1.) So contradictions do not entail everything: they entail nothing.

What other relevant arguments are there? We could spend much time talking about this, but I will not pursue the issue here. None that I know work.[8] It is hard enough to produce arguments for the LNC itself, but what we need in this context is not just an argument for the LNC, but one of a very strong kind. Consider, as an analogy, the arguments given by the early heliocentric astronomers for the centrality of the sun. These had force, but there were countervailing arguments; for example, the motion of the earth seemed to fly in the face of the accepted dynamics. In such a context, it was not irrational for someone not to accept the geocentric view. It would have been if the arguments for heliocentrism had rationally mandated their conclusion, something that later arguments were to do. In the same way, and returning to the issue of inconsistency, what we need in this case is not simply an argument for the LNC, but one that makes its conclusion rationally mandatory. This sets the bar very high, and I know of no argument, or raft of arguments, that even comes close to clearing it.

It might well be pointed out, quite correctly, that there is a possibility that I have been ignoring until now. There are certain things that one can believe rationally, even though one can give no reason for them. This is the case with perceptual reports, for example. I see a hand before my face. It is rational for me to believe this claim to be true, but I can give no reasons. My experience in some sense justifies my belief, but experience cannot be a premise in an argument. The Law of Non-Contradiction is obviously not a perceptual report, but could there be other sorts of examples where one may have a rational belief but no reason? Some have certainly thought so. For example, Wright (2004) suggests that we may have a rational entitlement to certain things, such as fundamental logical principles like *modus ponens*, even though no reason can be provided in any meaningful sense. Of course, certain conditions have to be satisfied—or we could take ourselves to be rationally entitled to the most absurd of views. How to formulate these conditions precisely we might argue about,

---

[8] Here is just one more. All contradictions are necessarily false. (See sect. 4.4.) But *one ought to reject things that are known to be false*. Hence one ought to reject all contradictions. The problem with this argument is clear. If one endorses dialetheism then one will reject the italicized claim (as we saw in sect. 6.2). It is not, then, obvious, and a dogmatic endorsement of it simply begs the question.

but crucial are that (a) justifications for the principle employ nothing better than that very principle, and (b) there are no grounds for doubting the principle.[9] Note that clause (b) is essential. Consider the principle *modus morons*: $\alpha \rightarrow \beta, \beta \vdash \alpha$. One may justify this as follows: Suppose that $\langle \beta \rangle$ and $\langle \alpha \rightarrow \beta \rangle$ are true. Then by the truth conditions for $\rightarrow$, if $\langle \alpha \rangle$ is true, so is $\langle \beta \rangle$. Hence, $\langle \alpha \rangle$ is true (by *modus morons*).[10] Now, whatever one thinks about the notion of ungrounded entitlement in general, the Law of Non-Contradiction does not satisfy clause (b). As I observed in the last section, various historical philosophers provided grounds for doubting the "Law"; and modern philosophers have added others—we will note one of these in section 7.5.[11]

In the end, I doubt that the rationality of individual logical principles is to be sought in this kind of entitlement. Individual principles are always part of whole logical theories. And a theory—and so the parts that comprise it—is the kind of thing for which it is possible to give meaningful reasons, as we are about to see.

7.4 RATIONALITY AND CONSISTENCY

Those who take consistency to be a *sine qua non* of rationality may well feel discomforted by all this. If the inconsistency of a view does not show it to be irrational, what does?! In fact, even if consistency is a constraint on rationality, it is a relatively weak one. It is possible to work many rationally bizarre views into consistent ones by a little massage. For example, the view that the earth is flat can be held quite consistently, by invoking suitable auxiliary hypotheses about the behaviour of light, the mendacity of the world's media, etc. It is irrational for all that. So how does rationality work? Anyone who expects a simple algorithm to determine whether a belief is rational or not is bound to be disappointed. This is a lesson of post-positivist philosophy of science, if, indeed, it was not already to be learned from Aristotle's account of phronesis. But this does not mean that one can say nothing.

Given a theory (in any area of human cognition—science, philosophy, logic, or whatever), there are many cognitive virtues, and, correlatively, vices, that it may have. Perhaps the most important is the adequacy of the theory to the data which it was proposed to handle. Does it really account for these? Any other criteria may be contentions, but familiar candidates include, for example:

- *Simplicity.* Is the theory clean and elegant, or it is complex and contrived?
- *Unity.* Does the theory have to invoke numerous *ad hoc* hypotheses, coming in from left field?
- *Explanatory Power.* Can the theory be used to explain other things in the same domain, or is it of limited applicability?
- *Parsimony.* Does the theory multiply entities beyond necessity?

[9] Thus (Wright (2004), sect. 2): 'The relevant kind of entitlement . . . may be proposed to be any proposition, *P*, of a cognitive project meeting the following two conditions: (i) there is no extant reason to regard *P* as untrue and (ii) the attempt to justify *P* would involve further presuppositions in turn of no more secure *a priori* standing . . .'   [10] See Haack (1976).
[11] More generally, see *In Contradiction*.

It is clear that all these criteria may come by degrees. And as even a quick perusal of some intellectual history demonstrates, they may pull in different directions. The early Copernican theory was simpler than the Ptolemaic theory, but it could deal with the dynamic problems of the motion of the earth only in *ad hoc* ways, at least until the invention of a new dynamics. By contrast, the Ptolemaic theory, though more complex, was not *ad hoc* in this way.

When is one theory rationally preferable to another? When it is sufficiently better than its rivals on sufficiently many of these criteria. That is, of course, vague. It can be tightened up in various ways. I will give one way in the next chapter. But in the end, I think, it is essentially so. Indeed, it is precisely this vagueness that allows for rational people to disagree. For legitimate disagreement is precisely a feature of the borderland of application of any vague predicate. People may legitimately disagree, for example, over whether the application of 'child' to a 14-year old is correct. This does not mean that there are no determinate facts concerning rationality and similar vague notions. Someone who calls a normal 30-year old a child is clearly mistaken. And one theory *can* be manifestly superior to its rivals, all things considered.

Is consistency a cognitive virtue? The natural answer is 'yes', but things are not as obvious as on might have supposed. For a start, certain sorts of consistency may be required by other virtues. For example, if the theory is an empirical one, adequacy to the empirical data is certainly a virtue. But at least for the most part, such data is consistent: as I argued in sections 3.4 and 3.5, contradictions are rarely perceived in the empirical world, and where they are, they are illusions. Hence, adequacy to the data requires consistency of observational content. The question, then, is whether consistency is a virtue when it is not required by other virtues.

One reason to suppose that it is, is that the very notion of a paradox seems to presuppose it. Paradoxes can usually be formulated as arguments that end in a contradiction of some kind. Maybe the view that contradictions are not acceptable at any price is wrong. But the very fact that the conclusion of a paradox is a contradiction gives us *some* reason to suppose that it is unacceptable, or it would not be a paradox. But again, things are not so clear. In many well-known paradoxes, the contradiction involved is an empirical one. In Zeno's paradoxes, the conclusions are things like 'Achilles never overtakes the tortoise', when we can see that he does; or in the sorites paradox, conclusions may be of the form 'This patch is red', when we can see that it is not. As I have just noted, there are independent reasons for rejecting contradictions of this kind. There are, of course, paradoxes which are not like this: the Liar is an obvious one such. And we do, in this case, take the contradiction to indicate that something has gone wrong. This, therefore, provides some reason to suppose that consistency, *per se*, is a cognitive virtue.[12]

Another reason can be found by considering another virtue, simplicity. Why simplicity—whatever, in fact, that comes to in the end—is a virtue is a tough question

---

[12] Even this is not entirely conclusive, however. People *do* take inconsistency in cases such as this to be a negative sign. But the question is whether they *ought*, rationally, to do so. Might not the common reaction simply be the product of an ungrounded ideology of consistency, or of a mistaken extrapolation from the observable case?

(to which I know no completely satisfactory answer). But an index of the fact that it is a virtue is that we tend to assign simpler hypotheses higher prior probabilities—for example, when curve-fitting. Something similar would appear to be the case with consistency. As I argued in *In Contradiction*, section 8.4, given an arbitrary situation about which we have little information, we would seem to be justified in taking its consistency to be a better bet than its inconsistency. This, therefore, indicates that consistency is a virtue: 'contradictions should not be multiplied beyond necessity'.[13]

Whether or not consistency is a virtue is, however, not centrally important for the present matter. If it is, it is simply one virtue amongst many. It is clear, then, how an inconsistent theory may be rationally acceptable; conversely, it is clear how an inconsistent theory may be rationally rejectable. It may simply be trumped by another theory.

Since this latter point is something of a stumbling block in discussions of para-consistency, let me just illustrate it. Let us suppose that you, an atheist, argue against the existence of (a Christian) god on the basis of the existence of suffering. God is omniscient, omnipotent, perfectly good, etc. Take some event which we know to have occurred, and which caused much gratuitous suffering, for example the torture and murder of a young child. The properties of God entail that had such a being existed, this event would not have occurred.[14] But it did; hence there is no God. Now consider the person who is prepared to accept a contradiction in this context: God exists and prevented the event; hence it did not occur; but it occurred too. This move is certainly out there in logical space. Is it a rational one? No: that the event both did and did not occur is an observable contradiction, and as we saw in section 3.5, there are good reasons to reject a contradiction of this kind. One could take on this claim as well, of course, but good luck to someone who does! I see no way of defending the view that the event both did and did not occur without invoking countless *ad hoc* hypotheses, and turning the situation into one of the flat-earth kind.

7.5 THE RATIONALITY OF INCONSISTENCY

So far, I have argued that the mere fact that someone's beliefs are inconsistent is not a definitive ground for rational criticism—and more, that to hold that it is, is itself irrational. I want to finish the chapter by arguing something stronger: that it is *irrational* to be consistent. I do not mean that it is irrational to be consistent about everything: just that there are some topics about which it is irrational to be consistent. Nor do I mean that it always has been and always will be irrational to be consistent about such topics: simply that in the present state of our knowledge, the rational belief is an inconsistent one.

The topic I have in mind here is that of truth. It seems to me that anyone weighing up the state of play concerning this notion, ought rationally to be inconsistent.

[13] *In Contradiction*, 90.
[14] Of course, one may dispute much of this: there is no such event; God had good reasons for letting it happen, etc. These moves are not on the agenda here.

A detailed argument for this would require its own book-length treatment, requiring as it would a systematic survey of all the theories of the semantic paradoxes with a detailed evaluation of their properties. So let me make the basic case and consider a few objections. I think it clear how one would go about filling in the details.[15]

A dialetheic account of truth accepts the T-schema: $\langle \alpha \rangle$ is true iff α, for every proposition, α. Assuming some basic principles of logic and self-reference, this entails contradictions in the shape, for example, of the Liar paradox. But because the underlying logic of the theory is paraconsistent, these contradictions are quarantined into singularities. Let us call this, or anything that endorses at least this much, the *naive account* of truth.

The most rational account at any time is, as I argued in the last section, the account which fares best according to the various epistemic virtues. So what other accounts are currently on the table? As most people who have even a passing acquaintance with the area will hardly need to be told, there is a plethora. Twentieth-century logic provided us with accounts by Tarski, Kripke, Gupta and Herzberger, Barwise and Etchemendy, and McGee, to name some of the major ones. So how do these fare in comparison to the naive account? It would be wrong to suppose that exactly the same considerations apply to all the theories; and in the end there is no substitute for examining the particular details of each one. In the present context, some broad brush strokes will have to suffice.[16]

Let us start with consistency. A dialetheic account is inconsistent; the other accounts are consistent—or at least, they appear to be; I will return to this in a moment. Here, then, and assuming consistency to be a virtue, the other accounts would appear to come out better. But what of all the other criteria?

Adequacy to the data is a singularly important virtue. And concerning this, the situation is reversed. Consistent accounts do not, generally speaking, endorse the T-schema in unrestricted form.[17] The schema is an overwhelmingly natural principle concerning truth. It is as ancient as Aristotle, and as modern as deflationist accounts of truth. The most celebrated truth-theorist of the twentieth century, Alfred Tarski, even called it a criterion of adequacy on any account of truth. Of course, one can have theoretical grounds for rejecting it—indeed, any solution to the paradoxes that rejects it must try to develop such an account. But the intuitive pull of the T-schema can hardly be denied. Even more telling, an important piece of data is that we find the paradoxical arguments intuitively *compelling*. If we did not, they would not be paradoxical. A dialetheic account explains this in the most natural way: the arguments are sound, and obviously so. Consistent accounts do not respect the data in this way.

So what of the other virtues? Take simplicity. The dialetheic account is simplicity itself. None of the other theories is in the same league. All involve hierarchical constructions, of various degrees of complexity, going into the transfinite.

---

[15] The matter is also discussed briefly in *In Contradiction*, sect. 7.4.

[16] For an analysis of Tarski, Kripke, Gupta and Herzberger, see *In Contradiction*, ch. 2. For Barwise and Etchemendy, see Priest (1993*b*); for McGee, see Priest (1994*b*).

[17] A notable exception is the account of Field (2003; and 2005). However, Field's account is subject to all the other problems I will mention. See Priest (2005b).

How about explanatory power? The paradoxes of self-reference appear to form a single family. They would seem to be manifestations of a single underlying phenomenon, in which case they ought to have a common solution: same kind of paradox, same kind of solution (the Principle of Uniform Solution). A naive account of truth obviously does not apply to all of these paradoxes: it can be readily extended to the other semantic paradoxes, but it has nothing to say about the set-theoretic paradoxes. However, it is a special case of a more general theory that applies to all the paradoxes of self-reference: one based on the Inclosure Schema.[18] This is decidedly not true of the other accounts of truth. At best, according to them, the set-theoretic and semantic paradoxes are a completely different phenomenon. At worst, what they have to say about truth is in tension with the usual treatment of the set-theoretic paradoxes.[19]

Of the other possible criteria, there is one more that is singularly relevant. What motivates all the consistent theories is an attempt to provide a consistent account of the semantic paradoxes of self-reference. This is the problem that they are meant to solve. If they do not solve this problem, this is a prime methodological failing. Do they? Not really; for all of them, the machinery deployed allows one to construct Liar-type arguments ending in contradiction (extended paradoxes). This is the reason that I said that the theories only *appear* to fare better on the virtue of consistency. In all cases, consistency can be enforced by quarantining the new machinery in a metalanguage, so making it illegitimate to deploy it in the paradox-producing way. But in all cases, the move (apart from being *ad hoc*) succeeds only in showing that the problem of consistency has not been solved, merely displaced. We may have a consistent account of truth, but a consistent account of the other semantic notions involved is still wanting.[20]

Now for the objections.

Objection 1: The comparison between the naive account and consistent accounts is unfair. For one needs different underlying logics for the two accounts, a paraconsistent logic for the dialetheic account and classical logic for the consistent account. One needs to evaluate the package deal (truth plus logic) in each case. And this changes the evaluation, since classical logic is much simpler than any paraconsistent logic, making the consistent package over-all simpler.

Reply. The point about the package deal is quite correct. It is also true that classical logic is simpler than all paraconsistent logics—but it is not *that* much simpler in many cases. For classical logic must be taken to include modal logic. We reason with modal sentences all the time, and we certainly need a theory of truth that applies to these. Now the simplest relevant logic is not much more complex than modal logic.[21] Its semantics diverges from that of $S5$ in two ways. First, the classical assumption that truth and falsity (at a world) are exclusive and exhaustive is dropped. This is a very minor change. Next, the class of worlds is extended to include not just possible

---

[18] See Priest (1995*a*), esp. part 3.

[19] For discussion, see Priest (1995*a*), esp. sects. 11.5–7 and 17.6 of the second edition. Field's account fails this test because its solution to the paradoxes of denotation—if, indeed, it has one—must proceed on different grounds.   [20] See the dilemma argument of sect. 4.6.

[21] I refer here to the logic N_4 of Priest (2001*a*), ch. 9.

worlds, but impossible worlds too (and conditionals are given suitable truth conditions as these). But again, impossible worlds are things we need to countenance anyway: they are needed, for example, to provide a suitable semantics for counterfactuals with logically false antecedents. Or, to put it another way, if modal logic is not extended in this way, a classical account of such conditionals must be given, and since this will give highly counter-intuitive results, extra complexities will have to be invoked to handle these. It is not clear, then, that the move to a relevant logic does increase complexity, all things considered. If it does, it is not of a kind that changes the over-all simplicity assessment.

Objection 2: Even if a certain amount of inconsistency is acceptable, too much is not. Thus, if inconsistencies spread into the empirical consequences of the theory of truth, the theory is not rationally acceptable. The consequences of a naive theory do spread into this area, due to Curry paradoxes. Specifically, given the inference of Contraction ($\alpha \rightarrow (\alpha \rightarrow \beta) \vdash \alpha \rightarrow \beta$), everything follows using the T-schema.

Reply. The point about the unacceptability of widespread contradiction is correct. However, with the appropriate logic, contradictions are appropriately restricted. Contraction is not valid in the simplest relevant logics. (Nor is its failure *ad hoc*. It is a simple consequence of the nature of impossible worlds.) Indeed, it can be shown that the inconsistencies in a naive theory of truth do not spread into the empirical realm, but are quarantined within those sentences that are not grounded (in the sense of Kripke).[22]

Objection 3: The employment of a non-classical logic means that the paraconsistent position concerning truth suffers from an important cognitive vice. For such a logic is weaker than classical logic. Hence, much classical reasoning must be accepted as invalid. This means that many of the important applications of classical logic must be given up, producing a significant loss of overall explanatory power.

Reply. It is true that many inferences that are classically acceptable must be acknowledged as invalid. This does not occasion an explanatory loss, however. For the only situations about which it makes sense to reason classically are consistent ones; and even paraconsistent logicians may employ classical logic in consistent situations (just as intuitionists may employ classical logic when reasoning about finite situations): it is a special case. The whole idea can be made formally rigorous and precise by the construction of an appropriate non-monotonic logic.[23]

Objection 4: A naive account of truth is just as susceptible to extended paradoxes as consistent accounts. For we may define an operator, $, by the conditions of classical negation (whether or not one calls this negation), and then use the T-schema to infer something of the form $A \wedge \$A$, giving rise to triviality. In the end, then, the naive account is no more acceptable than a consistent account.

Reply: No logical theory—of any kind—can allow unbridled licence in postulating connectives satisfying arbitrary conditions. The point was forcibly brought home by Arthur Prior in his discussion of *tonk*. From the point of view of the naive theory, any attempt to define a connective obeying the laws of classical negation will either

<hr>

[22] See Priest (2002*b*), sects. 8.1, 8.2.   [23] See, e.g. Priest (1991*b*).

produce a connective that does not satisfy these laws or will not succeed in specifying a meaningful connective at all. All this we saw in Chapter 5.

7.6 CONCLUSION

Whether or not one is persuaded by the details of the example of the last section, they illustrate at least the possibility that rationality may itself *require* inconsistency. It is a truism to point out that one of the greatest opponents of rationality has always been superstition, often of a religious nature. It is not a truism to note that one of the greatest superstitions in the history of Western thought has been that concerning consistency—as Wittgenstein put it, the 'superstitious dread and veneration in face of contradiction'.[24] Consistency has been taken to be the very cornerstone of rationality. But this view has itself no rational ground: it would seem to be simply the legacy of Aristotle. Indeed an inconsistent view may be the very embodiment of rationality.

So much for belief itself. What about change of belief? Does this provide more trouble for dialetheism? Let us see.

---

[24] Wittgenstein (1978), 122.

8

Belief Revision

8.1 INTRODUCTION

The rational person proportions their beliefs according to the evidence. This is, no doubt, a fundamental feature of rationality. But there is more to rationality concerning belief than that. The rational person is also one who *changes* their beliefs in the light of new information in an appropriate way. Sometimes, this will merely require the addition of the new information to the belief-set. At other times, this may require more drastic change, since old beliefs may have to be dropped. Though the topic of how one ought, rationally, to change one's beliefs is a venerable one in the history of Western philosophy, the application of formal methods to it is relatively recent. Yet these applications suffice to throw into relief various fundamental problems concerning belief-revision. It is one of these, concerning the role of consistency in the process, which I will address in this chapter. I will explain the problem in a moment. Let me first set the scene by saying something about one of the most common formal representations of belief-revision, the AGM account.

8.2 BACKGROUND: THE AGM CONDITIONS

In the AGM account, a set of beliefs is represented by a set of sentences, K, of some fixed language, $\mathcal{L}$. K is closed under deducibility. Hence, it is perhaps better to look on it as representing the set of *commitments* of an agent, rather than as their set of beliefs, since a real agent's explicit beliefs are not, as a matter of fact, closed under deduction. Given some information, α, expressed in $\mathcal{L}$, the AGM theory concerns three operations that may be effected on K in virtue of this.

The first is adding α to K. The result, written as $K + \alpha$ (and usually called 'expansion'), is easily defined. We simply put α together with K, and then form their logical closure (since belief-sets are closed under deducibility). Thus, $K + \alpha = \{\beta; K \cup \{\alpha\} \vdash_{CL} \beta\}$ (where $\vdash_{CL}$ denotes classical logical consequence).

The second operation is the result of taking α away from K, written as $K - \alpha$ (and usually called 'contraction'). Of course, α may not be in K at all, in which case, $K - \alpha$ is just K. But if it is, we cannot *simply* delete α from K. Since the result must be logically closed, we may have to delete other things as well. Depending on K, there may be no unique way of doing this. (Example: if K is the logical closure of $\{p, p \to q\}$, then if we remove q from K, one of p and $p \to q$ will have to be removed. But removing either of them will do the trick.) Possibly, other considerations will determine which deletions ought to be made, but it is not at all clear that simply being rational *does* define the result uniquely: *prima facie*, at least, rational people may well disagree about what ought to be given up. At any rate, the AGM account does not give an explicit definition of contraction; instead, it gives a set of axioms that $K - \alpha$ must satisfy. The conditions are well known, and I will not reproduce them here.[1]

A third operation on K, the one we are really interested in, revision, is the general result of revising K, given new information, α. This may be written as $K * \alpha$. Since revision may involve rejecting things, the same sort of considerations that apply to contraction apply to revision. Thus, AGM gives a set of conditions that $K * \alpha$ must satisfy. These are as follows:

K*1 $K * \alpha$ is logically closed
K*2 $\alpha \in K * \alpha$
K*3 $K * \alpha \subseteq K + \alpha$
K*4 $\neg \alpha \notin K \Rightarrow K + \alpha \subseteq K * \alpha$
K*5 $K * \alpha$ is inconsistent $\Rightarrow \alpha$ is a logical contradiction
K*6 α and β are logically equivalent $\Rightarrow K * \alpha = K * \beta$
K*7 $K * (\alpha \wedge \beta) \subseteq (K * \alpha) + \beta$
K*8 $\neg \beta \notin K * \alpha \Rightarrow (K * \alpha) + \beta \subseteq K * (\alpha \wedge \beta)$

K*2 is usually called the *success* condition: revising by α produces a belief-set that contains α. K*5, which will be of particular importance in what follows, may be called the *consistency* condition. (Its converse is given by the success condition.)

A natural thought at this point is that revision may be defined in terms of the other two operations: $K * \alpha = (K - \neg \alpha) + \alpha$. This is often called the *Levi identity*. We will come back to it later, but at any rate, if revision is defined in this way, it can be shown that the AGM conditions for $+$ and $-$ entail those for $*$.

Note that one feature of the AGM account of revision is that $K * \alpha$ is a set of sentences of the same language as that with which we started. Thus, it provides no account of revision that involves *conceptual innovation*. This is a highly important form of revision, not perhaps a common form, but arguably the most profound. At any rate, AGM has nothing to tell us about this.

The AGM axioms themselves are rather abstract. There are many concrete models of them; these characterize revision (uniquely) in terms of other things. One of the nicest models is in terms of "spheres". A simple way of thinking of this is as follows. A set of beliefs, K, can be identified with the set of its models (in the model-theoretic sense). Let us write K^+ for the set of all interpretations that make K true (its models). I will write α^+ for $\{\alpha\}^+$. $K + \alpha$ is then simply the theory whose models are $K^+ \cap \alpha^+$. To define the other two operations, we suppose that K comes furnished with a set of "spheres": $K^+ = S_0 \subseteq S_1 \subseteq \ldots \subseteq S_n = I$ (the set of all interpretations of $\mathcal{L}$). To keep things simple, we suppose that there is a finite number of spheres, though this is inessential. Each sphere may be thought of as a "fallback" theory. Thus, if any

---

[1] For details of these, and of all the features of the standard AGM theory mentioned in what follows, see Gärdenfors (1988).

S_i is shown to be untenable, the agent's next choice is S_{i+1}. For any non-empty set, $X \subseteq I$, there must be a smallest sphere, S_X, that intersects it (and if X is empty, let $S_X = I$). $K * \alpha$ may be defined as the theory whose models are $S_{\alpha^+} \cap \alpha^+$. That is, it is the largest portion of the most preferred fallback theory that entails α. The definition of contraction need not concern here.[2] Let us just note that it can be shown that the operations, defined in terms of spheres, satisfy the AGM conditions.

8.3 INCONSISTENT BELIEF

Now to the problem posed by inconsistency. In the standard AGM account, as we saw, it is assumed that the logical consequence relation employed is classical. In particular, then, an inconsistent belief-set is trivial. Thus, adding to a belief-set something that is inconsistent with it produces triviality. Moreover, revising a belief-set with something inconsistent also gives triviality, because of the success condition.

Now, here is the problem. People often have inconsistent commitments. The persons whose beliefs are consistent is, in fact, a rarity. Yet it is absurd to suppose that a person who has inconsistent commitments is thereby committed to everything. If, by oversight, I believe both that I will give a talk on campus at noon, but also that I will be in town at noon, this hardly commits me to believing that the Battle of Hastings was in 1939.

It might be suggested that the theory of belief revision is one of an ideally rational agent, and that such an agent never has inconsistent beliefs. But this is a confusion. The theory of belief revision is a theory of how an ideally rational agent *changes* their beliefs. It is quite possible that such an agent should find themself with inconsistent beliefs in the first place (maybe through their education). Indeed, one thing we should expect of a theory of belief revision is an account of what it is rational to do if we do find ourselves in this situation.

Worse, it is not at all clear that an ideally rational agent must have consistent beliefs. Sometimes there is overwhelming evidence for inconsistent beliefs. The evidence points mercilessly to the fact that either a committed the crime or that b did. But I have known both a and b for years. Both are of impeccable moral character; neither is the kind of person who would do such a thing. This sort of situation seems to be a not uncommon one in science. For example, in the late nineteenth century, the evidence that evolution had occurred, and that the age of the earth was hundreds of millions of years, was overwhelming. But the thermodynamic evidence concerning the age of the sun showed that the earth could not possibly be that old. Nor is this simply a matter of history: it is well known that presently the general theory of relativity and quantum theory are mutually inconsistent. Indeed, as many philosophers of science have noted, most accepted scientific theories face contradictions and anomalies.[3] For

---

[2] For the record again, if we write α^- for the set of all interpretations that do not make α true $K - \alpha$ is defined as the theory whose models are $K^+ \cup (S_{\alpha^-} \cap \alpha^-)$.

[3] e.g., Lakatos (1970), Feyerabend (1975), ch. 5.

this reason, we cannot simply *suspend* belief in theories facing inconsistency. If we did, we would have no science left.

Further, as we saw in section 6.2, there are, in fact, good grounds for supposing that an ideally rational agent *must* have inconsistent beliefs. Such an agent would not believe something unless the evidence supported its truth. Hence, every one of their beliefs, $\alpha_1, \ldots, \alpha_n$, is rationally grounded. But the rational agent also knows that no one is perfect, and that the evidence is overwhelming that everyone has false beliefs (rational agents included: rationality does not entail infallibility). Hence, they believe $\neg(\alpha_1 \wedge \ldots \wedge \alpha_n)$. So their beliefs are inconsistent.[4] And even if, for some reason, this argument fails, one would hardly want to rule out *a priori* the *possibility* that rational belief is fallible in this way.

Of course, a rational agent can hardly believe everything. Hence, whether one takes the agent of the theory to be simply a rational reviser, or to be a rational believer as well, a theory of belief revision must allow for the possibility of agents having inconsistent but non-trivial beliefs.

8.4 PARACONSISTENCY

Possibly, there are a number of ways that one might try to solve this problem, but the most obvious is simply to employ a relation of logical consequence that is paraconsistent, that is, in which inconsistencies do not entail everything. An agent's commitments may then be inconsistent without being trivial.[5] There are many paraconsistent logics, and we do not need to go into details here.[6] Using such a logic, pretty much the whole of the AGM theory goes over intact. Just replace $\vdash_{CL}$ with the appropriate paraconsistent notion of consequence. The sphere modelling, too, works the same way. We just replace classical models with the models of the paraconsistent logic employed. There is only one major and inevitable casualty amongst the AGM postulates: the consistency postulate.[7] This must fail: $K * \alpha$ may be inconsistent, even if α is quite consistent, and for reasons that have nothing to do with α. But this is entirely what one should expect in the current context.[8]

---

[4] This is a version of the "preface paradox". For references and further arguments to the effect that if may be rational to have inconsistent beliefs, see Chapter 7 and *In Contradiction*, sect. 7.4.

[5] It might be suggested that triviality may be avoided by chunking beliefs into a number of consistent but mutually inconsistent parts. It should be noted that this is not an alternative to a paraconsistent strategy. Non-adjunctive paraconsistent logics effectively employ a chunking procedure of exactly this kind.   [6] These can be found in, e.g. Priest (2002*b*).

[7] There are a number of somewhat sensitive issues that I am sliding over, but nothing that affects what I have to say here. Details can be found in Tanaka (1996).

[8] Since the standard AGM account employs classical logic, there is no difference between inconsistency and triviality. Hence, the consistency condition is sometimes expressed with 'trivial' replacing 'inconsistent'. Both the consistency condition and its converse may then fail. For the latter: revising by a logical inconsistency will certainly produce an inconsistent set—assuming the success condition—but this will not, in general, be trivial. The possible failure in the opposite direction is not so obvious, but follows from a result that I will mention in a moment.

But now we face another problem. If we are allowing for the possibility of incon-sistent beliefs, why should revising our beliefs with new information ever cause us to reject anything from our belief-set at all? Why not simply add the belief to our belief-set, and leave it at that?[9]

The problem comes out sharply in the sphere modelling of the AGM postulates. In many standard paraconsistent logics, there is a trivial interpretation, ∞, one that makes everything true. *A fortiori*, it is a model of every theory. Given such an interpretation, for any α and K, $\infty \in K^+ \cap \alpha^+$. Thus, S_{α^+} is just K^+ itself, and so $S_{\alpha^+} \cap \alpha^+ = K^+ \cap \alpha^+$. Revision and expansion are exactly the same thing![10] ∞ is just a technical way of saying that when you can believe any contradiction, revision requires nothing but addition. Note, however, that in a paraconsistent context there is no reason to suppose the Levi identity holds (unless, of course, one uses it to *define* revision). For example, let K be the set of logical consequences of $\neg p$. Then $\neg p$ is not in $(K - \neg p) + p$, but it is in $K + p$.

8.5 MULTIPLE CRITERIA

But this is too fast. Suppose that we use a paraconsistent logic. If we revise our beliefs in the light of new information, α, there is nothing now in logic that will force us to delete $\neg \alpha$ (and some of the things that entail it) from our beliefs. But just because this is a *logical* possibility, it does not follow that it is a *rational* possibility. There is a lot more to rationality than consistency. Many quite consistent beliefs are irrational; for example, the belief that I am a fried egg. I may even hold this belief consistently with the rest of my beliefs, if I make suitable adjustments elsewhere (by jettisoning, e.g. the belief that I was born, and not laid). This makes it no more rational.

As I discussed in section 7.4, and as epistemologists have often noted, there are many features of a set of beliefs that may speak against its rational acceptability. Inconsistency

[9] One answer to this is provided by Bayeseanism. We suppose that belief is not an all-or-nothing matter, but comes by degrees which operate according to the laws of probability. If a belief, α, is assigned the probability $P(\alpha)$ and information β arrives, we assign α a new probability, $P'(\alpha)$, determined by conditionalisation: $P'(\alpha) = P(\alpha/\beta)$. (Of course, once it is granted that our beliefs may be inconsistent—that is, that we may give probability greater than 0.5 to each of contradictory propositions—we can no longer use standard probability theory, but we can use an apprparite paraconsistent probability theory—as given, for example, in *In Contradiction*, sect. 7.6).) If $P(\alpha) >$ 0.5, and we are given that $\neg \alpha$, then $P'(\alpha) = P(\alpha/\neg \alpha)$ may not be 0, but it may well be below 0.5.

Bayeseanism of this kind has a number of problems. It works best for beliefs that have a well-defined probability distribution. When applied to appraising rival scientific theories, such as Ptolemaic astro-nomy and Copernican astronomy, it is not clear how to deploy it. Moreover, as even Bayseans admit, there is consistent information on which one cannot conditionalize, and so on which this model breaks down. (More of this in sect. 11.9.) Perhaps most importantly in the present context, Baysean-ism puts many beliefs beyond the scope of revision. For given the information that α, its posterior probability is just $P(\alpha/\alpha) = 1$. And once something has probability 1, no conditionalization will change this. α is a belief that cannot be revised. There are ways around this problem. For example, Jeffrey (1983), ch. 11, suggests that given information β, the posterior probability of α should satisfy not Bayes' condition, but: $P'(\alpha) = P(\alpha/\beta) \cdot P'(\beta) + P(\alpha/\neg \beta) \cdot P'(\neg \beta)$. Unlike Bayesean conditionalization, this does not determine a unique posterior probability distribution at all.

[10] This shows that the consistency condition fails in this model when 'inconsistent' is replaced by 'trivial'. If K is the trivial set, then, whatever α is, $K * \alpha = K + \alpha = K$, and so is trivial.

may perhaps do this, but so, for example, does a high level of *ad-hoc*ness—which is presumably what goes wrong in the case of the person who gerrymanders their beliefs into a consistent set containing one to the effect that they are a fried egg. Conversely, there are many features of a set of beliefs that speak in favour of its rational acceptability. Simplicity is a traditional such virtue; so are: a low degree of *ad-hoc*ness, fruitfulness, explanatory power, unifying power.[11] What, exactly, all these criteria—except consistency—amount to, is a thorny issue: they are all notoriously difficult to spell out. It may even be the case that some of them, when properly understood, come to the same thing, but certainly not all of them. Moreover, how one is to justify these epistemic virtues is a very difficult question.[12] But it is also a different one: as with moral virtues, people can agree that something, say kindness, is a virtue, whilst disagreeing in their theoretical accounts of why this is so. Indeed, that kindness is a virtue is a datum much firmer than any moral theory will ever be.

We need not go into any of these questions further here, though. For, again as noted in section 7.4, it is simply the multiplicity of the criteria that is presently relevant. As long as there is a multiplicity, there is the possibility of conflict between them.[13] One set of beliefs may be the simplest, have the highest explanatory power, but be inconsistent. Another may be consistent and fruitful, but highly *ad hoc*. What is it rational to believe in such circumstances? There may be no determinate answer to this question. But, as argued in section 7.4, it would seem clear that (vaguely) if one set of beliefs scores sufficiently better on a sufficient number of these criteria than another, it is rationally preferable. This is how an inconsistent set of beliefs can be rationally acceptable: it scores highly on many of the other criteria. Conversely, and to return to the problem at hand, this is why an inconsistent set of beliefs may not be rationally acceptable. Its inconsistency may speak against it; and so may many other criteria. In particular, if we always revise simply by adding on the new information, we are likely to lose in simplicity, economy, unity. So the result may be quite irrational.

Looking at things in this way, consistency is no longer a necessary condition for rational belief; at best, it is merely one of a list of (potentially conflicting) desiderata. But we conceded this once we conceded the possibility that it might be rational to have inconsistent beliefs anyway. The important point is that simply tacking on new information to our beliefs, rendering the whole belief-set inconsistent, though it may be a logical option, may not be the rational course of action.[14]

8.6 FORMAL MODELS

Let me now outline a formal model of belief revision incorporating this insight. Suppose, as before, that our belief-set is K, and that new information, α, arrives. What is the new rational set of beliefs? There are a number of possibilities. One is

---

[11] See, e.g. Quine and Ullian (1970), ch. 5, Kuhn (1977), Lycan (1988), ch. 7.
[12] For one account, see Lycan (1988), ch. 7.
[13] The point is made in Kuhn (1977) and Lycan (1988), 130.
[14] The matter is discussed further in *In Contradiction*, ch. 7, and Priest (1998*b*).

simply the addition, $K + \alpha$. Another is something obtained by the Levi operation: $(K - \neg\alpha) + \alpha$, where $-$ is some suitable notion of contraction.[15] Another is a theory obtained by reversing the operations involved: $(K + \alpha) - \neg\alpha$. (There is no reason to suppose that, in general, this gives the same result. For example, it may not satisfy the AGM success condition.) Recall that the AGM conditions do not specify contraction uniquely; there may therefore even be many theories of the forms specified by the Levi identity and its reversal. And there may well be other possibilities as well. For example, one rational course of action may simply be to reject the new information, and write it off on the grounds of experimental error or whatever—though in this case one will presumably add to the belief-set something like 'it seemed that α', or 'our instruments reported that α'—in which case, again, the success condition will clearly fail.[16] More profoundly, the new information may occasion conceptual innovation, and thus there may be sets of beliefs in a new language.[17] Let us call the collection of all options, whatever they are, K^α.[18]

We know that there is a set of criteria, C, which can be used to evaluate sets of belief. These criteria are not all-or-nothing matters. (Given a paraconsistent logic, even inconsistency comes by degrees.) So let us suppose that for each $c \in C = \{c_1, \ldots, c_n\}$ there is a scale of how well a belief-set fares according to that criterion. Specifically, for each belief-set, $k \in K^\alpha$, there is a real number, $\mu_c(k)$, measuring how good that set is. (The higher the number, the better the set.) One might prefer some other scale, perhaps some subset of the real numbers, such as [0, 1]. But since the matter is largely conventional, this is not a crucial issue.

Next, we need a way of amalgamating the various criteria. A simple way of doing this is by taking their weighted average.[19] Let $\rho(k)$, the "rationality index" of k, be defined thus:

$$\rho(k) = w_1\mu_{c_1}(k) + \cdots + w_n\mu_{c_n}(k)$$

The weights, w_i, reflect the relative importance of each of the criteria. I will have a little more to say about these later. $K * \alpha$ can now be defined as the member of K^α

[15] Fuhrmann (1991) defines such a notion in terms of base contraction (i.e. revising a theory via revising its axioms). This approach does not obviate the need for the use of a paraconsistent logic, as Fuhrmann notes. Note, also, that the existence of an appropriate $(K - \neg\alpha) + \alpha$ does nothing on its own to solve the problem of why one should not revise simply by expanding.

[16] Further on this, see Hansson (1997).

[17] If we have a theory containing sentences of the form $P(\beta) = r$, stating a probability distribution, another candidate for membership of K^α might be obtained by replacing each of these with its Bayesean conditionalization, $P'(\beta) = r'$, where $r' = P(\beta/\alpha)$ (or, alternatively, by its "Jeffrey conditionalization"). A theory given by conditionalization may, then, give the rational successor theory of K, but it may also be trumped by a theory with better credentials.

[18] How to determine the totality of theories in K^α is an interesting question. It is not to be supposed that all logical possibilities—whatever that might mean in this context—are in K^α. K^α may comprise simply those theories which it has occurred to people (so far) to put on the table in response to the new circumstances.

[19] A similar proposal is mooted by Levi (1967), 106.

with the largest rationality index.[20] If there is more than one, $K * \alpha$ is one of these, non-deterministically. (Believers have a free choice.)

The model I have just described is simple, but obviously unrealistic in a number of ways. One of these is that, given a criterion, c, the assignment of a unique real number, $\mu_c(k)$, to a theory, k, is not really to be expected. About the best we can hope for is to assign k a range of numbers. (And probably a vague range, at that. But how to handle vagueness poses a whole new set of problems that would take us far away from the present problem.)

A second feature of the model is that, according to it, all theories are comparable as to the rationality of their acceptability. The ordering is a linear one.[21] This seems quite unrealistic. Rational people may well disagree about the best thing to believe when different criteria rank theories radically differently.[22] Thus, suppose that there are two criteria, c_1 and c_2; c_1 ranks k_1 high, but k_2 low, and c_2 vice versa. Then there may just be no comparing the two theories. The best we can hope for is a determinate answer when most of the criteria give similar results (and that's vague too). Thus, the ordering *ought* to be a partial one.

By a small modification of the construction, we can solve both of these problems at once. We now take each μ_c to assign each k, not a single value, but a non-empty range of values, $[\mu_c^-(k), \mu_c^+(k)]$. (The first figure is the lower bound; the second figure is the upper bound.) When we amalgamate these, the result is also going to be a range of values. The highest value a belief-set can hope for is clearly realized when it obtains the highest value under each component, and similarly for the lowest. So we can take $\rho(k)$ to be the range $[\rho^-(k), \rho^+(k)]$, where:

$$\rho^-(k) = \sum_{1 \leq i \leq n} w_i \mu_{c_i}^-(k)$$

$$\rho^+(k) = \sum_{1 \leq i \leq n} w_i \mu_{c_i}^+(k)$$

An overall ranking, $\sqsubset$, may now be defined on belief-sets. One belief-set, k_1, is rationally preferable to another, k_2, if it is clearly better, that is, if any value that k_1 can have is better than any value k_2 can have:

$$k_1 \sqsubset k_2 \Leftrightarrow \rho^-(k_1) > \rho^+(k_2)$$

It is easy to check that this is a partial ordering. It is not, in general, a total ordering. For example, if $\rho(k_1) = [3,7]$ and $\rho(k_2) = [2,4]$, then neither $k_1 \sqsubset k_2$ nor $k_2 \sqsubset k_1$.

[20] In certain traditions, it is common to talk about the coherence of a set of beliefs (see, e.g. sect. 2.6). It is usually assumed that consistency is a necessary condition for coherence, but not a sufficient one. The issue of what *are* sufficient conditions, though, is a tough one, and answers are hard to find. One way of understanding the notion is simply to define the degree of coherence of a theory to be its rationality index. If one does this then consistency is, of course, no longer a necessary condition for (a high degree of) coherence.

[21] In many ways, it might be more natural to take the range of each μ_c to be some partial (non-numerical) ordering. One then has to face the question of how to amalgamate all these orderings into a single partial ordering with the appropriate properties. There may well be ways of doing this, but I do not presently know of a suitable way.

[22] For an excellent discussion, see Kuhn (1977).

Thus, it may be that the rationality ordering, $\sqsubseteq$, provides a clear judgment concerning two theories sometimes, but not others. Rational disagreement is possible.

We can now define $K * \alpha$ to be any belief-set in K^α maximal in the ordering. If there is more than one, this is non-deterministic. For it is easy to see that there may be more than one distinct maximum. For example, suppose that $\rho(k_1) = [3, 7]$ and $\rho(k_2) = [4, 6]$, but for every other $k \in K^\alpha$, $\rho(k) = [1, 2]$. Then k_1 and k_2 are rationally preferable to all the other ks, except each other, and neither is preferable to the other.

Let me illustrate this definition of revision with a toy example. Suppose that K is the set of logical consequences of $\{p, q\}$ (p and q being logically independent of each other) and that α is $\neg p$. We suppose that the only members of K^α are $k_1 = K + \alpha$, the set of logical consequences of $\{p, q, \neg p\}$, and the Levi revision $k_2 = (K - p) + \neg p$, the set of logical consequences of $\{q, \neg p\}$. Suppose, now, that there are two criteria, consistency, c_1, and explanatory power, c_2, and that the values of μ are (for the sake of illustration) as follows:

$$\mu_{c_1}(k_1) = [2, 2] \qquad \mu_{c_1}(k_2) = [8, 8]$$
$$\mu_{c_2}(k_1) = [4, 5] \qquad \mu_{c_2}(k_2) = [3, 4]$$

There is no room for disagreement about which theory is the more consistent! Finally, suppose that $w_1 = 1$, and $w_2 = 2$. Thus, we think that explanatory power is more important than consistency. Computing, we determine that:

$$\rho(k_1) = [10, 12] \quad \rho(k_2) = [14, 16]$$

Thus, $k_1 \sqsubset k_2$, and $K * \alpha = k_2$. In particular, note, revision has occasioned the dropping of a belief.

This more complex model is clearly more realistic, but it is still a very idealized model. For a start, is there any reason to suppose that the criterion-weights, w_i, are uniquely and precisely determined? None that I can see. Moreover, it might well be the case that there could be rational disagreement about what their values ought to be.[23] A solution here is to treat weights as we treated the single-criterion values. That is, instead of taking them to be single values, we take them to be a range of values, broad enough to encompass differences of opinion. When we amalgamate, $\rho^+(k)$ is computed using the maxima of the weight-values; $\rho^-(k)$ is computed using the minima.

The account, thus modified, is still just a model. If it were ever to be applied in practice, the question of how to determine the values of the ws and the μ-values of each theory would become an important one. Of course, the *absolute* values are unimportant: the scales are almost completely arbitrary. It is the *relative* values (within scales and across scales) that are important. It can be hoped that a community of investigators could reach consensus on appropriate figures, particularly since it is only a *range* of values that has to be agreed upon. We may be able to set limits that keep everybody happy.

---

[23] This is, again, well illustrated in Kuhn (1977).

Note, also, that there might well be grounds for revising the weights themselves in the light of philosophical and scientific developments. Clearly, weight-revision cannot be done arbitrarily. Someone cannot declare, for example, that empirical adequacy is to be weighted 0. The result—on pretty much most other assumptions—would be that the trivial theory would come out as the most rational. However, there is a rational procedure for changing weights. The theory of rationality that I have laid out in this chapter, *including the weights of the different criteria*, is just that: a theory. It can therefore be revised in the way that I have described. In particular, the sentence to the effect that the weight of such and such a criterion is so and so might well be revised in the process. Maybe we come to believe, for example, that the world is just not the sort of place that is likely to be simple—in which case, the weight for simplicity would be decreased. (Indeed, the project of this book might be seen as part of an argument for lowering the weight traditionally assigned to consistency.) This raises the spectre that the revised theory might not be rationally acceptable given the revised weights, and so would need to be revised again. There is nothing, *per se*, wrong with this possibility. Revision, after all, should be expected to be an ongoing process.[24] There clearly might be a problem if the process went round in some kind of vicious loop. However, this fact itself, once realized, would be new information which would, presumably, provide the impetus for a revision that takes things out of the loop.

8.7 THE AGM CONDITIONS REVISITED

Since we started the chapter with a discussion of the AGM axioms, let me finish by briefly discussing to what extent $K * \alpha$, as defined here, satisfies them. Take them one by one.

K*1: $K * \alpha$ is logically closed.

$K * \alpha$ is a theory, and so logically closed; but under which logic? As argued, we may expect it to be a paraconsistent logic. But note that the construction does not require the logic to be any particular logic. Indeed, the different members of K^{α} may well be closed under logics that are different from each other, and from that of K too. For, as I will discuss in Chapter 10, one thing that we may wish to revise under the influence of recalcitrant information is exactly our logical theory. Thus, e.g. under the weight of counter-examples to the material conditional, it might be (indeed it is!) rational to move to a relevant logic. Quite unlike standard AGM constructions,

---

[24] Foundationalist accounts of rationality prescribe *a priori* criteria for what it is rational to accept. I think that such accounts are fundamentally misguided. Rationality is essentially and unavoidably *situated*. We all find ourselves in a pre-existing state of information. We do not have the luxury of going back to some *tabula rasa* postion. Indeed, it is not even clear what this possibility would amount to. We simply start where we find ourselves and do the best we can from there.

then, this account shows us how, and in what way, our logic may be revised too. The rational choice, $K * \alpha$, simply has a different logic from K.[25]

K*2: $\alpha \in K * \alpha$.

The success postulate need not be satisfied by $K * \alpha$, as has already been discussed.

K*3: $K * \alpha \subseteq K + \alpha$.

This postulate may not be satisfied either. For α may occasion conceptual revision. And if it does, there may be beliefs in $K * \alpha$ that cannot even be expressed in the language of K, and so are not in $K + \alpha$ at all. For this reason, the revision of phlogiston chemistry under the recalcitrant results obtained by weighing, occasioned beliefs employing quite new concepts, like *oxygen*.

K*4: $\neg \alpha \notin K \Rightarrow K + \alpha \subseteq K * \alpha$.

For similar reasons, this postulate fails. Old beliefs, such as that there is a substance called phlogiston, may get ditched in the process of revision.

K*5: $K * \alpha$ is inconsistent $\Rightarrow \alpha$ is a logical contradiction.

The failure of this postulate needs no further discussion.

K*6: α and β are logically equivalent $\Rightarrow K * \alpha = K * \beta$.

There is no reason to suppose that this postulate holds either. Nor should it. For α and β may be logically equivalent under the logic of K, but they may occasion different revisions of logic. For example, the existence of a counter-example to the law of excluded middle is equivalent to the existence of one to distribution (of $\wedge$ over $\vee$) in classical logic, since these are both tautologies. Yet the first may occasion a rational move to a three-valued logic (in which distribution, but not the law of excluded middle, holds), whilst the second might occasion a rational move to a quantum logic (in which the law of excluded middle, but not distribution, holds).

K*7: $K * (\alpha \wedge \beta) \subseteq (K * \alpha) + \beta$.

This postulate fails too. Suppose that, $\alpha \notin K$, and that, given K, α is incredible. So if α arrives as new (*prima facie*) information, the best thing to do is write it off to experimental error. Then $\alpha \notin K * \alpha$. Now suppose that β is something that does not entail α (even in conjunction with $K * \alpha$), so $\alpha \notin (K * \alpha) + \beta$, but that in the light of β, α is acceptable. In particular, given α and β together, α does become acceptable. That is, $\alpha \in K * (\alpha \wedge \beta)$.

K*8: $\neg \beta \notin K * \alpha \Rightarrow (K * \alpha) + \beta \subseteq K * (\alpha \wedge \beta)$.

This postulate fails for similar reasons. Choose some β such that neither β nor $\neg \beta$ is in K. Suppose that, given K, α, β and—*a fortiori*—$\alpha \wedge \beta$, are incredible. Their

---

[25] Indeed, the model will work just as well if we do not insist that the members of K^{α} be closed under their appropriate logic. Realistically, we have at our disposal at any time only a finite fragment of any theory, and it is really this that we evaluate.

arrival as *prima facie* new information then have no substantial effect on K. Then $\neg\beta \notin K = K * \alpha, \beta \notin K = K * (\alpha \wedge \beta)$, but $\beta \in (K * \alpha) + \beta$.

In summary, then, given the construction of this section, all the AGM postulates may fail. They do so because the model shows how to operate in a much more general class of revisions than the simple ones envisaged by AGM. This, indeed, is one of its strengths.[26]

8.8 CONCLUSION

The model of belief revision give here is, as we have seen, a much more general and flexible one than AGM. I do not think that, in real life, disputes over what belief-set (theory) it is rational to adopt proceed explicitly in the way prescribed by the model. Rational belief change is a much less cleanly articulated business than this. But I do think that the model captures, at least roughly, the qualitative features of what goes on implicitly in such contexts. And it suffices to give the lie to an objection often raised against those who think that it may be rational to believe a contradiction.[27] This is to the effect that there can be no rational debate with a person who will accept contradictions, since they may accept anything. They may do nothing of the kind.

---

[26] There is another solution to the main problem of this chapter that is worth noting here. In (1997), ch. 4, and (1999) Fuhrmann gives ways of defining an operation which merges two sets of information, A and B, to form a consistent set $A \circ B$. ($A \circ B$ is offered as the way to revise A given a whole set of new information, B.) Fuhrmann observes that if we have premise sets A and B, which may be inconsistent, and define $A, B \vdash \alpha$ as $A \circ B \vdash_{CL} \alpha$—or, alternatively, define $A \vdash \alpha$ as $A \circ A \vdash_{CL} \alpha$—then $\vdash$ is a paraconsistent notion of inference. Given that it is paraconsistent, it could well be the notion of inference employed in the construction of this paper. But there is a way of applying the construction more directly (though not one mooted by Fuhrmann himself). Suppose that *whenever* we acquire new information, α, we simply add it; but we allow the consequences to be determined by $\vdash$. Thus, the inference engine itself determines the resolution of contradictions. This construction is less satisfactory than the one described here. The question to ask is: which set is it that represents our beliefs (commitments)? Is it our total information, or is it its $\vdash$-consequences? If it is the first, then we never drop any beliefs at all, which certainly seems wrong. If it is the second, then our set of beliefs would never be inconsistent; as argued, this is wrong too. Another drawback of the suggestion is that it is much less general than the account given here: it allows for neither conceptual innovation nor for revision of the underlying logic of a belief-set.

[27] Versions of it can be found in Lewis (1982), 434, and Popper (1963), 316 f.

9

Consistency and the Empirical Sciences

9.1 INTRODUCTION

What role does, or should, inconsistency play in the empirical sciences? This is the question that is to be addressed in this chapter. The question is hardly a new one, but the development of modern formal paraconsistent logics has a profound impact on the subject. Paraconsistent logicians have realized that their subject has important implications for the empirical sciences and the philosophy thereof,[1] but discussions of the applications of paraconsistent logic have focused largely on non-empirical areas, such as semantics and metaphysics. It therefore seems appropriate to address the question directly.

I will first address the issue of the specificity of the empirical sciences: observation. Next, we will look at the role that inconsistency has played in science (henceforth in this chapter, I will often take the qualifier 'empirical' for granted), and the relation of this to paraconsistent logic. This will raise the question of how inconsistent information *ought* to be treated in science: what criteria, for example, may lead us to accepting an inconsistent theory? And should such an acceptance ever be more than provisional? These topics will be addressed in the next sections. An outcome of this discussion will be that, in the light of developments in paraconsistent logic, we may well have to change our attitude to inconsistencies of certain kinds; such a change would open whole new possibilities in science itself.

9.2 INCONSISTENCY AND OBSERVATION

Before we can address the issue of the role of inconsistency in empirical sciences, it will be important to discuss how such sciences differ from similar inquiries (which are often intricately connected with them), such as mathematics and metaphysics. The standard answer to this question is that in the empirical sciences, but not the others, observation plays a role. In the more developed sciences such observations are obtained through active experimentation. The observations serve to provide the ultimate *explananda* for science, as well as providing important inputs into the evaluation of scientific theories. This standard answer is not entirely unproblematic: the role of empirical data in science has often been overrated, and its role in areas such as philosophy

---

[1] See, e.g. Priest and Routley (1989*a*), 367–79, and Priest and Routley (1989*b*), 494 ff.

underrated—for example, by positivists and empiricists. However, that it plays a much more central role in science than in other inquiries can hardly be denied.

The distinction between what is observable and what is not, is not, itself, entirely unproblematic. Some states of affairs are certainly observable (such as the colour of an insect) and some are certainly not (such as the colour of a quark). But it is impossible to draw a sharp boundary between what is, and what is not. What is observable may depend on what aids to perception (such as a microscope) are used; or on how we interpret our sensory input in the light of accepted theories (such as theories that tell us that when we witness the tracks in a bubble chamber, we are seeing the tracks of charged particles). However, as with all vague or context-dependant distinctions, the fact that it is impossible to draw a neat line between its two sides does not mean that there is not an important distinction to be drawn. (Compare: being a child and being an adult.)

Let us now revisit the discussion of observation in section 3.5 with this new context in mind. What can one see?[2] For a start, seeing, in the sense relevant to explanation and confirmation, is propositional. We see *that* something is the case. We see that the stars appear to be in a certain position and ask for an explanation, or use this against a theory according to which they should appear somewhere else. As we noted in section 3.5, some have thought that one cannot see that something is *not* the case. We always see that something *is* the case, and then infer that something else is not the case. For example, we see that something is red and infer that it is not black. Whilst one may certainly do this, one need not: one can see directly that something is not the case. Try a thought experiment. I show you an ordinary apple and ask: is this black? You compare its colour with a mental paradigm of blackness, and it does not match; you say no.[3] Or again, you enter a room; the whole room is visible from where you stand; there is no one there. You can see that Pierre is not in the room. You do not have to say: the things in the room are a chair, a table . . .; Pierre is not a chair, Pierre is not a table . . .; therefore, etc.[4] The very distinction between seeing what is the case and what is not the case is a false one. Some seeings are both. When talking of actual physical objects, to be transparent is not to be opaque and vice versa. But you can see that something is transparent and you can see that something is opaque.

It should be remembered that seeing is not simply a matter of light rays hitting the retina. Certainly, the eyes are involved in seeing; but one needs more than eyes to see. If what one sees is to play a role in one's cognitive functioning, one must also understand one's visual input. Hence, the categories of the understanding play a role. To see is to interpret ones visual stimuli, by applying these categories, either consciously or preconsciously; and there is no reason why truth functions such as negation or disjunction should not enter into the process of interpretation directly. For example, I can see that this is a photograph of either Ned or Ted, identical twins such that I cannot tell the difference, without seeing that it is a photograph of Ned, and inferring the disjunction.

---

[2] In what follows, I will restrict myself to discussing vision, since this is by far the most important sensory modality in science; but similar comments apply to the other senses.

[3] I am not suggesting that all vision is paradigm-based in this way, as should become clear in a moment.　　　　　　　　　　　　[4] The example comes from Sartre (1943), ch. 1, sect. 2.

Now, suppose that α and β are states of affairs observable at the same time and place, from the same perspective, etc., as I discussed in section 3.5; then, as argued there, so is their conjunction. We can see that something is a unicorn; we can see that it is green. Hence, we can see that it is a green unicorn. Thus, if α and $\neg\alpha$ are observable states of affairs, so is $\alpha \wedge \neg\alpha$. Of course, this is not to say that the conjunction is observed; merely that it is observ*able*—that is, it is of a kind such that if it were to be the case, it could be seen.

In reply to the suggestion that it might be impossible to see inconsistent states of affairs because our perceptual apparatus imposes some "consistency filter", it suffices to note, as we saw in section 3.5, that we perceive impossible situations in various visual illusions. Thus, there are many well-known impossible figures (of the kind, for example, employed by Escher in his drawings); there are perceptual sets where people report seeing things as simultaneously red and green; there are situations where things appear to be moving and not moving. Let me just remind the reader of one of these, the last.[5] This is commonly known as the waterfall illusion. After conditioning the visual field by showing it constant motion of a certain kind, say a spinning spiral, one then looks at a stationary scene. The scene appears to move in the opposite direction, but nothing in the scene changes its position; for example, an object at the top of the visual field does not move round to the bottom. What we see appears to be both moving and stationary; this is the natural way of describing one's visual sensations. Of course, perception in the cases I have described is not veridical;[6] these are illusions, and things are not really thus; but that is how they would appear if things were thus. There is therefore nothing about our visual system that requires perception to be consistent.

9.3 TYPES OF INCONSISTENCY

Let us now turn to the issue of inconsistency in science. The inconsistencies in question here are inconsistencies in what are accepted scientific beliefs. Many historians and philosophers of science have observed that there are such inconsistencies—indeed that they are common—even in contemporary science.[7] If we distinguish between observation and theory (what cannot be observed), then three different types of contradiction are particularly noteworthy for our purposes: between theory and observation, between theory and theory, and internal to a theory itself.[8] Let us look at these three in more detail.

Inconsistency between theory and observation is the most obvious example. We have a well-received theory, T, with a certain observable consequence, α. We then run

---

[5] Details of examples such as this can be found in most books on vision and visual illusions, e.g. Robinson (1972). Examples of this kind are further discussed in Feyerabend (1975), 258 ff.

[6] Which is not to say that a perception of a contradictory state of affairs *cannot* be veridical. But as we saw in sect. 3.5, there are good reasons to suppose that those I have described are not.

[7] For example, Lakatos (1970), Feyerabend (1975), ch. 5, which can be consulted for details of many of the following examples.

[8] A good general discussion of kinds of problem situations in science, including those involving various kinds of contradictions, can be found in Laudan (1977), chs. 1, 2.

an experiment and observe that $\neg\alpha$. Simple-minded falsificationists would suggest that this shows that T is wrong and is to be ditched. But many philosophers of science have pointed out that this does not necessarily happen.[9] The contradiction may be treated as the site of an anomaly: both T and $\neg\alpha$ may be accepted *pro tem*. T will not be jettisoned until we have a better alternative; $\neg\alpha$ will not be jettisoned until we have an explanation of why our observation was incorrect. Examples of this kind in the history of science are many. The precession of the perihelion of Mercury, at odds with received facts about the heavenly bodies and Newtonian dynamics, was known for a long time before the rejection of Newtonian dynamics in favour of special relativity. Prout's hypothesis was widely accepted by many chemists even though it was known to be at odds with empirical data (much of which was subsequently rejected). And so on.[10]

The second kind of inconsistency, between theory and theory, is less frequently noted, but certainly occurs. This is when we have two well-accepted theories, T_1 and T_2, which have inconsistent consequences. Again, though this may be noted as the site of a problem, both T_1 and T_2 are retained until a suitable replacement theory for one or both is found. An example of this concerns the age of the earth in late nineteenth-century science. According to evolutionary theory (which was, by that time, well accepted), the age of the earth had to be hundreds of millions of years; but according to received thermodynamics, the sun—and so the earth—could not possibly be that old. (The issue was resolved only in the twentieth century with the discovery of radioactivity, a hitherto unsuspected form of heat-generation.) Another, contemporary, example: the theories of relativity and quantum theory are known to be mutually inconsistent.[11]

The third example of an inconsistency is when a theory is self-inconsistent. This could arise because a theory has inconsistent observational consequences, though I know of no interesting cases of this in the history of science. What there certainly have been are inconsistent theories where the inconsistencies are located internally, away from observational consequences. For example, for over a hundred years Newtonian dynamics was based on the old calculus, in which infinitesimals had inconsistent properties (being both non-zero, at one point in computations, and zero at others). Another, particularly striking, example is Bohr's theory of the atom, which included both classical electrodynamic principles and quantum principles that were quite inconsistent with them. Though the theory was certainly considered as problematic, its empirical

[9] e.g. Kuhn (1970), Lakatos (1970), Feyerabend (1975). This literature is quite old now, and many aspects of the philosophy of Kuhn, Feyerabed, *et al.* have been subject to telling criticism. Much of the brunt of the criticim has fallen on the Kuhn/Feyerabend claims about incommensurability. This is irrelevant to the present matter.

[10] In such situations, scientists may well, of course, have ideas about how to resolve the contradiction. But investigating possible ways of making a belief revision is not the same thing as making a revision. Revisions in accepted wisdom are not made until one of these ways looks as though it will work.

[11] This is not to say that individual scientists will endorse things of the form α and $\neg\alpha$, much less $\alpha \wedge \neg\alpha$. As I will we note in a minute, scientific knowledge is chunked, the chunks often belonging to different experts. α may well belong to one chunk, and $\neg\alpha$ to another.

predications were so much better than those of any other theory at the time that it had no real competitor.[12]

9.4 HANDLING INCONSISTENCY

As we have seen, the corpus of scientific beliefs may, or is even likely to be, inconsistent at any time. But from things accepted, scientists infer other things to be accepted, and they do not infer arbitrary conclusions. It follows that the inference procedure employed here must be a paraconsistent one (where an arbitrary α and $\neg\alpha$ do not entail an arbitrary β). What paraconsistent inference procedure is employed in inconsistent cases is another question; there is no *a priori* reason to suppose that it must be one of the standard monotonic paraconsistent logics, or even that it must be monotonic at all. Nor should one suppose that it must be the same in every case. What is guaranteed is that there must be some systematic procedure for drawing conclusions, and which does not permit drawing an arbitrary conclusion from a contradiction. What procedure is or was employed in any given case is a matter for detailed investigation.

I do not intend to discuss detailed examples here; but for what follows, it will be important for us to distinguish between two different kinds of paraconsistent logic: adjunctive and non-adjunctive. In adjunctive paraconsistent logics, such as standard relevant logics and da Costa's C systems, the rule of adjunction, $\alpha, \beta \vdash \alpha \wedge \beta$, is valid. In non-adjunctive systems, such as discussive logics, it is not. Non-adjunctive paraconsistent logics often employ some chunking procedure. Because of the failure of adjunction, one cannot simply put arbitrary premises together and draw conclusions. If the inference procedure is not to be impoverished, it is usually necessary to be able to put *some* premises together (into a chunk). A simple procedure is to put together any bunch of premises that are mutually consistent; but there are more sophisticated ones.[13]

One thing that is clear from a fairly cursory consideration of the scientific handling of inconsistent information is that the inference procedure employed is often of a non-adjunctive, chunking, variety. For example, given the dispute about the age of the earth at the end of the nineteenth century, no one conjoined the views that the earth was hundreds of millions of years old, and that it was not, to infer that the earth

---

[12] It might be suggested that in the situations mentioned the scientific community did not really accept inconsistencies. Rather, they had degrees of belief in various propositions, and their degrees of belief in the contradictory α and $\neg\alpha$ were less than 1. Now, it may well be the case that there are degrees of belief, and that acceptance is to be understood as having a sufficiently high degree; but this suggestion will really help. For example, given the inconsistency between the theory of evolution and thermodynamics, it would follow that one or both of these theories was believed to degree ≤ 0.5, which is to say that one or both of these was not accepted at all, which is untrue. Or if both were accepted to degree 0.5, and one sets the level of acceptance at this figure, then inconsistencies *were* accepted, as claimed.

[13] For a general account of paraconsistent logic, see Priest (2002*b*). On non-adjunctive strategies, see, especially, sect. 4.2. A non-adjunctive strategy which seems particularly apt for handling many historical examples is described in Brown and Priest (2004).

really had a contradictory age.[14] Similarly, in the Bohr theory of the atom, the drawing of conclusions was restricted to well-defined consistent chunks, possibly in accordance with some pragmatically determined—but still determinate—considerations.[15] A conclusion drawn may then have been fed into another consistent chunk which contained information inconsistent with that in the first chunk.[16] Whether adjunctive paraconsistent logics have, historically, ever been used in handling inconsistencies is a different matter, and is rather doubtful. At any rate, I know of no examples where this is clearly the case.

9.5   ACCEPTING INCONSISTENT INFORMATION

We have seen that inconsistent information has sometimes been accepted in the history of science; we have also seen, at least in outline, why this does not lead to disaster. None of this shows that the inconsistent information *ought* to have been accepted (even provisionally). But the situation seems to have arisen so frequently that it is implausible to level at the scientific community charges of blatant and frequent irrationality. This, therefore, raises the question of the conditions under which it is reasonable to accept an inconsistent theory or other body of information.

The question of what makes it reasonable to accept any theory is a familiar one in contemporary philosophy of science, and a very difficult one. Neither do I intend to advance a detailed answer to that question here. But let us recall the account of rational belief developed in the previous two chapters.

The doxastic goodness of a theory may be evaluated under a number of orthogonal criteria. A major criterion is empirical adequacy. For any observational consequence, α, that a theory entails, if α is observed, this is a good mark. If it is not, this is a black mark. Empirical adequacy is, perhaps, the most important criterion in science. It is, at least, the one that mainly distinguishes the empirical sciences from similar investigations. But it is certainly not the only one; nor can it be. It is at least theoretically possible to have different theories that are both empirically adequate; more commonly, it happens that no theory in the field is entirely empirically adequate. Hence other criteria have also to be employed. There is a multitude of these;[17] philosophers may disagree both about what they are, and about how, exactly, to understand them, but the following have certainly been suggested, and are very plausible. Good-making features include: simplicity, ontological leanness (Occam's razor), explanatory power, a low degree of *ad hoc*ness, unity, fruitfulness. The converse features are bad: complexity,

[14] Which is not to say that people did not notice that the theories together entail something of the form $\alpha \wedge \neg\alpha$, and so conclude that there was a problem here; merely that the corpus of accepted beliefs was not closed under an adjunctive logic.

[15] Many non-monotonic (paraconsistent) logics incorporate pragmatic features of this kind; for example, in the ordering relation with respect to which minimization is defined. See sect. 11.10.

[16] For a more detailed discussion, see Smith (1988), Brown (1990) and, especially, Brown (1993) and Brown and Priest (2004).

[17] See, e.g. Quine and Ullian (1970), ch. 5, Kuhn (1977), Lycan (1988), ch. 7.

ontological extravagance, explanatory poverty, much *ad hoc*ness, fragmentation, barrenness.[18]

The exact number of, and details concerning, criteria of these kinds, though a highly important and interesting question, need not detain us here. The important points are (a) that there is a multitude, and (b) that the criteria do not necessarily hang together. One theory, say Bohr's theory of the atom, may have a high degree of empirical adequacy, be very fruitful, but inconsistent. Another may be consistent, have a lesser degree of empirical adequacy, and be rather *ad hoc*. As I have argued in the previous two chapters, one theory is rationally preferable to another if it is sufficiently better on a sufficient number of criteria.

This account, rough as it may be, is sufficient to demonstrate a number of things. It shows why theory choice is a messy business: there is no simple algorithm. It shows why, within certain limits, there may be room to disagree over which theory is better: if no theory is overall best, people may reasonably disagree. All this is familiar from standard philosophy of science. As we noted in previous chapters, it shows two further things. First, it shows how and when it may be rational to accept an inconsistent theory: when, despite its inconsistency, it is markedly better than its rivals on sufficiently many other criteria. Secondly, it shows when it may be right to reject an inconsistent theory, even when inconsistency may be rationally tolerable: when a rival theory scores higher on sufficiently many criteria. That is, it shows how theories may be "falsified", even if inconsistencies are sometimes tolerable.

9.6   INCONSISTENCY AND TRUTH

But should an inconsistent corpus of belief be accepted only provisionally, until a better one can be found; or can it be accepted as a candidate for the final truth? Several comments are pertinent here. First, there is no such thing as certainty about anything in science. Any theory or set of theories, whether consistent or inconsistent, should be endorsed fallibly. All theories go beyond the data—which is itself, in any case, "theory laden". In this sense, the acceptance of anything is only ever provisional.

But is there something special about inconsistency in this regard? Here, it seems to me, the nature of the inconsistency is relevant. Note, first, that if a theory is empirically inadequate, however acceptable it is, the received information is not a candidate for the truth, at least as things stand. If a theory entails an observable consequence α, and α is not perceived, something is wrong, either with our theory or with our perceptions; something needs to be fixed. In particular, then, if a theory entails $\beta \wedge \neg \beta$, where β is some observation statement, then if such a contradiction is not observed, something is wrong. As I have already argued, $\beta \wedge \neg \beta$ is a perfectly observable state of affairs.[19] Moreover, if the inconsistency in the scientific corpus is between a theory and an

---

[18] The question of whether consistency/inconsistency should be on these lists is not as obvious as it might seem. See sect. 7.4.

[19] Thus, even if one suggested that one contradictory perceptually occluded the other, as discussed in sect. 3.5, we would need some (presumably psychological) explanation of why this is the case.

observation, something needs to be revised. For if theory T entails α, but $\neg\alpha$ is observed, not α, we again have an empirical inadequacy. It may be retorted that if inconsistencies are acceptable, maybe $\alpha \wedge \neg\alpha$ is true after all. But again, since $\alpha \wedge \neg\alpha$ is an observable state of affairs, and one that is not observed in the situation described, we have an empirical inadequacy: if $\alpha \wedge \neg\alpha$ were true, so would α be, and this is precisely what is not observed.

What if a contradiction is one between theory and theory, or internal to a theory, not spilling over into observation? Here, the situation is more complicated. Suppose, first, that one is an instrumentalist; then all one cares about is the empirical adequacy of a theory; if a contradiction is located deep in the heart of theory, this is of no moment. But if, as I think correct—though I shall not argue it here—one should, in general, be a realist about scientific theories, the matter is different, and depends crucially on how this inconsistency is handled. If it is handled by a chunking strategy, then the theory is not a candidate for the truth. If α is true and $\neg\alpha$ is true, then so is their conjunction. If a theory refuses to allow this move then the theory cannot be correct, and we know this.[20]

If, on the other hand, the inconsistency is handled with an adjunctive paraconsistent logic, there is no reason, as far as I can see, why we should not suppose the theory or theories in question to be correct. In particular, then, a theoretical inconsistency that is handled adjunctively is not, in itself, a reason to suppose that the theory cannot, in the long run, be allowed to stand. Any argument to the effect that such inconsistencies are ultimately unacceptable must be a quite general and *a priori* defence of the Law of Non-Contradiction in the appropriate form: any contradiction is known, in advance, to rule a theory out as a candidate for the truth. I know of no such argument that works. All fail, usually by simply begging the question in some way.[21] Thus, if we are realists, we will let our best theory, provided that it is not ruled out as a candidate for truth on other grounds, inform us as to what reality is like; and if our theory is inconsistent, there is no reason to suppose that the theory does not get it right: reality itself is inconsistent. In other words, inconsistencies of *this* kind in science do not mandate that the acceptance of the theory or theories in question be provisional in any special way.[22]

9.7 INCONSISTENT MATHEMATICS

It is here that the impact of paraconsistent logic is revisionary—indeed, revolutionary. The Law of Non-Contradiction has been well entrenched in Western thought—and

[20] More generally, if the inconsistency is handled with an inference mechanism that does not respect truth-preservation, such as that of Brown and Priest (2004), the same conclusion follows.

[21] The major arguments are those advanced or inspired by Aristotle in *Metaphysics* Γ. We saw why these fail in Chapter 1.

[22] This raises the following question. Suppose that we have a theory based on a non-adjunctive logic. This, as I have argued, is not an ultimately acceptable theory. Why can we not turn it into one, simply by changing the underlying logic to an adjunctive (truth-tracking) one? This may be a possibility, though not if changing the logic results in the theory being empirically inadequate—which is normally why a non-adjunctive procedure is used in the first place.

so science—since the canonization of Aristotle, whose defence of the law has rarely been challenged. Hence, scientists and philosophers have not been prepared to brook the thought that an inconsistent theory of any kind might be true. But subscribing to the Law is not rationally mandatory, as I argued in Chapter 7, and as the development of paraconsistent logics has played a large role in showing. Once this fact is digested, scientists may well—justifiably—take a different attitude to inconsistent theories of the appropriate kind. Indeed, they may even develop inconsistent theories, if these have the right empirical consequences, just as paraconsistent logicians have articulated inconsistent theories of semantics to handle the paradoxes of self-reference.

In modern science, the inferentially sophisticated part is nearly always mathematical. An appropriate mathematical theory is found, and its theorems are applied. Hence, a likely way for an inconsistent theory to arise now in science is via the application of an inconsistent mathematical theory. Though the construction of inconsistent mathematical theories (based on adjunctive paraconsistent logics) is relatively new, there are already a number: inconsistent number theories, linear algebras, category theories; and it is clear that there is much more scope in this area.[23] These theories have not been developed with an eye to their applicability in science—just as classical group theory was not. But once the paraconsistent revolution has been digested, it is by no means implausible to suppose that these theories, or ones like them, may find physical application—just as group theory did. For example, we might determine that certain physical magnitudes appear to be governed by the laws of some inconsistent arithmetic, where, for example, if n and m are magnitudes no smaller than some constant k, $n + m = k$ (as well as its being the case that $n + m \neq k$).[24] There are, after all, plenty of episodes in the history of science in which we came to accept that certain physical magnitudes have somewhat surprising mathematical properties (being imaginary, non-commuting, etc.). Why not inconsistency?[25]

9.8 CONCLUSION

I believe that the development of modern formal paraconsistent logics is one of the most significant intellectual developments of the twentieth century. In challenging entrenched Western attitudes to inconsistency that are over 2,000 years old, it has the potential to ricochet through all of our intellectual life—and empirical science wears no bullet-proof vest. As we have seen, empirical scientists have always tolerated, and operated within, inconsistency in certain ways. One of the liberating effects of paraconsistency should be to allow us to understand better exactly how this proceeded.

[23] For inconsistent arithmetic, see Priest (1997a) and (2000c). On inconsistent mathematics in general, see Mortensen (1995).
[24] I will return to this idea in sect. 10.7. There is even one place where an inconsistent mathematics might possibly find an application already. In the two-slit experiment in quantum mechanics, the causal anomaly can be resolved by supposing that the photon does the impossible, going through the two slits simultaneously, and handling this with an adjunctive paraconsistent probability theory. For details, see Priest and Routley (1989a), 377 f.
[25] Which is not to say that an inconsistent mathematical theory *must* be interpreted realistically. Such theories may have instrumental uses, just as much as consistent theories.

Such an understanding is bound to reflect into our understanding of the rationality of theory-choice, in the ways that I have indicated. Perhaps most importantly of all, paraconsistency may open the gate to important new kinds of theory within science itself. Where this will all lead, one cannot even begin to speculate.

One branch of science—though perhaps not empirical science—as traditionally conceived, is logic. The nature of this brings us to the fourth part of the book. And about the nature of logic, one can do a lot more than speculate.

PART IV
LOGIC

10

Logic and Revisability

10.1 INTRODUCTION

In the first three parts of this book, we have looked at the relevance of dialetheism to three core notions of philosophy—and vice versa—truth, negation, and rationality. In this last part of the book we take on a fourth: logic itself.

If dialetheism is correct, then—unless one is a trivialist—one must subscribe to some form of paraconsistent logic. The orthodox logic of our time is not a paraconsistent logic, and so dialetheism requires us to revise our beliefs about which logic is correct. This is often described as revising our logic; but this is a very misleading way of putting the matter. The process is one of belief-revision of a kind discussed in Chapter 8. I indicated in that chapter how belief-revision in general operates; and this account applies to our beliefs and theories about logic, as much as anything else.

Still, it might be thought that there is something special about logic which makes it different. In this chapter I will argue that there is not. Logic is revisable in just the same way that any other theory is. For comparison, I will also discuss the situation concerning geometry and arithmetic. The chapter also discusses some ramifications and implications of the revisability of logic. In particular, we will look at what the rivalry of logical theories amounts to, and at Quine's remarks concerning rivalry and the possibility of "deviant logics".

Paraconsistent logic is not, of course, the only "deviant" logic. Many formal non-classical logics were developed in the twentieth century, including intuitionist logic, various many-valued logics, quantum logics, etc. All of these provide potential rivals for classical logic, and many of the considerations posed by paraconsistent logics are quite general. I will therefore discuss the question of logical revision in the more general context of non-classical logics. The central concern, however, will remain paraconsistent logic.

10.2 LOGICS, GEOMETRIES, AND ARITHMETICS

The earliest formal non-classical logics to be developed in the twentieth century was many-valued logic. *Principia Mathematica* was hardly off the press before Łukasiewicz was formulating various logics of this kind.[1] In producing these, Łukasiewicz had the model of non-Euclidean geometries very much in mind. For example, he wrote:[2]

It would perhaps not be right to call the many-valued systems of propositional logic established by me 'non-Aristotelian' logic, as Aristotle himself was the first to have thought that the law of bivalence could not be true for certain propositions. Our new-found logic might rather be termed 'non-Chrysippean', since Chrysippus appears to have been the first logician to consciously set up and stubbornly defend the theorem that every proposition is either true or false. The Chrysippean theorem has to the present day formed the most basic foundation of our entire logic. It is not easy to foresee what influence the discovery of non-Chrysippean systems of logic will exercise on philosophical speculation. However, it seems to me that the philosophical significance of the systems of logic treated here might be at least as great as the significance of non-Euclidean geometry.

The analogy between non-standard logics and non-Euclidean geometries is an important and interesting one, though several people have denied it. For example, the Kneales (1962), 575, say:

Even from a purely formal point of view the ordinary two-valued system has a unique status among deductive systems which can plausibly be called logic, since it contains all the others as fragments of itself. In short, they are not alternatives to classical logic in the sense in which Lobachevski's geometry is an alternative to Euclid's.

Now this is just factually wrong. There are, for example, connexivist systems of logic that contain logical truths that are not classical logical truths, such as $(\alpha \rightarrow \beta) \rightarrow \neg(\alpha \rightarrow \neg\beta)$.[3] But even if it were not, the conclusion would hardly follow. From the fact that a logic is maximal in some sense, it does not follow that another cannot be an alternative. The maximal logic might entail *too much*.

Some have insisted that classical logic has some kind of priority over other systems, since metatheoretic reasoning must be classical.[4] Even if this were to entail some disanalogy, the claim is, again, just false. Intuitionist metatheory for intuitionist logic makes perfectly good sense.[5] Even Rescher (1969), 219, who has a good deal more sympathy for the claim than many others, denies the analogy, on the ground that the articulation of a logical system requires the employment of a metalogic (normally an informal one, and not necessarily classical), whereas the articulation of a geometric system does not require the employment of a metageometry. Rescher's observation seems correct. But again, it is difficult to see it as having significant import for the question. The formulation of a grammar for a language requires the employment of a metalanguage, and so a metagrammar. But this hardly entails that there cannot be rival grammars for a language, or that the question of which is correct is not a fallible and revisable matter. The same could be true of logic.

[1] Brouwer's intuitionism was being developed about the same time. But formal intuitionistic logic, as developed by Heyting, was about a decade later.
[2] Łukasiewicz (1930), quotation taken from p. 63 of the English translation.
[3] See, e.g. Anderson and Belnap (1975), sect. 29.8.
[4] e.g. Linke. See Rescher (1969), 229.
[5] It is illustrated in Dummett (1977). See esp. p. 214.

In fact, the analogy between non-Euclidean geometries and non-classical logics is a close one, as we will see. To facilitate the comparison of geometry and logic, we will also look at an important half-way house, arithmetic. Logic, arithmetic, and geometry are the three great *a priori* sciences of Kant's *Critique of Pure Reason*. According to Kant, the mind has certain cognitive structures which, when imposed on our "raw sensations" produce our experiences. The first two, space and time, are dealt with in the Transcendental Aesthetic. The third, the categories, is dealt with in the Transcendental Analytic. In the case of all three, a certain body of truths holds good in virtue of these *a priori* structures; and these constitute the three corresponding sciences; geometry in the case of space, arithmetic in the case of time, and logic in the case of the categories. As the difference in location in the *Critique* indicates, the sciences are not entirely on a par: geometry and arithmetic are synthetic; logic is analytic. Nonetheless, each, as a science, is certain and, essentially, complete. This gives us Euclidean geometry, (standard) arithmetic, and Aristotelian logic.

10.3   NON-EUCLIDEAN GEOMETRY

There are few now who would agree with the Kantian picture of these three sciences—at least in its entirety. It has disintegrated, not just under the pressure of philosophical criticism, but under the pressure of developments in science itself. This is clearest in the case of geometry.

Until the nineteenth century, 'geometry' just meant Euclidean geometry; but in the first part of that century some different geometries were developed. Initially, these were obtained by Lobachevski and Bolyi simply by negating one of the postulates of Euclidean geometry in order to try to find a *reductio* proof of it. But under Riemann, the subject developed into one of great generality and sophistication. In particular, he developed a highly elegant theory concerning the curvature of spaces in various geometries. Whether non-Euclidean geometries were to be called geometries *in stricto sensu* might have been a moot point; after all, they did not describe the structure of physical space. But they were at least theories about objects called 'points', 'lines', etc., whose behaviour bore important analogies to that of the corresponding objects in Euclidean geometries. Moreover, Riemann realized that it might well be an empirical question as to which geometry should be applied in physics.[6]

Within another fifty years, and even more shocking to Kantian sensibilities, Riemann had been vindicated. The General Theory of Relativity postulated a connection between mass and the curvature of space (or space-time) which implied that space may have non-zero curvature, and so be non-Euclidean. Predictions of this theory were borne out by subsequent experimentation, and the Theory is now generally accepted.

These developments have forced us to draw a crucial distinction. We must distinguish between geometry as a pure mathematical theory and geometry as an applied

[6]   On the history of non-Euclidean geometry, see Gray (1994); and on Riemann in particular, see Bell (1937), ii. ch. 26.

theory. As pure mathematical theories, there are many geometries. Each is perfectly well-defined by some axiomatic or model-theoretic structure. What holds in it may be *a priori*. By contrast, which to apply to the cosmos as a physical geometry is neither *a priori* nor incorrigible. Each pure geometry, when applied, provides, in effect, a theory about spatial (or spatio-temporal) relations; and which is correct is to be determined by the usual fallible scientific criteria.

This by no means resolves all pertinent philosophical issues. In particular, how to understand the status of applied geometry is still contentious. The simplest interpretation is a realist one.[7] Physical geometry is a theory about how certain things in physical space, i.e. points, lines, etc., behave; and a non-Euclidean geometry gets it right. The alternative to realism is non-realism, of which there are many kinds. One is reductionism: talk of geometric points and lines is to be translated without loss into talk of relationships between physical objects. This is the view traditionally associated with Leibniz, but has found few modern adherents. Another kind of non-realism is instrumentalism.[8] Geometry has no descriptive content, literal or reductive. It is merely auxiliary machinery for the rest of physics. As such, we may choose whatever geometric machinery makes life easiest elsewhere; and a non-Euclidean geometry does just that. One notable version of instrumentalism is that according to which, once we have chosen a geometry, its claims become true by convention. Such conventionalism is often associated with the name of Poincaré.[9]

10.4   NON-STANDARD ARITHMETICS

Is the situation concerning different logics the same as that concerning different geometries, at least in principle? *Prima facie*, it might well be thought not. A crucial difference would appear to be that logic, unlike geometry, is analytic, not synthetic. Thus, logic is not about the world in any interesting sense; consequently, the question of changing logic to provide a better description of the world, as geometry was changed, does not arise.

Before we consider this issue, it will be illuminating to consider the case of arithmetic, which is a halfway house. Kant, it is true, considered both geometry and arithmetic to be synthetic. The received view in the twentieth century was more influenced by Frege, however.[10] Geometry may be synthetic, but arithmetic is analytic.

Let us start by asking if there could be alternative pure arithmetics in the sense that there are alternative pure geometries. Normal arithmetic is the set of sentences of the usual first-order language that are true in the standard model, the natural numbers, $0, 1, 2, \ldots$, as subject to the usual arithmetic operations. We may take an alternative arithmetic simply to be one that is inconsistent with this. In other words,

---

[7] This is endorsed by Nerlich (1976).   [8] This is endorsed in Hinckfuss (1996).
[9] See, e.g. Poincaré (n.d.).
[10] For example, Wright (1983) shows that standard arithmetic may be derived in second-order logic augmented by "Hume's Principle": if X and Y are in one-to-one correspondence then the number of Xs is the same as the number of Ys. This certainly looks as though it could be analytic.

we form an alternative arithmetic by throwing in something false in the standard model. Naturally, if consistency is to be preserved, other things must be thrown out. There are two possibilities here.

The first is that we retain all the axioms of Peano Arithmetic, but add the negation of something independent of Peano Arithmetic but true in the standard model. We then have a theory that has a classical non-standard model.[11] As a rival arithmetic, such theories are a little disappointing, however. For as is well known, any model of such a theory must have an initial section that is isomorphic to the standard model. In a sense, then, such theories are not rivals to standard arithmetic, but extensions.

The second, and more radical, way of obtaining a non-standard arithmetic is to add something inconsistent with the Peano axioms, and jettison some of these. (This is the analogue of how non-Euclidean geometries were initially produced.) In principle, this could produce many different systems, but I know of only one to be found in the literature. This jettisons the axiom which says that numbers always have a successor, and adds its negation, producing a finite arithmetic.[12] Although there are such systems, then, there is no well worked-out theory of their general structure.

10.5 MODELS OF THE INCONSISTENT

A more radical way still of producing a non-standard arithmetic, for which there is now a general theory, is to drop the consistency requirement. We may then add the negation of something true in the standard model and jettison nothing. Let us approach the issue via a little history.

A driving force behind the development of mathematics can be seen as the extension of the number system in such a way as to provide solutions to equations that had no solution. Thus, for example, the equation $x + 3 = 2$ has no solution in the natural numbers. Negative numbers began to be used for this purpose around the fifteenth century. Or consider the equation $x^2 = -1$, which has no solution in the domain of real numbers. This occasioned the introduction of complex numbers a little later. In each case, the old number system was embedded in a new number system in which hitherto insoluble equations found roots.

Now consider Boolean equations. A Boolean expression is a term constructed from some of an infinite number of variables, $p, q, r, \ldots$ by means of the functors $\wedge, \vee$ and $-$ (complementation). A Boolean equation is simply an equation between two Boolean expressions. The simplest interpretation for this language is the two-element

---

[11] In this model there may even be solutions to diophantine equations that have no solution in the standard model—by the solution to Hilbert's tenth problem—though these solutions will have no name in the standard language of arithmetic.

[12] See Van Bendegem (1987). Goodstein (1965) gives an arithmetic where a number can have more than one successor, though it would be more accurate to describe this as an arithmetic in which there is more than one successor function.

Boolean algebra, $\mathcal{B}_2$, whose Hasse diagram is:

$$\top$$
$$\uparrow$$
$$\bot$$

($\wedge$ is interpreted as meet, $\vee$ as join, and $-$ as order inversion). Within this interpreta-tion many Boolean equations have solutions. For example, the equation $p \vee -p = q$ is solved by $q = \top$ and $p = \top$ (or $\bot$). But many equations have no solutions, e.g. $p = -p$. It is natural, then, to extend the algebra to one in which all equations have solutions. The simplest such one is that whose Hasse diagram is as follows:

$$\top$$
$$\uparrow$$
$$\mu$$
$$\uparrow$$
$$\bot$$

(where operations are interpreted in the same way; in particular, μ is a fixed-point for $-$). In this structure the equation $p = -p$ is solved by $p = \mu$. More generally, it is not difficult to check that if every variable is assigned μ, any Boolean expression evaluates to μ. Hence every Boolean equation has a solution.

The construction here is a special case of a more general one. The three-element algebra just given, $\mathcal{D}_3$, is a De Morgan lattice with a fixed point for negation. By the same argument as before, every Boolean equation has a solution in an algebra of this kind. The general result is that every De Morgan algebra (and *a fortiori*, every Boolean algebra) can be embedded in such an algebra.[13] The result is analogous to one of the fundamental theorems of algebra, that every field can be extended to one over which all equations have solutions (i.e. all non-constant polynomials have roots), an algebraic closure. (The algebraic closure of the reals is, of course, the field of complex numbers.)

Algebras have many applications. The most obvious application of $\mathcal{D}_3$ in a philo-sophical context is to provide a structure of truth-values for a propositional language. In this context, the fact that every Boolean expression can be evaluated to μ means that, provided we take the designated values of our logic to be those $\geq \mu$, every

---

[13] The following proof is due to Peter Milne. Take any De Morgan algebra. Add top and bottom elements, 1 and 0 (such that $-1 = 0$) if the algebra does not have them. Let an *interval* $[a, b]$, be any set of the form $\{x : a \leq x \leq b\}$. Define the operations on intervals as follows:

$$[a, b] \vee [c, d] = [a \vee c, b \vee d]$$

$$[a, b] \wedge [c, d] = [a \wedge c, b \wedge d]$$

$$-[a, b] = [-b, -a]$$

The set of intervals with these operations is a De Morgan algebra. The map which sends a to $[a, a]$ is an embedding, and $-[0, 1] = [-1, -0] = [0, 1]$. See Milne (2004).

sentence is satisfiable; as, more generally, is every set of sentences. (The interpretation where everything takes the value μ is, of course, a rather uninteresting one. But there will be many others. The point is simply to demonstrate the existence of models.)

In terms of logics, the above algebraic structure is exactly the logic LP,[14] and the value μ is normally thought of as *both true and false*. The truth-value μ might seem a rather odd one. One might be tempted to call it an imaginary truth-value, for the same reason that $\sqrt{-1}$ was called imaginary. But there is nothing really imaginary about imaginary numbers. Mathematically speaking they are just as *bona fide* as real numbers. Indeed, they even have applications in physics. Leave quantum mechanics out of this; even in classical physics, magnitudes such as impedance are given by complex numbers. Similarly, mathematically speaking, there is nothing imaginary about μ. And like imaginary numbers, μ may even have important applications, for example, as the truth-value of paradoxical self-referential sentences, α (for which we often appear to have $\alpha \leftrightarrow \neg\alpha$).

Anyway, as we have now seen, every set of sentences, even inconsistent ones, has a model in the logic LP (at least the trivial one, where everything takes the value μ, but in general many non-trivial models too).[15] In particular, and to return to the main issue, so do inconsistent arithmetics.

10.6 INCONSISTENT ARITHMETICS

The fact that there are *logical* models of inconsistent arithmetics does not tell us anything about their *arithmetical* structure. In fact, they have an interesting common structure. What is this? I will restrict myself here to describing the situation for the simplest finite models. The general case (even the general finite case) is more complex.[16]

In every such model there is a tail, T, of numbers, $0, \ldots, n - 1$, that behave consistently. The numbers from n onwards form a cycle with some period, $p(> 0)$, so that for any $i \geq n, i + p = i$. (But since this is a model of arithmetic $i + p \neq i$ also.) These models may therefore be characterized by two parameters: the tail, T, and the period, p. The trivial model is the special case in which $T = \phi$ and $p = 1$.

Every structure of the kind described is a non-standard arithmetic, and the numbers in it are analogous to the points and lines in a non-standard geometry. Since each of the non-standard arithmetics extends ordinary arithmetic, every equation that has a solution in standard number theory has a solution in it. But, as might be expected, there are equations that have no standard solution but which have solutions in non-standard arithmetics. Let a numerical expression be any term formed from variables,

---

[14] See, e.g. *In Contradiction*, ch. 5.

[15] Strictly speaking, we have seen this only for sentences of a propositional language. The result extends in a natural way to a full first-order langauge, however. The details of this can safely be left as an exercise.

[16] A complete characterization of the finite case is given in Priest (1997*a*). Details of the general case can be found in Priest (2000*c*).

$x, y, \ldots$, and the constant **0**, using the functors $+$, $\times$ and $'$ (successor).[17] (I will use **m** for the numeral of m.) An equation is any identity of the form $s = t$, where s and t are arithmetic expressions. It is not difficult to establish that in the trivial model, every arithmetic equation has a solution (viz. $x = y = \ldots = 0$.) But many families of equations have general solutions in non-trivial models. For example, any equation of the form **m** $=$ **n** has a solution in a model where $m, n \notin T$ and $m = n$ (mod p). And any equation of the form $s(x) = t(x)$, where x occurs in s and t, has a solution in every model where $p = 1$ (namely the least inconsistent number).[18]

10.7 EMPIRICAL APPLICATIONS

We have seen that there are alternative pure arithmetics, in the same sense that there are alternative pure geometries: abstract mathematical structures dealing with objects (numbers or points) that behave in a way recognizably similar to the corresponding objects of the standard theories. But, it might be suggested, this is as far as the similarity goes. There is no possibility of applying a non-standard arithmetic to an empirical situation in the same way. There could be no such thing as applied non-standard arithmetic in the same way that there is applied non-Euclidean geometry. Is this so? I take the answer to be 'no'. There are theoretical arguments for this; we will come to these when I turn to logic. For the present I will demonstrate the point by telling a story to show how we might come to replace a standard application of ordinary arithmetic with a different one. There are a few such stories already in the literature, notably, those of Gasking (1940). But I will give one which might motivate the adoption of one of the inconsistent arithmetics that we met in the last section.[19] I do not want to claim that the situation described is a possibility in any real sense: it is merely a thought experiment. But if it succeeds it will show the required conceptual possibility.[20]

Let us suppose that we come to predict a collision between an enormous star and a huge planet. Using a standard technique, we compute their masses as x_1 and y_1, respectively. Since masses of this kind are, to within experimental error, the sum of the masses of the baryons (protons and neutrons) in them, it will be convenient to take a unit of measurement according to which a baryon has mass 1. In effect, therefore, these figures measure the numbers of baryons in the masses. After the collision, we

[17] Other functional expressions, e.g. exponentiation, could be added to the list. However, others, such as subtraction, cause problems.

[18] Likewise, families of equations that have no simultaneous solution in standard arithmetic can have one in inconsistent arithmetics. The case of families of linear equations, with an application to control theory, is discussed in Mortensen (1995), ch. 8.

[19] There are certainly others. For example, even if arithmetic is not the form of the intuition of time, as Kant thought, one might tell a story where circumstances suggested the possibility of calibrating time with a non-standard arithmetic. In virtue of the cycles in the finite inconsistent arithmetics, stories of time travel would appear to be particularly fruitful here.

[20] It is worth noting that Gasking is criticized by Castañeda (1959), who argues that if we use a different arithmetic and preserve our standard practices of counting, we end up with either a simple change of terminology or inconsistency. I will not discuss Castañeda's argument here. Even if he is right, this is clearly no objection in the present context.

measure the mass of the resulting (fused) body, and obtain the figure z, where z is much less than $x_1 + y_1$. Naturally, our results are subject to experimental error. But the difference is so large that it cannot possibly be explained by this. We check our instruments, suspecting a fault, but cannot find one; we check our computations for an error, but cannot find one. We have a puzzle. Some days later, we have the chance to record another collision. We record the masses before the collision. This time they are x_2 and y_2. Again, after the collision, the mass appears to be z (the same as before), less than $x_2 + y_2$. The first result was no aberration. We have an anomaly.

We investigate various ways of solving the anomaly. We might revise the theories on which our measuring devices depend, but there is no obvious way of doing this. We could say that some baryons disappeared in the collision; alternatively, we could suppose that under certain conditions the mass of a baryon decreases. But either of these options seems to amount to a rejection of the law of conservation of mass(-energy), which would seem to be a rather unattractive course of action.

Then someone, call them Einquine, fixes on the fact that the resultant masses of the two collisions were the same in both cases, z. This is odd. If mass has gone missing, why should this produce the same result in both cases? An idea occurs to Einquine. Maybe our arithmetic for counting baryons is wrong.[21] Maybe the appropriate arithmetic is one where z is the least inconsistent number, and p (the period of the cycle) $= 1$. For in such an arithmetic $x_1 + y_1 = x_2 + y_2 = z$, and our observations are explained without having to assume that the mass of baryons has changed, or that any are lost in the collisions! Einquine hypothesizes that z is a fundamental constant of the universe, just like the speed of light, or Planck's constant.[22]

While she is thus hypothesizing, reports of the collisions start to come in from other parts of the galaxy. (The human race had colonized other planets some centuries before.) These reports all give the masses of the two new objects as the same, but all are different from each other. Some even measure them as greater than the sum of their parts. Einquine is about to give up her hypothesis, when she realizes that this is quite compatible with it. Even if the observer measures the mass as z', provided only that $z' > z$ then $z = z'$, and their results are the same!

But this does leave a problem. Why do observers consistently record result that differ from each other? Analysing the data, Einquine sees that values of z (hers included), are related to the distance of the observer from the collision, d, by the (classical) equation $z = z_0 + kd$ (where z_0 and k are constants). In virtue of this, she revises her estimate of the fundamental constant to z_0, and hypothesizes that the effect of an inconsistent mass of baryons on a measuring device is a function of its distance from the mass. Further observational reports bear this hypothesis out; and Einquine starts to consider the mechanism involved in the distance effect.

We could continue the story indefinitely, but it has gone far enough. For familiar reasons, there are likely to be theories other than Einquine's that could be offered for the

[21] We already know that different sorts of fundamental particles satisfy different sorts of statistics.
[22] The revision of arithmetic envisaged here is a local one, in that it is only the counting of *baryons* that is changed. It would be interesting to speculate on what might happen which could motivate a global change, i.e. a move to a situation where everything is counted in the new way.

data. Some of them might preserve orthodox arithmetic by jettisoning conservation laws, or by keeping these but varying some physical auxiliary hypotheses. Others might modify arithmetic in some other, but consistent, way.[23] And each of these theories might become more or less plausible in the light of further experimentation, etc. But the point is made: it is quite possible that we might vary our arithmetic for empirical reasons. There can be alternative applied arithmetics, just as there are alternative applied geometries.[24]

An applied arithmetic is, in effect, a theory concerning certain relations of magnitude. As with geometry, there are various ways in which one might understand such a theory. One can tell a realist story: collections of physical objects have a certain physical property, namely size; and sizes, together with the operations on them, have the same objective structure as the numbers and corresponding operations in the non-standard arithmetic. Hence, facts about the mathematical structure transfer directly to the physical structure, and this is why it works. Or one could tell instrumentalist stories of various obvious kinds. For example, Gasking (1940), runs a conventionalist line on arithmetic that is similar to Poincaré's on geometry. We need not pursue these matters further here, though.

10.8 REVISING LOGIC: THE CASE OF SYLLOGISTIC

We have seen that there are numerous pure geometries and arithmetics. We have also seen that, when applied, a geometry or arithmetic is a corrigible theory of some kind. Let us now turn to the question of whether the same is true of logic. I will argue that it is. Indeed, it may fairly be pointed out that I have already assumed this, since the argument concerning arithmetic was partly based on arithmetics whose underlying logic is non-classical.

First, there are numerous pure logics. This point I take to be relatively uncontentious. There are the many-valued logics that Łukasiewicz invented, not to mention others such as intuitionism, quantum logic, and paraconsistent logic (one of which, *LP*, we met in the preceding sections). Possibly, a purist might say that they are not logics since they are not the *real* logic. But that would be like saying that non-Euclidean geometries are not geometries since they are not the *real* geometry. In both

---

[23] An obvious suggestion here is that we might use, instead, a finite consistent arithmetic, with maximum number z_0, which is its own successor. For all we have seen of the example so far, this would do just as well. However, there might well be reasons that lead us to prefer the inconsistent arithmetic. Notably, this arithmetic gives us the full resources of standard arithmetic, whilst the finite arithmetic does not. For example, in the inconsistent arithmetic it is true that for any prime number there is a greater prime, which is false in the finite arithmetic. This extra strength might cause us to prefer it. Alternatively, the difference might even occasion different empirical predictions, which verify the inconsistent arithmetic.

[24] Some of the philosophical issues surrounding inconsistent arithmetics are aired in Priest (1994a). There it is argued that our ordinary arithmetic might be an inconsistent one. A critique of this is to be found in Denyer (1995), with replies in Priest (1996a). Denyer's criticisms are not relevant here. For present purposes, I concede that our ordinary arithmetic is the usual one. My concern is with inconsistent arithmetics as revisionary.

cases we have a family of structures (logics or geometries) that are perfectly well-defined mathematical structures; and, as far as that goes, all on a par.

The more contentious question is whether in logic, as in geometry and arithmetic, which one we apply may be a corrigible matter. Of course, a pure logic can have many applications (as may pure geometries and arithmetics). For example, standard propositional logic may be used to test inferences or simplify the design of electrical circuits; and for some of these applications (e.g. the latter) the question of which logic is correct may well be a theory-laden and corrigible matter. But when talking of application here, what we are talking about is what one might call the canonical application. The canonical application of geometry is in physical geometry; the canonical application of arithmetic is to counting and measuring; the canonical application of logic is to reasoning.

Now, there is a well known and very famous argument to the effect that all applied theories are revisable in principle, and so corrigible. I refer, of course, to that contained in Quine's celebrated paper 'Two Dogmas of Empiricism' (1951). The argument is to the effect that there is no principled way of drawing a line between the revisable and the unrevisable theories; and hence the sciences traditionally thought of as *a priori*, such as geometry and arithmetic are just as revisable as psychology and physics.[25] Quine also mentions logic explicitly in this context, but does not pursue the matter at great length.[26] Different arguments for similar conclusions were put forward by Putnam in (1962). Moreover, Putnam went on to develop the conclusion for logic. In (1969), drawing on the example of non-Euclidean geometry explicitly, Putnam argued that the situation in quantum physics might well occasion the replacement of classical logic by quantum logic—at least in reasoning about the micro-world.

We need not work through the details of Putnam's example here. To show that the received logic may change it is not necessary to argue for the *possibility* of this. One can point to a place where it has *actually* happened.[27] When Kant defended the incorrigibility of logic in the *Critique of Pure Reason*,[28] he defended Aristotelian logic—by which I mean, here, not Aristotle's logic, as found in the *Organon*, but the somewhat pathetic remnants of medieval logic, based on the theory of the syllogism, which was orthodox in the eighteenth and nineteenth centuries.[29] Within 150 years, this had been replaced by the entirely inappropriately called 'classical logic' of Frege and Russell.

That Aristotelian and classical logic are distinct will hardly be denied. But it might well be suggested that the adoption of classical logic did not revise Aristotelian logic in any interesting sense: Aristotelian logic was perfectly correct as far as it went; it was

---

[25] Interestingly enough, exactly the same argument was used some ten years earlier at the end of Gasking (1940).

[26] The consequences for logic are drawn out clearly in Haack (1974), ch. 2.

[27] The theme is developed in Priest (1989*a*).

[28] 'That logic has already, from the earliest of times, proceeded upon this sure path is evidenced by the fact that since Aristotle it has not required to retrace a single step . . . It is remarkable also that to the present day logic has not been able to advance a single step, and is thus to all appearance, a closed and completed body of doctrine.' B viii. Kemp Smith (1964), 17.

[29] For an excellent summary of this, see Prior (1967).

just incomplete. Classical logic simply extended it to a more complete theory. Such a suggestion would be false. It is a well-known fact, often ignored by philosophers (though not, perhaps, historians of philosophy) that Aristotelian logic is incompatible with classical logic in just the same way that non-Euclidean geometries are incompatible with Euclidean geometry. A central part of Aristotelian logic is syllogistic, and the most natural translation of the syllogistic forms into classical logic is as follows:

AaB	All As are Bs	$\forall x(Ax \supset Bx)$
AeB	No As are Bs	$\neg\exists x(Ax \wedge Bx)$
AiB	Some As are Bs	$\exists x(Ax \wedge Bx)$
AoB	Some As are not Bs	$\exists x(Ax \wedge \neg Bx)$

Given this translation, Aristotelian syllogistic gives verdicts concerning the validity of some syllogisms that are inconsistent with classical logic. Consider the inferences called by the medievals *Darapti* and *Camestros*, which are, respectively:

All Bs are Cs
All Bs are As
Hence some As are Cs

All Cs are Bs
No As are Bs
Hence some As are not Cs

Both of these are valid syllogisms. Both are invalid in classical logic.

The problem is, of course, one of existential import. Some syllogisms seem to presuppose that various categories are instantiated.[30] It is sometimes suggested that the problem can be repaired by adding the import to the translations explicitly. Specifically, we add the clause $\exists xAx$ to each of the a and e forms. (It would be redundant in the other two.) This is, indeed, sufficient to render all the syllogistic forms classically valid, but the problem with this is that it invalidates other central parts of Aristotelian logic, notably, the square of opposition. The square is:

AaB	AeB
AiB	AoB

where the claims on the top line are contraries; on the bottom line are sub-contraries; and on both diagonals are contradictories. Now it is clear that, once the a form is augmented with existential import, a and o are not contradictories: both are false if there are no As. For the same reason, neither are e and i.

Another suggested repair is to add existential import to the a form (but not the e), and take the o form to be its negation ($\exists x(Ax \wedge \neg Bx) \vee \neg\exists xAx$). This validates all the syllogisms and the square of opposition. The oddity of taking 'some As are not Bs' to

[30] For the record, these are the inferences Darapti and Felapton in the third figure, and all the medieval subaltern moods: Barbari, Celaront, Cesaro, and Camestros. A discussion of the problem of existential import can be found in Kneale and Kneale (1962), 54–61.

be true if there are no *A*s is clear enough. But more importantly, this repair invalidates another part of the traditional logic: the inferences of obversion. Specifically, obversion permits the inference from 'no *A*s are *B*s' to 'all *A*s are non-*B*s'; which fails if the *e* form is not existentially loaded. Obversion is not in Aristotle, but it is a perfectly standard part of traditional logic.

It is sometimes suggested that, rather than adding existential import to the translations explicitly, we should take the instantiation of all the categories involved to be a global presupposition. This is a move of desperation. If it is correct, then we cannot use syllogistic to reason, e.g. in mathematics, where we certainly do not make such presuppositions. I don't think that the traditional logicians who endorsed syllogistic believed this. Moreover, if we were to allow validity to have contingent presuppositions, pretty much *anything* could be made to be valid.[31]

More importantly, the suggestion really will not save syllogistic.[32] All winged horses are horses, and all winged horses have wings. Applying Darapti, we may infer that there are some winged horses. The argument clearly generalizes. All *A*s are *A*s.[33] *A fortiori*, all *AB*s are *A*s; and symmetrically, all *AB*s are *B*s. By *Darapti* it follows that there are some *AB*s. Thus syllogistic allows us to prove that any two categories intersect. And if it be replied that this is just one of the global presuppositions, take *B* to be $\overline{A}$, the complement of *A* (non-*A*). It can hardly be maintained that Aristotelian logic globally presupposes contradictions. This argument requires the use of compound terms. Again, these are not in Aristotle, but are an established part of traditional logic.[34]

What we have seen is that, however one interprets traditional logic in classical logic, *something* has to be given up. Moreover, this is quite essential. For as the last argument shows, traditional logic is, in fact, inconsistent. At any rate, classical logic is not (just) a more generous framework subsuming traditional logic. Prevarication aside, modern logic has given the thumbs-down to *Darapti* and its ilk.

10.9 QUINE AND MEANING-VARIANCE

As Quine insisted, then, there can be rival logics for canonical application, just as there can be rival geometries and arithmetics for their canonical applications. Some years after writing 'Two Dogmas', Quine developed his views on radical translation, with some corollaries for logic. And many commentators have viewed these as a partial reneging on his earlier radical views concerning logic.[35] The views are spelled out first

---

[31] It is worth noting that classical logic has its own contingent presuppositions, notably that something exists, and its own Darapti: $\forall x Fx \vdash \exists x Fx$.

[32] The following argument is due to Len Goddard. For a further discussion see his (2000).

[33] One might, of course, deny this. But then one has to reject another standard part of traditional logic: the Law of Identity.

[34] They are omitted in Łukasiewicz' (1957) formalization of syllogistic, which allows it to be consistent.　　　[35] For example, Haack (1974), ch. 1, Dummett (1978), 270.

in *Word and Object* (1960), section 13; but they are put most pithily in *Philosophy of Logic*, thus:

> To turn to a popular extravaganza, what if someone were to reject the law of non-contradiction and so accept an occasional sentence and its negation as both true? An answer one hears is that this would vitiate all science. Any conjunction of the form '*p.~p*' logically implies every sentence whatever; therefore acceptance of one sentence and its negation as true would commit us to accepting every sentence as true, and thus as forfeiting all distinction between true and false.
>
> In answer to this answer, one hears that such full-width trivialisation could perhaps be staved off by making compensatory adjustments to block this indiscriminate deducibility of all sentences from an inconsistency. Perhaps, it is suggested, we can so rig our new logic that it will isolate its contradictions and contain them.
>
> My view of the dialogue is that neither party knows what he is talking about. They think that they are talking about negation, '~', 'not'; but surely the notion ceased to be recognisable as negation when they took to regarding some conjunctions of the form '*p.~p*' as true, and stopped regarding such sentences as implying all others. Here, evidently, is the deviant logician's predicament: when he tries to deny the doctrine he only changes the subject.[36]

Quine has paraconsistent logic in his sights here, but the context makes it plain that the point is meant to be a general one; and the point would seem to be that a change of logic occasions a change of meaning of the connectives concerned (though Quine might not put it this way because of his scepticism about meaning).

The claim has been denied by some,[37] and I think that it would be wrong to suppose that the connectives of different logics *must* have different meanings. However, I think that it must be agreed that the connectives of different pure logics often do have different meanings. Consider, for example, negation in intuitionist and classical logics. Given a possible-world interpretation for a propositional language, the truth conditions of classical and intuitionist negation are, respectively:

$\neg\alpha$ is true at world w iff α is not true at world w
$\neg\alpha$ is true at world w iff for all w' such that $w \leq w'$, α is not true at w'

It is clear that the truth conditions are quite distinct. Since identity of meaning would certainly seem to entail identity of truth conditions, it follows that the two negations mean something different. An intuitionist would say that the first truth conditions do not succeed in defining a meaningful connective at all. I do not think that this is right; but even if it were, it would still follow that the two connectives do not mean the same: one is meaningful; the other is not.

It would be wrong, however, to suppose that Quine takes the meaning variance of connectives across different logics to be an argument against his earlier view concerning the revisability of logic. A few pages after the passage just quoted, he says (p. 83):

> By the reasoning of a couple of pages back, whoever denies the law of excluded middle changes the subject. This is not to say that he is wrong in so doing. In repudiating '*p* or *~p*' he is indeed giving up classical negation, or perhaps alternation, or both; and he may have his reasons.

---

[36] Quine (1970), 81.   [37] For example, Putnam in (1962) and (1969).

And summing up some of the lessons learned in the book he reiterates explicitly the revisability of logic (p. 100):

> ... I am committed to urge the empirical nature of logic and mathematics no more than the unempirical character of theoretical physics; it is rather their kinship I am urging, and a doctrine of gradualism ... A case in point was seen ... in the proposal to change logic to help quantum mechanics. The merits of the proposal may be dubious, but what is relevant now is that such proposals have been made. Logic is in principle no less open to revision than quantum mechanics or the theory of relativity.

Moreover, Quine is absolutely correct to insist that the views concerning meaning-change do not render rivalry and revision impossible. One way to see this is to recall that a number of influential writers in the philosophy of science, such as Kuhn (1962) and Feyerabend (1975), argued for a version of meaning variation for scientific theories. According to them, the meanings of terms in scientific theories are defined by the scientific principles in the theory, and thus, e.g. 'mass' in Newtonian mechanics means something different from 'mass' in relativistic mechanics. They concluded from this that the theories are incommensurable, i.e. that no direct comparison of content is possible between them. But they did not infer that the theories are not rivals. They obviously are: they give different and incompatible accounts of, e.g. motion, to the point of making inconsistent predictions.[38]

So, if Quine is not arguing against the possibility of rivalry in logic, what point is he making? Let us return to that in a moment. It will pay us, first, to look more closely at how rivalry in logic manifests itself.

10.10 RIVALRY

As pure logics, no logic is a rival of any other. They are all perfectly good abstract theories. It is only when we apply them that a question of rivalry occurs. To give a theory canonical application, it is crucial that we forge some link between it and the practices that give the application life.[39] In the case of geometry, we need to relate the objects of the theory to our practices of measuring lines and angles; in the case of arithmetic, we need to relate the objects of the theory to our practices of counting. And in the case of logic, we need to relate the theory to our practices of inferring.

Inferring is a practice carried out in the vernacular; maybe the vernacular augmented with a technical vocabulary (such as that of chess, physics or whatever); maybe the

---

[38] In a passage just before the first one quoted, Quine raises the possibility of someone who uses 'and' as we use 'or', and vice versa, and notes, quite correctly, that there is no real rivalry between the respective views, merely a trivial linguistic one. This is because there is a translation manual between their idiolect and ours, which is precisely what is impossible when we have a case of incommensurability.

[39] The link may, of course, be coeval with the theory itself, as it was in the case of Euclidean geometry and Aristotelian logic.

vernacular augmented with mathematical apparatus; but the vernacular nonetheless.[40] Hence, to apply a logic, we must have some way of identifying structures in the formal language with claims in the vernacular. (Whether these are sentences, propositions, thoughts or whatnot, we need not go into here.) Notoriously, in the case of logic, the mode of identification is largely tacit. It is a skill that good logicians acquire, but no one has ever spelled out the details in general. It is simple-minded, for example, to suppose that every sentence with a 'not' in is adequately represented in the language of a logical theory by whatever represents the sentence with 'not' deleted, and prefixed with '¬'. For a start, the negation of 'All cows are black' is not 'All cows are not black'. And as we have had a couple of occasions to observe earlier in the book, English uses 'not' for functions other than negation (as in 'I'm not British; I'm Scottish'). Similar points can be made concerning '∧' and 'and', and '∨' and 'or'.[41]

Rivalry in geometry, arithmetic or logic, occurs when different theories, each relative to the way it is applied, deliver different, incompatible, verdicts. In the case of logic, this happens when incompatible verdicts are given concerning the validity of some inference. For example, consider the inference 'If there is not a greatest prime number then there is a greatest prime number. Hence there is a greatest prime number.' Given the usual identifications, classical logic says that it is correct to draw this conclusion; intuitionist logic that it is not. Or take the inference '107 both is and is not the greatest prime number. Hence Fermat's Last Theorem is true.' Classical logic says that this is a correct conclusion to draw; paraconsistent logic that it is not.

10.11   QUINE IN DEFENCE OF CLASSICAL LOGIC

Let us now return to Quine's observations and ask, assuming them to be correct, what their point is supposed to be. The deviant's logician's 'predicament' is that if they change the logic they change the subject; but if this does not rule out rivalry in logic, why, exactly, is it a predicament? I take the answer to be this. The deviant logician may want to change logics and meanings—and may be justified in doing so—but what they cannot do is say that the principles of (the received) logic are *false*. If someone denies one of the principles, then either their words mean something different, or what they say is (logically) false.

The observation is clearly made in defence of classical logic against its rivals. It is, after all, supposed to be a predicament for the *deviant* logician, not the classical one.[42] But the first thing to note about the above point is that it is entirely symmetrical. The

---

[40] This is not to say that portions of the reasoning may not be formalized in the language of some logical theory. But this is already to apply the theory, since it presupposes the adequacy of the formalization.

[41] See Strawson (1952), 78–93. My own favourite example is due to John Slaney: 'One move and I shoot'.

[42] There is no doubt who the deviant logician is supposed to be. Introducing the topic, Quine says: '[In previous chapters] we did not consider any inroads on the firm area [logic] itself. This is our next topic: the possible abrogation of the orthodox logic of truth functions and quantifiers in favour of some deviant logic' (1970), 80.

classical logician is in exactly the same situation with respect to the rival logic: when they deny the principles of that, they, too, mean something different, or what they say is (logically) false.

So why does Quine think that the observation tells against non-classical logic? The answer is that he *assumes* that the logical constructions of the vernacular *are* those of classical logic. This is demonstrated by the passage in the original quotation where he lists negation, '∼', and 'not' as the same thing, without further comment. Even granting that negation and 'not' are the same (which they are not, as I have already observed), '∼' is a sign of a formal language with a certain semantics (classical for Quine), whereas negation is a notion from vernacular reasoning.[43]

But Quine's assumption is exactly what a partisan of a logic other than classical is likely to take issue with. Someone who rejects classical logic, say a paraconsistent logician, need not deny that the (classical) meaning of '∼' is sufficient to guarantee the validity of inference $p.\sim p \vdash q$ in classical logic (the pure abstract theory);[44] what they will certainly deny is that this is the meaning of negation, as it occurs in vernacular reasoning, about, say, the claim 'This sentence is not true'. According to them, the semantics of their pure logic is the correct semantics for vernacular negation. Seen in this way, a dispute between rival logics is, then, exactly a dispute over meanings.[45] This may surface, for example, as a dispute over the truth conditions of vernacular negation. It is therefore entirely open to someone who holds that our theory of logic is revisable to hold that the correct logical principles are analytic, that is, true solely in virtue of the meanings of the logical connectives employed;[46] it is just that which principles are analytic is a corrigible and theory-laden issue.

At any rate, as we see, Quine's defence of classical logic completely begs the question, as does any logician who claims that classical logic is right *by definition*.[47] The question is: which definition? And this is to be settled by investigations of the kind standardly engaged in in trans-logical debates.

10.12 LOGIC AND TRANSLATION

As I observed earlier, what underlies Quine's views about the meaning-variance of connectives in different logics are certain of his views concerning radical translation. These are brought to bear on the issue explicitly in the section in *Philosophy of Logic* immediately following the one I have just been discussing. Here, Quine appeals to aspects of radical translation to try to establish that one cannot attribute to a speaker any view incompatible with classical logic.

---

[43] Quine's identification of logic with classical logic is also manifest in the following passage. 'It would seem that the idea of a deviation in logic is absurd on the face of it. If sheer logic is not conclusive, what is? What higher tribunal could abrogate the logic of truth functions or quantification?' (1970), 81.   [44] Though they may, as we saw in ch. 5.
[45] Which is the way that Dummett sees it. See (1978), 288.
[46] For example, as in Priest (1979).   [47] e.g. Slater (1995).

The argument is to the effect that when we translate the utterances of another, it is a constraint on correct translation that we cannot take them to be denying things that we take to be obvious (since they must be equally obvious to them). But logic is obvious. Hence we cannot attribute to them beliefs we take to be logically false. As he sums up the argument ((1970), 83):

> . . . logical truth is guaranteed under translation. The canon 'Save the obvious' bans any manual of translation that would represent the foreigners as contradicting our logic (apart perhaps from corrigible confusions in complex sentences).

In the present context, several comments on this argument are pertinent. First, even if the argument is right, the situation concerning classical and non-classical logicians is entirely symmetrical. If a classical logician ("we") cannot impute the denial of a classical logical truth to an intuitionist or paraconsistent logician (a "foreigner"), then they cannot impute a denial of what they take to be a logical truth to a classical logician. The argument cannot, therefore, be used as an argument for classical logic.[48]

Secondly, the argument is, in any case, badly deficient. There are two reasons for this. The first is that the claim that logic is obvious is mind-numbingly false. That certain principles hold in various pure logics may well be obvious. That they are so in the vernacular is not at all true—or what is the debate between rival logics all about? From a modern perspective, it may *seem* obvious that Darapti is invalid. It was not obvious to logicians for the previous 2,000 years that this was so—or if it was, they kept very quiet about it. History has taught us that what seems obvious may well not be so. Indeed, it may be false. Quine can assume that logic is obvious only because he has tacitly identified logic with the received theory[49]—an error I have already commented on.

The second failure of the argument is due to the fact that the rule that the obvious should be built into translation is only a defeasible rule, and may be defeated by other aspects of the context. Someone standing in the pouring rain may yet deny that it is raining, since they may believe that they are in a virtual-reality machine. Less fancifully, people in the fifteenth century took it to be obvious that the earth is stationary (apart from occasional quakes and tremors). When Galileo said otherwise, they did not translate his beliefs away: they showed him the thumbscrews. Similarly, and closer to home, when writers such as Hegel and Engels explicitly endorse contradictions, we do not automatically say that they cannot mean, or believe, what they say. In the light of the rest of what they say, we may well conclude that this is exactly what they believe.[50]

---

[48] One might also observe that even if the argument is correct, it is wrong to say, as Quine does, that logical truth is guaranteed under translation. What is guaranteed is *belief* about logical truths. (The methodology of translation requires us to ascribe to others those of our beliefs that we take to be obvious.) The fact that we believe something to be a logical truth does not make it so, in logic as elsewhere.

[49] '. . . every logical truth is obvious, actually or potentially. Each, that is to say, is either obvious as it stands or can be reached from obvious truths by a sequence of individually obvious steps. To say this is in effect just to repeat some remarks of Chapter 4: that the logic of quantification and identity admits of complete proof procedures . . .' Quine (1970), 82 f.

[50] The point is well made by Dancy (1975), 34 ff.

For all these reasons, appeal to radical translation will not help, one iota, in defending classical logic.

10.13 REALISM VS. INSTRUMENTALISM IN LOGIC

We are now finished with Quine. Let us return to the analogy between logic, geometry, and arithmetic. An applied geometry is, in effect, a theory of spatial relations; an applied arithmetic is a theory of relations of magnitude; and an applied logic is a theory of logical relations. In particular, then, when we change our logical theory, it does not follow that what principles of logic are valid also changes, any more than when we change our theory of geometry, the geometry of the cosmos changes. The fact that we may use the word 'logic' to apply both to our theory and the concerns of that theory may encourage this confusion.[51] The word 'geometry' is similarly ambiguous; but in a post-Kantian age only the naive would suffer from the corresponding confusion.

What, though, makes a theory of logic correct? Just as with geometry and arithmetic, one may tell both realist and non-realist stories here. In the next chapter I will argue for a realist account. But for the present, I will just chart some of the positions in conceptual space.

According to a simple instrumentalist story, logic is a tool that we use for inferring; and what makes a logical theory right is that, combined with our other theories, it produces the right results. 'Right' here is to be understood as meaning that the things that we deduce which are subject to relatively direct testing, test positive. Thus, for example, if I deduce the existence of something satisfying a certain condition (an atomic particle, or a number), and investigation fails to find such a thing, then the prediction would appear to be dubious. Of course, as Quine (of 'Two Dogmas') would have pointed out, we can decide to hold on to any predictions our theory makes if we make suitable changes elsewhere—which we may well determine to do. What settles the most appropriate theory, then, is simply that which is overall simplest, most adequate to the data, least *ad hoc*, and so on.[52]

As in geometry and arithmetic, this simple instrumentalism may be augmented by some kind of conventionalism. Even though the correct logic is a matter of choice, one may still regard claims of logic as true or false. What makes them so is the convention of our choice. This is conventionalism in logic, of the positivist variety.

The realist story is different. What makes a theory the right theory is that it correctly describes an objective, theory-independent, reality. In the case of logic, these are logical relationships, notably the relationship of validity, that hold between propositions (sentences, statements, or whatever one takes truth-bearers to be). But what are these logical relationships? Several answers are possible here. Perhaps the simplest is one according to which logical truths are analytic, that is, true solely in virtue of the meanings of the connectives, where these meanings are Fregean and objective. Logical relationships are therefore platonic relationships of a certain kind.

---

[51] See, further, *In Contradiction*, ch. 14.
[52] This is the view of logic endorsed by Haack (1974), ch. 2, and also Rescher (1969), ch. 3.

A different, and more common story, which avoids reification of meanings, is Tarski's.[53] Interpretations are set-theoretic structures of a certain kind; truth (or maybe satisfaction) in an interpretation is given a recursive definition; and validity is defined as truth-preservation in all interpretations. The facts of validity are then defined by general facts about what interpretations there are. Depending on one's views, this may or may not be a partly empirical question—and if it is, logic turns out to be an *a posteriori* subject (in the traditional sense), as well as corrigible.

If a realist account of the nature of logical relations is given, then, whatever that is, the question arises as to the criteria one should use to determine which theory is correct. The answer to this, as explained in the previous part of the book, is that one decides on the basis of which theory is overall simplest, most adequate to the data, least *ad hoc*, and so on. These are, of course, exactly the same criteria as are used by the instrumentalist. Thus, although there are profound ontological differences between instrumentalists and realists, when it comes to the decision as to which logic is correct, all parties may appeal to the similar considerations. This is why the debates between various logical theories may well be, and often are, conducted largely independently of the ontological issue.

10.14 LOCALISM VS. GLOBALISM

Let me finish by commenting on another issue, that of whether the correct logic is global or local. Is the same logical theory to be applied in all domains, or do different domains require different logics? This question is orthogonal to the realist/instrumentalist issue. Since instrumentalists are guided purely by pragmatic concerns, localism sits well with it; but it is quite possible for an instrumentalist to insist that logic is, by its very nature, domain-neutral, and so be a globalist. For example, Ryle (1954) argues that topic-neutrality is a necessary condition for a construction to be the concern of formal logic. Globalism is probably the more natural position for a realist, but it is quite possible for a realist to insist that the nature of the logical relationships between statements about one domain is different from that between statements concerning another. Thus, it is quite possible for a realist to be a localist.

In the end, I doubt that there is a serious issue here. Even if modes of legitimate inference do vary from domain to domain, there must be a common core determined by the syntactic intersection of all these.[54] In virtue of the tradition of logic as being domain-neutral, this has good reason to be called *the* correct logic. But if this claim is rejected, even the localist must recognise the significance of this core. Despite the fact that there are relatively independent domains about which we reason, given any two domains, it is always possible that we may be required to reason *across* domains, for

[53] Tarski (1956). Tarski's account has recently been criticized by Etchemendy (1990). For some defence of Tarski, see Priest (1995c).

[54] It could be, I suppose, that this intersection is empty, but I have never heard a plausible argument to this effect.

example about the relationship between the macro-domain and the micro-domain, or between mathematical objects and physical objects. Now, if α is a statement about one domain, and β about another, the only logical relationships that we can count on, e.g. $\alpha \wedge \beta$ or $\alpha \rightarrow \beta$ satisfying are those that are common to the two domains.

But conversely, even a globalist may admit that when applying logic to certain domains, the generally valid inferences may legitimately be augmented by others. An intuitionist, for example, may agree that it is permissible to use all of classical logic to reason about the finite (or at least, the decidable); and a paraconsistent logician may hold that it is permissible to use all of classical logic when reasoning about the consistent. Thus, there would seem to be no significant disagreement between localists and globalists about the facts; only about how to describe them.

10.15 CONCLUSION

We started our discussion of geometry, arithmetic, and logic with Kant. For him, these were the three great *a priori* sciences. The appearance of non-Euclidean geometries, and, in particular, the adoption of one of them as a physical geometry early in the twentieth century made it impossible to subscribe to the Kantian picture. There are many pure geometries; each, when applied, provides a theory of corrigible status. We have seen that exactly the same is true of arithmetic and logic. There are many pure arithmetics and logics; any one of these may be applied to provide a theory of some appropriate kind; and no theory can claim incorrigibility in this matter. Łukasiewicz' analogy between non-Euclidean geometries and non-standard logics is therefore a highly apt one.

Logics, then—that is, our theories of logic—are fallible theories. As we noted in 10.13, this raises the question of how such theories should be interpreted. Should one understand them instrumentally, or realistically, or perhaps in some other way? And if realistically what is the reality in question? This is the topic to which we turn in the next chapter.

11

Validity

11.1 INTRODUCTION

What is logic? Uncontroversially, logic is the study of reasoning. Not all the things that might fall under that rubric are logic, however. For example, the way that people actually reason may, in some profound sense, be part of the ultimate answer to the question of the nature of logic (think of Wittgenstein in the *Investigations*), but logic is not about the way that people actually think. The reason for this is simple: as a rich literature—if not common sense—now attests, people frequently reason illogically.[1] Logic does not tell us how people *do* reason, but how they *ought* to reason. We should cede the question of how people actually reason to psychology (and I will return to the question of normativity later).

The study of reasoning, in the sense in which logic is interested, concerns the issue of what follows from what. Less cryptically, some things—call them *premises*—provide reasons for others—call them *conclusions*. Thus, people may provide others with certain premises when they wish to persuade them of certain conclusions; or they may draw certain conclusions from premises that they themselves already believe. The relationship between premise and conclusion in each case is, colloquially, an argument, implication, or *inference*. Logic is the investigation of that relationship. A good inference may be called a *valid* one. Hence, logic is, in a nutshell, the study of validity.

But what is validity? Beyond a few platitudes, it is not at all clear how one should go about answering this question. It is not even clear what notions may be invoked in an answer: truth, meaning, possibility, something else? In this chapter I will provide an answer. In a nutshell, I will argue that validity is the relationship of truth-preservation-in-all-situations. *Exactly* how that relationship behaves is a question that can be answered only by the articulation of a logical theory of the kind discussed in the last chapter. As I argued there, each pure logic, when given its canonical interpretation, can be thought of as a theory concerning the behaviour of certain notions; specifically, those notions that are standardly deployed in logic. Validity is undoubtedly the most important of these—to which all the others must relate in the end. (We have looked at another of these, negation, in Chapter 4.) Though the account leaves many details to be filled in, it is at least sufficient to answer the question of what logical theories are theories *of*—truth preservation of the appropriate kind—and so, as we will see, to show that they sustain a realistic interpretation.

---

[1] See, e.g. Wason and Johnson-Laird (1972), esp. the places indexed under 'fallacies'.

11.2 VALIDITY: A FIRST PASS

What, then, is validity? Doubtlessly, a valid inference is one where the premises provide some genuine ground for the conclusion. But what does that mean? Traditionally, logic has distinguished between two notions of validity: deductive and non-deductive (inductive). A valid deductive argument is one where, in some sense, the conclusion cannot but be true, given the premises; a valid inductive argument is one where there is some lesser degree of support. Standard examples illustrate the distinction clearly enough. One might well ask why the notion of validity falls apart in this way, and what the relationship is between the two parts. I will come back to the whole issue of inductive inference later in the chapter, and give a uniform account of validity, both deductive and inductive. For the present, let us simply accept the distinction between the two notions of validity as a given, and focus on deductive validity.

11.3 PROOF-THEORETIC CHARACTERIZATION

What, then, is a deductively valid inference? Modern logic standardly gives two, very different, sorts of answer to this question: proof-theoretic and model-theoretic (semantic). In the proof-theoretic answer, one specifies some basic rules of inference syntactically. A valid inference is then one that can be obtained by chaining together, in some syntactically characterizable fashion, any of the basic rules. The whole process might take the form of a Gentzen system, a system of natural deduction, or even (God help us) an axiom system.

Such a characterization may undoubtedly be very useful. But as an answer to the main question it is of limited use, for several reasons. The first is that there seem to be languages for which the notion of deductive validity is provably uncharacterizable in this way. Second-order logic is the obvious example. This has no complete proof-theoretic characterization. Given certain assumptions, the same is true of intuitionistic logic too.[2]

Possibly in these cases—especially the intuitionistic one—one might simply reject the semantic notion of validity with respect to which the proof-theory is incomplete. But even if one does this, there is a more profound reason why a proof-theoretic characterization is unsatisfactory as an ultimate characterization of validity. We can clearly give any number of systems of rules. Some may have nothing to do with logic at all; and those that do may give different answers to the question of which inferences are valid. The crucial question is: *which system of rules is the right one?* The natural answer at this point is to say that the rules are those which hold in virtue of the meanings of certain notions that occur in the premises and conclusions. This appears to take us into the second characterization of validity, the semantic one. Some independent account of those meanings is given, and the appropriate proof-theory must answer to

---

[2] See McCarty (1991).

the semantics by way of a suitable soundness proof (and perhaps, also, completeness proof). And indeed, I think this way of proceeding is correct.

One may, however, resist this move for a while. One may suggest that it is a mistake to understand meaning in some independent way, but that the rules themselves *specify* the meanings of certain crucial notions involved. For example, one might say that the introduction and elimination rules for a connective in a system of natural deduction, specify its meaning. The problem with this was pointed out by Prior (1960). One cannot claim that an arbitrary set of rules specifies the meaning of a connective. Suppose, for example, that one could characterize a connective, $*$ (*tonk*), by the rules: $\alpha \vdash \alpha * \beta$ and $\alpha * \beta \vdash \beta$. Then everything would follow from everything—hardly a satisfactory outcome.

Some constraints must therefore be put on what rules are acceptable. One might attempt some purely syntactic constraint. For example, as we noted in section 5.3, it has been suggested[3] that the rules in question must give a conservative extension. This, however, will not solve the problem. Conservativeness is always relative to some underlying proof theory. For example, as we also noted Chapter 5, adding the rules for Boolean negation to a complete proof theory for positive "classical" logic is conservative; adding them to one for positive intuitionist logic is not. One needs, therefore, to justify the underlying proof theory. Possibly, one might try to justify the rules for one of the connectives of this by considerations of conservativeness. We are obviously then in a regress situation. Given that there is a finite number of connectives, this will ground out. If the ground itself has rules of inference, nothing has been gained. Perhaps, though, the ground will contain no rules of inference. Maybe the ground is just constituted by a vocabulary of atoms, with no rules of proof.

Even in this case, however, the problem of justification does not vanish. This is for two reasons. The first is that, as we noted in section 5.4, conservativeness is not invariant under the order in which notions are added. Each of classical negation and truth is conservative with respect to an appropriate positive relevant logic (and self-reference), but once one is added, the addition of the other is no longer conservative. This makes the order in which notions are added crucial; but there would seem to be no way of justifying a non-arbitrary order.

Less obviously, perhaps, justifying the individual rules is not enough. A proof-theory allows us to put together rules in a certain way, e.g. by chaining together. There are various possibilities here, which themselves need justification. The point comes out most clearly when the proof-theory is formulated as a sequent-calculus. I will return to the issue in a moment.

A different attempt to state justificatory constraints on a proof-theory (which rules out *tonk*-like connectives) takes us back to the discussion of section 5.5. Suppose that we are working in a natural deduction system, and suppose that we take the introduction rule for a connective to provide a direct account of its meaning. This needs no justification: *any* introduction rule may serve to do this. The corresponding elimination rule is then justified by the fact that it is conservative with respect to the introduction rule. In the words of Dummett, one of the people to whom this idea is

---

[3] e.g. by Belnap (1962).

due, the introduction and elimination rules are in harmony.[4] The idea can be cashed out in terms of a suitable normal-form theorem: whenever we have an introduction rule followed by the corresponding elimination rule, both can be eliminated.

Even if this strategy can be made to work, it can provide only a partial justification for the proof-theory. For the introduction and elimination rules are superimposed on structural inferential rules; for example, the transitivity of deducibility (deductions may be chained together to make longer deductions). Such structural rules are not inevitable,[5] and the question therefore arises as to how *these* rules are to be justified. This becomes patently obvious if the proof-theory is formulated as a Gentzen system, where the structural rules are quite explicit, and for which there is now a well-advanced study of logics with different structural rules: sub-structural logics.[6] One needs to justify which structural rules one accepts (and which one does not), and there is no evident purely proof-theoretic way of doing this.

If, as the foregoing discussion suggests, one cannot justify every feature of a proof-theory syntactically, the only other possibility would seem to be some semantic constraint to which the rules must answer.[7] We are thrown back to the other kind of characterization of validity, the model-theoretic one. So let us turn to this.

11.4 MODEL-THEORETIC CHARACTERIZATION

A deductively valid inference is, we said, one where the premises cannot be true without the conclusion also being true. A crucial question here is how to understand the 'cannot'. Modern logic has produced a very particular but very general way of understanding this. When we reason, we reason about many different situations; some are actual—what things are like at the centre of the sun; some are merely possible—what things would have been like had the German Axis won the Second World War; and maybe even some that are impossible—what things would be like if, *per impossibile*, someone squared the circle. We also have a notion of what it is to hold in, or be true in, a situation. In talking of validity, necessity is to be explicated in terms of holding in all situations. Let us use lower-case Greek letters for premises and conclusions,[8] upper-case Greeks for sets thereof, and write $\vdash$ to indicate valid inference. Then we may define $\Pi \vdash \kappa$ as:

for every situation in which all the members of Π hold, κ, holds

There is also a corresponding notion of logical truth: κ is logically true iff it holds in all situations.

---

[4] For full references, see Sundholm (1986).
[5] For example, there is "harmony", but not transitivity in the logic of Tennant (1987).
[6] See Schroeder-Heister and Došen (1993), Slaney (1990), and especially Restall (2000).
[7] In the context of *tonk*, this was suggested by Stevenson (1961).
[8] I shall not be concerned with what *sort* of thing premises and conclusions are, sentences, statements, propositions, or whatnot. As far as this chapter goes, they can be anything as long as they are truth-bearers, that is, the (primary) kind of things that may be true or false.

So far so good. But what is a situation, and what is it to be true in it? One could, I suppose, take it that these notions are indefinable, but this is not likely to get us very far; nor is it the characteristic way of modern logic. Using mathematical techniques, both notions are normally defined. A situation is taken to be a mathematical structure of a certain kind, and holding in it is defined as a relationship between truth-bearers and structures. Both structures and relation are normally defined set-theoretically.

No one would suppose that situations are mathematical entities, such as ordered *n*-tuples—at the very least, in the case of actual situations. Strictly speaking, then, set-theoretic structures *represent* situations. They do this, presumably, because the situations have a structure (or, at least, a pertinent structure) that is isomorphic to that of the mathematical structure. How to understand this is a question in the philosophy of mathematics. Indeed, how to understand this sort of question is *the* central question of the nature of applied mathematics. I shall not pursue the matter here.[9]

In the case of the standard account of validity for (classical) first order logic (without free variables), a structure is a pair:

$$\mathcal{A} = \langle D, I \rangle \tag{Q}$$

where D is the non-empty domain of quantification, and I is the denotation function. Truth in $\mathcal{A}$ is defined in the usual recursive fashion. Or in a Kripke semantics for modal logics, a structure is a 4-tuple:

$$\mathcal{A} = \langle W, @, R, I \rangle \tag{K}$$

where W is a set of worlds, $@$ is a distinguished member of W (the "base world"), R is a binary relation on W satisfying certain properties (to be employed in stating the truth conditions of $\Box$), and I is the denotation function, which assigns each atomic formula a subset of W (namely, those worlds at which it is true). Truth at a world $w \in W$ is again defined in a recursive fashion. And truth in $\mathcal{A}$ is defined as truth at $@$.

Once the notions of a structure and holding-in are made precise, the definition of validity can be spelled out exactly. Let us write $\mathcal{A} \models \alpha$ to mean that α holds in structure $\mathcal{A}$. We may also say that $\mathcal{A}$ is a *model* of α. $\mathcal{A}$ is a model of a *set* of truth bearers if it is a model of every member of the set. Then α is a logical truth iff every structure is a model of α. And:

$$\Pi \vdash \kappa \text{ iff every model of } \Pi \text{ is a model of } \kappa \tag{DV}$$

I take this to be the best answer to the question of when an inference is deductive valid presently on offer.

More needs to be said about this, however. Given any proof-theory of a certain kind, there is a well-known way that a semantics of the kind just described can be obtained. We simply construct a sound and complete many-valued semantics from the Lindenbaum algebra of the logic. A situation is an assignment of values

[9] For a discussion, see Priest (2005a), ch. 7.

in the algebra to sentences, and a sentence holds in a situation just if its value is a designated one. This semantics is clearly too cheap. More generally, it reminds us of the fact that we need to distinguish those semantics that are of a kind to be genuinely informative about the meanings of the notions involved, and those that are not. Truth-functional semantics for first-order logic are of this kind, as are Kripke semantics for modal logics. The semantics obtained from the Lindenbaum algebra are not; neither are these the only ones: many logics have topological, algebraic, or many-valued semantics which, though they are useful in establishing various things about the proof-theory—especially various independence results—are of a purely "technical" nature.

The distinction between "informative" semantics and "technical" semantics is obvious enough in principle, though it is not an easy one to draw cleanly. However, for an informative semantics, we need something like this: the notions employed in the semantics must have some intuitive meaning; and it should be clear why these notions, with the properties that the semantics attributes to them, may naturally be involved with a specification of the meanings of the logical notions that occur in the proof-theory. Thus, the notion of a possible world—though contentious enough—clearly has intuitive purchase, and it is quite clear why such a notion might be used to state the truth conditions of modal operators. By contrast, given, say, a many-valued interpretation of the kind used to prove the independence of some axiom in an axiom system, the values involved may have no intuitive meaning whatever; nor, therefore, can it be clear why giving recursive conditions for a connective in terms of these values can tell us anything about the meaning of the connective.

However one finally cashes out the details, it is essential that the semantics involved in the project of giving an account of validity be of the informative kind. If they are not, then they are vulnerable to exactly the same charge of arbitrariness that I levelled against a simple proof-theoretic characterization of validity. If they are, however, they can be taken to provide an account of the meanings of the logical notions involved, of the kind required. Given an appropriate soundness proof, the semantics will provide a justification of the proof-theory—in a way that the proof-theory does not provide a justification of the semantics.

As Dummett puts it:

When soundness . . . fails, the remedy . . . must of course be sought in a modification of either the syntactic or the semantic notion of logical consequence, and, on occasion, it might be the semantic notion rather than the syntactic one that is altered. Nevertheless, the semantic notion always has a certain priority: the definition of the syntactic notion is required to be responsible to the semantic notion, rather than the other way about. The syntactic relation is defined by devising a set of primitive rules of inference, and a corresponding notion of formal deduction. If a semantic notion can be defined with respect to which a soundness proof can be given, we then have a reason for regarding the primitive rules of inference as valid: until then, we have only an intuitive impression of their validity.[10]

---

[10] Dummett (1975*b*), 201.

11.5   FILLING IN THE DETAILS

(*DV*) is the *form* of a definition of validity. It leaves many details to be filled in. These depend, for a start, on the language employed in formulating the premises and conclusions. More importantly, as I indicated in section 11.1, the details cannot be filled in without constructing an adequate logical theory for that language, and hence without resolving philosophical issues of a very substantial kind. This is not the place to go into these, but let me just point out some of the things at issue in the process.

A major question to be answered is: how, exactly, are situations structured? This question cannot be divorced from that of how to define the relation of being true in a structure.[11] For example, should the truth conditions of the conditional employ an ordering relation on worlds, as occurs in Kripke semantics for intuitionist logic, a ternary relation, as occurs in many relevant logics, or none of these, as in classical logic? If either of the first two of these is correct, then the relation will have to be a part of the structure. Another example: assuming that the truth/falsity conditions for a predicate are to be given in terms of its extension (those things it is true of) and anti-extension (those things it is false of), are we to suppose that these are exclusive and exhaustive of the relevant domains (as classical logic assumes) or not (as more liberal logics may allow)? Issues of the above kind pose deep metaphysical/semantical issues of a highly contentious nature.

Many of the relevant considerations here are familiar from the literature debating intuitionist, paraconsistent, and other non-classical logics. Theoretical issues concerning meaning, truth, and many other notions, certainly enter the debate. There is also a question of adequacy to the data. We have intuitions about the validity of particular inferences. (We may well have intuitions about the validity of various *forms* of inference as well, though because of the universality implicit in these, they are much less reliable.) These act like the data in an empirical science: if the theory gives the wrong results about them, this is a black mark against it. But as with all theorization, the fact that a theory has desirable theoretical properties (e.g. simplicity, non-*ad-hoc*ness), may well cast doubt on any data that goes against it—especially if we can explain how we come to be mistaken about the data. (We will see an example of this concerning

---

[11]   Let me (again; see sect. 4.5) note that *being true in* is quite distinct from *being true* (*simpliciter*). The latter notion is a property, or at least, a monadic predicate, and has nothing, in general, to do with sets. One might be interested in it for all kinds of reasons, which it is unnecessary to labour. The former is a relation, and a set theoretic one, at that; and the only reason that one might be interested in it is that it is a notion necessary for framing an account of validity. The two notions are not, of course, entirely unrelated. One reason we are interested in valid inferences is that they preserve truth, *actual* truth. Hence it is a desideratum of the notion of truth-in-a-structure that there be a structure, call it the actual structure, such that truth (period) coincides with truth in it. The result is then guaranteed. No doubt this imposes constraints on what one's account of structure should be, and on how the truth-in relation should behave at the actual structure. But one should not suppose that just because the actual structure possesses certain features (such as, for example, consistency or completeness), other structures must share those features: we reason about many things other than actuality. Similarly, recursive truth conditions may collapse to a particularly simple form at the actual structure because of certain privileged properties. But that is no reason to think that they must so collapse at all structures.

enthymemes a little later.) The dialectical juggling of theory against data is always a matter of good judgment (which is not to say that all judgments are equally good), and always fallible.[12]

The situation is, in fact, even more prone to dispute than I have so far said. This is because (*DV*) itself is couched in terms whose behaviour is theory-laden, such as the logical constant 'every'; and if one parses the restricted quantifier 'every *A* is *B*' in the usual way as 'everything is such that if it is an *A* it is a *B*', then the conditional is getting in on the act too. The meanings of such notions, especially 'if', are philosophically contentious.[13]

Another way of looking at the matter is this: it is not just the definition (*DV*) itself that is at issue, but—as I observed with respect to truth conditions in section 5.9—what does and what does not follow from it. This depends on the behaviour of the "logical constants"; that is, the valid principles that such constants satisfy; which is part of what is at issue in an account of validity; which is what (*DV*) gives. The issue is therefore a circular one. This does not mean that it is impossible to come up with a solution to the whole set of matters. It just means that there is no privileged point of entry: we are going to have to proceed by bootstrapping. Certainly, one can do this with "classical logic"; one can equally well do it with intuitionist logic or a paraconsistent logic. In the end, we want a theory that, *as a total package,* comes out best under "reflective equilibrium". There is no short way with this.

11.6   THE TARSKIAN ACCOUNT

Before we leave deductive validity and turn to inductive validity, it will be illuminating to compare the account of validity I have given with the celebrated account given by Tarski in his essay (1956).[14] In a nutshell, this is as follows. Certain words of the language are designated *logical constants*. Given a sentence, its *form* is the result of replacing each non-logical-constant with a parameter (variable). An *interpretation* is

[12] It is sometimes said that there is no determinate answer to the question of whether or not an inference is (deductively) valid. An inference may be valid in one semantics (proof theory, logic, system, etc.) but not another. Maybe this is just a way of saying that it is valid according to some particular theories or accounts of validity but not others, in which case it is unproblematic. But it is, I think, often meant as stronger than this: there is no fact of the matter as to which theory gets matters right. And if it means this, it would certainly appear to be false. Either it is true that 'Socrates had two siblings' gives a (conclusive) ground for 'Socrates had at least one sibling' or it is not. This fact is not relative to anything—unless one is a relativist about truth itself. I will take up the issue of pluralism in logic at length in the next chapter.

[13] The notion of set employed in (*DV*) may also be up for grabs. The nature of workaday sets, such as the null set and the set of integers, may not be problematic; but the definition of validity concerns *all* structures of a certain kind; and the behaviour of such totalities is a hard issue. Even if you suppose that the totality of sets is exhausted by the cumulative hierarchy, how far "up" this extends is still mathematically moot, as is the question of whether we may form totalities that are not, strictly speaking, sets. Throw in the possibility that there may be sets that are, e.g. non-well-founded, let alone inconsistent, and one starts to see the size of the issue.

[14] It should be noted that this is not the orthodox model-theoretic account, which occurs in Tarski's later writings. For a discussion of Tarski's views and their history, see Etchemendy (1988).

a function that assigns each parameter a denotation of the appropriate type (objects for names, extensions for predicates, etc.). A relationship of *satisfaction* is defined between interpretations and forms, standardly by recursion. An inference is valid iff every interpretation that satisfies the form of each premise satisfies the form of the conclusion. (Correspondingly, a sentence is logically true if its form is satisfied by all interpretations.)

If we identify interpretations with what I have been calling structures, and write the satisfaction relationship as $\models$, then the form of the Tarskian definition of validity is exactly (DV). It is therefore tempting to think of the two accounts as the same. And indeed they may, in some cases, amount to the same thing; but as accounts, they are quite distinct. For a start, an interpretation, as employed in the definition, is normally only *part* of a structure, e.g. the I of (Q) or (K). In all but the simplest cases, structures carry more information than that, e.g. the domain, D, in (Q), and the binary relation, R, in (K). This will, in general, make an important difference as to what inferences are valid. For example, consider the sentence $\exists x \exists y \, x \neq y$. At least as standardly understood, this contains only logical constants. According to the Tarskian account it is therefore either logically true or logically false. In fact, it is the former, since it is true (*simpliciter*). But given standard-model theory, it holds in some structures and not others, hence it is not logically true.[15]

In (1990) Etchemendy provides an important critique of the Tarskian account. It will be further illuminating to see to what extent the account offered here is subject to the same problems. Etchemendy provides two sorts of counter-examples to the Tarskian account. These concern under-generation and over-generation.

According to the Tarskian account, any valid inference is, by definition, formally valid; that is, any inference of the same form is valid. This seems to render certain intuitively valid inferences invalid. For example, given the usual understanding of logical form:

This is red;
hence this is coloured

is invalid, since its form is:

x is P;
hence x is Q

which has invalid instances.

This argument is not conclusive. One may simply agree that the original inference is invalid, but explain the counter-intuitiveness of this by pointing out that the inference is an enthymeme. It is an instance of the valid form:

x is P;

---

[15] This fact is picked up by Etchemendy (1990) who points out, quite correctly, that the Tarskian account of validity has to be doctored by "cross term restrictions" for a more orthodox result. A slightly different way of doctoring it, by making the parametric nature of quantifiers explicit, is given in Priest (1995).

everything that is P is Q;
hence x is Q

and the instance of the suppressed premise here is 'everything that is red is coloured', which is obviously true.[16]

I shall not discuss the adequacy of this move here. I wish only to use the example to contrast the account of validity given here with the Tarskian one. For, modulo an appropriate account of logical form, the present account may, but *need not*, make validity a formal matter. This just depends on what structures there are. In the case at point, for example, there may be no structures where there is something in the extension of 'red' that is not in the extension of 'coloured'. We might, for example, eliminate such structures from a more general class with "meaning postulates", in the fashion of Carnap and Montague.[17] If this is the case, the inference in question is valid, though not formally so. Of course, this path is not pursued in standard-model theory, where the more general notion of structure is employed; the result of this is that the notion of validity produced is a formal one. If one takes this line, then the model-theoretic account of validity also has to employ the enthymematic strategy.

Etchemendy's second sort of counter-example to the Tarskian approach concerns over-generation. In such examples, Tarski's account gives as valid, inferences that are not so; or if perchance this does not happen, this is so only by "luck". Consider the sentence: there are at most two cats: $\forall x \forall y \forall z((Cx \land Cy \land Cz) \supset (x = y \lor y = z \lor z = x))$. Provided that there are at least three objects *in toto*, this is not a logical truth; but if not, it is. In this case, presumably, the account gets the answer right. But if the universe is finite, with, say, $10^{10^{10}}$ objects, the account is going to give the wrong answer for: there are at most $10^{10^{10}}$ cats. Moreover, whether or not something is a logical truth ought not to depend on such accidental things as the size of the universe.

One may meet Etchemendy's criticism by pointing out that the totality of all objects is not restricted to the totality of all physical (actual) objects, but comprises *all* objects, including all mathematical objects, all possible, and maybe all impossible, objects too. Not only is this so large as to make every statement of the form 'there are at most i cats' (where i is any size, finite or infinite) not a logical truth; but this result does not arise because of some "lucky contingency". There is nothing contingent about the totality of all objects.[18]

An objection similar to Etchemendy's might be made against the account of validity offered here. An inference is valid if it is truth-preserving in all situations. Couldn't this give the wrong answer if there are "not enough situations to go around"; and even if there are, should such a contingency determine validity? The answer to this is the

---

[16] See Priest (1995*c*).
[17] See Carnap (1952), and Montague (1974), esp. p. 53 of Thomason's introduction. In fact, orthodox model theory, in effect, employs meaning postulates for the logical constants. The recursive truth conditions select one denotation for each logical constant from amongst all the syntactically possible ones.
[18] See Priest (1995*b*), 289–91. Etchemendy has some other examples of over-generation, but these are less persuasive, ibid.

same, and even more evident. The totality of situations is the totality of *all* situations: actual, possible, and maybe impossible too. It doesn't make sense to suppose that there might not be enough. Nor is the result contingent in any way. The totality of all situations is no contingent totality.

But the point may be pressed. The official definition is given, not in terms of situations, but in terms of the mathematical structures that represent them. Might there not be enough structures to "go around". One might doubt this. Structures need not be "pure sets". Any situation is made up of components; and it is natural to suppose that these can be employed to construct an isomorphic set-theoretic structure. Yet the worry is a real one. One of the situations we reason about is the situation concerning sets. Yet in Zermelo Fraenkel set theory, there is no structure with the totality of sets as domain. Hence this set theory cannot represent that situation. This does not show that (*DV*) is wrong, however. It merely shows that *ZF* is an inadequate vehicle for representation. A set theory with at least a universal set is required. There are many other reasons for being dissatisfied with *ZF* as a most general account of set.[19]

Before we turn to the matter of inductive validity, let me end this section by returning to the question of logical realism. The account of validity offered here is a realistic one. Its realism operates on two levels. First, if one takes a logic to be specified by an appropriate proof-theory (axiom system, natural deduction system, or whatever), one can take this as an attempt to characterize the appropriate notion of truth-preservation. That is what the theory is about. A soundness proof establishes partial success in the enterprise; a completeness proof the other half. But at a deeper level, the model-theoretic account of validity can itself be thought of as an applied mathematical theory which attempts to characterize a certain relationship between situations themselves. That is what *it* is about. The ontological status of these situations, we might argue about. Are they physical objects of a Lewisian kind, abstract objects such as sets of propositions, or non-existent objects of a Meinongian kind? We need not go into this issue here.[20] Whatever kind of thing they are, the situations themselves are what the model theory is supposed to represent.

11.7 INDUCTIVE VALIDITY

We have seen that the model-theoretic account of validity that I have offered is different from the Tarskian account. But, so far, we have not seen any definitive reason to prefer it to that account. The model-theoretic account is more powerful and more flexible, for sure, but as long as the enthymematic move is acceptable, we have seen no cases where this extra power and flexibility *must* be used. However, an argument for this may be found by looking at the question of inductive validity. In due course, I will also give a model-theoretic definition of inductive validity. But let us approach these issues via a different question.

Theories of deductive validity took off with Aristotle, and are now *highly* articulated. Theorization about inductive validity is, by comparison, completely underdeveloped.

---

[19] See *In Contradiction*, ch. 2.
[20] Priest (2005a), ch. 7, argues for a Meinongian account.

Why? A standard answer, with a certain plausibility, is as follows. Deductive validity is a purely formal matter. Hence it is relatively easy to apply syntactic methods to the issue. By contrast, if an inference is inductively valid, this is not due to its form, but to the *contents* of the claims involved, a matter which is susceptible to no such simple method.

The issue is, however, not that straightforward. For a start, as we have seen, it may not be the case that deductive validity is a matter of form. That just depends on how other details of the account pan out. Moreover, it is not immediately clear that inductive validity is not a matter of form either. The inference:

x is *P*;
most *P*s are *Q*s;
hence *x* is *Q*

is a pretty good candidate for a valid inductive form. (It is certainly not deductively valid.) It is true that an inference such as:

Abdul lives in Kuwait;
hence Abdul is a Moslem

is frequently cited as a valid inductive inference, and one that is not formally valid on the usual understanding of what the logical constants are. But it is not at all clear that this is so. Just as in the deductive case, we may take it to be an enthymeme of the above form with suppressed premise: most people who live in Kuwait are Moslems.

Despite this, inductive validity is not, in fact, always a formal matter. This, I take it, is one of the lessons of Goodman's new "riddle of induction".[21] Consider an inference of the following form (plausibly, one for enumerative induction):

$$\frac{Ea_1 \wedge Ga_1, \ldots, Ea_n \wedge Ga_n}{\forall x(Ex \rightarrow Gx)}$$

If *E* is 'is an emerald' and *G* is 'is green', this inference seems quite valid. If, on the other hand, *G* is 'is grue' (that is, a predicate which, before some (future) time, *t*, is truly applicable to green things, and truly applicable to blue things thereafter), it is not. It is well known that there is no syntactic way of distinguishing between the two inferences. For though 'grue' is, intuitively, a defined predicate, 'green' can be defined in terms of grue and bleen (a predicate which, before *t*, is truly applicable to blue things, and truly applicable to green things thereafter). Hence any syntactic construction may be dualized. What breaks the symmetry is that 'emerald' and 'green' are natural properties (are projectible, in Goodman's terminology), whereas 'grue' is not. But there is no syntactic characterization of this. Hence, inductive validity is not, in general, a formal matter. It follows, then, that no version of the Tarskian account of validity is going to be applicable to inductive validity. For as we have seen, Tarskian validity is formal validity.

---

[21] As explained, for example, in ch. 3 of Goodman (1979).

11.8 PROBABILITY

How, then, are we to get a grip on the notion of inductive validity? A natural suggestion is that we should appeal to a suitable notion of probability. (Probability assignments are not, except in a very few cases, a formal matter.) Now there certainly seem to be intimate links between inductive validity and probability, but it is not clear that one can use the notion to formulate a satisfactory theory of inductive validity.

Let us restrict ourselves, for simplicity, to the one-premise case, and let us write the conditional probability of α given β in the usual way, as $p(\alpha/\beta)$. Then a first suggestion for defining inductive validity is as follows: an inference from premise β to conclusion α is valid if β raises the probability of α, i.e. if $p(\alpha/\beta) > p(\alpha)$. This will not do, however. Just consider a case where β raises the probability of α though this is still small, as in, e.g.:

John used to be a boxer;
so John has had a broken nose

This seems quite invalid. (Most boxers have never had broken noses.)

A more plausible suggestion is that the inference is valid if $p(\alpha/\beta)$ is "sufficiently high"—where this is to be cashed out in some suitable fashion. But this, too, has highly counter-intuitive results. Consider the case, for example, where β *decreases* the probability of α, even though the conditional probability is still high, as in:

John used be a boxer;
so John has *not* had his nose broken

This inference is of dubious validity.[22]

Could an appeal to Bayesianism solve the problem at this point? According to Bayesians, the relevance of a premise, β, is simply that if we learn—or were to learn—that β, we (would) revise our evaluation of the probability of any statement, α, to $p(\alpha/\beta)$, where p is our current probability function. I do not wish to deny that we sometimes revise in this way, but this cannot provide a satisfactory account of inductive inference for two reasons. First, if there is nothing more to the story than this, it is tantamount to giving up on the notion of inductive inference altogether. Inference is concerned with the question of when, given certain premises, it is reasonable to accept certain conclusions. In other words, we want to be able to *detach* the conclusion of the argument, given the premises. Conditionalization does not, on its own, give an answer to the question of when this is possible.[23] More conclusively, even Bayesians concede

---

[22] It might be thought that what is causing the problem here is that we are trying to make inductive validity an all-or-nothing matter, when it is really a matter of degree. Hence, we may simply take the degree of validity of the inference from β to α to be $p(\alpha/\beta)$. But this does not seem to help. According to this account, the inference is still an inductive inference of high degree of validity, which seems odd.

[23] It might be replied that we never simply accept things: we always accept things to a certain degree. The question of detachment does not, therefore, arise. But this is just false: acceptance may be a vague notion, but there are clear cases of things that I accept, *simpliciter*, for example that Brisbane is in Australia (though I would not give this unit probablity, for standard, fallibilist, reasons).

that there is information upon which one cannot conditionalize.[24] For example, if α is anything such that $p(\alpha) = 1$, and if the probability function that will result from our next revision is q, then we cannot conditionalize coherently on, e.g. $q(\alpha) \leq 0.5$. For the result of conditionalization is $q(\alpha) = 1$ (still). Yet information of this form can certainly be the premise of an inductive argument; for example, one whose conclusion is that $q(\alpha) < 0.5$. Hence inference outstrips conditionalization.

Even if there were some way of analysing inductive validity satisfactorily in terms of probability, a more fundamental problem awaits us. Deductive validity and inductive validity would seem to have something to do with each other. They are both species of *validity*. If deductive validity is to be analysed in terms of preservation of truth in a structure, and inductive validity is to be analysed as something to do with probability, they would seem to be as different as chalk from cheese.

Maybe there is some deeper connection here, but it is not at all obvious what this could be. One might try *defining* a deductively valid inference from β to α, as one where $p(\alpha/\beta) = 1$. This has nothing to do with model theory, but one might hope that, by making suitable connections (for example, by considering a probability measure on the space of models), the definition could be shown to be equivalent to (*DV*). One might even jettison the model-theoretic definition of deductive validity entirely, and attempt a uniform account of validity in terms of probability. Such moves face further problems, however. For example, consider:

John chose a natural number at random;
hence John did not choose 173

On the usual understanding of probability theory, this satisfies the probabilistic account of deductive validity, but it is hardly deductively valid: the conclusion might turn out to be false. There are ways that one might try to get around this problem too, but if would certainly seem much more satisfactory if an account of inductive validity could be found which made the connection with deductive validity obvious, and which did not depend upon probabilistic jiggery-pokery.

11.9 NON-MONOTONIC LOGIC

Such an account is now available, thanks to recent developments in non-monotonic logic. An inference relation, $\vdash$, is *monotonic* if $\Pi \vdash \kappa$ entails $\Pi \cup \Sigma \vdash \kappa$. Deductively valid inferences are monotonic. For suppose that $\Pi \vdash \kappa$. If all the premises in $\Pi \cup \Sigma$ hold in a structure, then certainly all those in Π do. In which case, so does κ. On the other hand, inferences traditionally accounted inductively valid are well known not to be monotonic. Consider only:

Abdul lives in Kuwait;
Abdul went to mass last Sunday;
hence Abdul is a Moslem

[24] See, e.g. Howson and Urbach (1993), 99 ff.

The study of non-monotonic inferences, quite independently of probability theory, is one that has seen rapid and exciting developments in the last 25 years, mainly from amongst logicians in computer-science departments. There are many distinctive approaches to non-monotonic inference, of various degrees of mathematical sophistication. But it is now becoming clear that at the core of theories of non-monotonicity there is a canonical construction.[25]

Let me illustrate. Consider Abdul again. What makes it plausible to infer that he is a Muslim, given only that he lives in Kuwait, is that, if he were not, he would be rather abnormal. (*Qua* inhabitant of Kuwait, and not, of course, in any evaluative sense.) Although the inference may not be truth-preserving, it is certainly truth-preserving in all "normal situations".

We can formulate this more precisely as follows. Let us suppose that we can compare situations (or the structures that represent them) with respect to their normality. Normality, of course, comes by degrees. Let us write the comparison as $\mathcal{A} \succ \mathcal{B}$ ($\mathcal{A}$ is more normal than $\mathcal{B}$). $\succ$ is certainly a partial order (transitive and anti-symmetric); but it is not a linear order. There is no guarantee that we can compare any two structures with respect to their normality. Let us say that $\mathcal{A}$ is a *most normal* model of a set of sentences, Π, $\mathcal{A} \models_n \Pi$, iff:

$$\mathcal{A} \models \Pi \text{ and for all } \mathcal{B} \text{ such that } \mathcal{B} \succ \mathcal{A}, \mathcal{B} \not\models \Pi$$

Then if we write inductive validity as $\vdash_i$, we can define:

$$\Pi \vdash_i \kappa \text{ iff every most normal model of } \Pi \text{ is a model of } \kappa \qquad (IV)$$

This captures the idea that an inference is inductively valid if the conclusion holds in all models of Π that are as normal as Π will let them be. Notice how this gives rise to non-monotonicity in a very natural way. κ may well be true in all situations most normal with respect to Π, but throw in Σ, and the most normal situations may be more abnormal, and not necessarily ones where κ holds.[26]

11.10 CONSEQUENCES OF THIS ACCOUNT

The definition (IV) is the one I wish to offer. It is exactly the same as (DV), except that where (DV) has 'model' (IV) has 'most normal model'. The connection between the two notions is therefore patent. Where deductive validity requires truth preservation over *all* structures, inductive validity requires truth preservation over *all normal* structures (with respect to the premise set). Deductive validity is the same as inductive validity except that we don't care about normality. This is equivalent to taking $\succ$ to be the minimal ordering that relates nothing to anything. We therefore

---

[25] See, e.g. Shoham (1988), Katsuno and Satch (1995). For an application of the construction in a paraconsistent context, where normality is cashed out in terms of consistency, see Priest (1991*b*).

[26] An additional condition, sometimes called the smoothness constraint, is often imposed on the ordering $\prec$: for any α and $\mathcal{A}$, if $\mathcal{A} \models \alpha$ then there is $\mathcal{B} \succ \mathcal{A}$ such that $\mathcal{B} \models_n \alpha$ (see, e.g. Katsuno and Satch (1995), Gabbay (1995)). This prevents finite sets of premises that are non-trivial under deduction from exploding under induction—obviously a desirable feature.

have a generic account of validity. Validity is truth-preservation in all structures of a certain kind. Deductive validity is the limit case where we are talking about *all* structures, period. Otherwise put: validity is about truth preservation in all normal structures. Deductive validity is the limit case where *every* situation is to be considered normal.[27]

This account of inductive validity extends the model-theoretic account of deductive validity. Hence, all the comments that I made about filling in its details carry over to it, also. In this respect they are the same. The major technical difference between the two notions, is the fact that inductive validity makes use of the ordering $>$, whilst deductive validity does not. This, therefore, focuses the major conceptual difference between the two. Although the question of what structures there are is open to theoretical debate, whatever they are, they are invariant across all contexts in which we reason. The definition (*IV*) also gives us a core of universally inductively valid inferences, namely those that hold for *all* orderings.[28] But when we employ the notion of inductive validity in practice, we do not argue relative to all orderings, but with respect to one particular ordering. The ordering is not *a priori*, but is fixed by external factors, such as the world and the context. For example, the fact that to be green is more normal (natural) than to be grue is determined by nature. Or what is to count as normal may depend on our interests. In the context of discussing a religious question, a resident of Kuwait who goes to mass is not normal. In the context of discussing biological appendages, such as noses, they are (normally) quite normal.[29]

This is, I think, the heart of the difference that people have sensed between inductive and deductive validity. It is not really a matter of the difference between form and content—or if it is, what this comes down to is exactly the dependence of inductive validity on an *a posteriori* feature, the ordering $>$.

11.11 NORMATIVITY AND INFORMATION PRESERVATION

Let me conclude by tying up a couple of loose ends; and let us start by returning to the question of the normativity of logic. Validly, I said, is how people ought to reason. Why? The answer is simple. We reason about all kinds of situations. We want to know what sorts of things hold in them, given that we know other things; or what sorts of things don't hold, given that we know other things that don't. If we reason validly then, by the definition of validity, we can be assured that reasoning forward

[27] It is fair to ask what happens to the boxer examples of sect. 11.8 on this account. Both, given reasonable assumptions, turn out to be invalid, since there are normal situations where boxers get their noses broken and normal situations where they do not.
[28] A version of this is given a proof-theoretic characterization in Kraus, Lehmann, and Magidor (1990). The semantics include the smoothness constraint.
[29] The ordering may even be subjective in a certain sense. For example, a natural thought is to take $A \prec B$ to mean that situation A is less probable than situation B (assuming this to make sense), where the probability in question is a subjective one. An ordering relation plays an important role in the semantics of conditional logics—which are, in fact, closely related to non-monotonic logics. (See, e.g. Gabbay (1995), Katsuno and Satch (1995).) The *a posteriority* of this is well recognized. See, e.g. Stalnaker (1981).

preserves the first property, and that reasoning backwards preserves the second. Validly is how one ought to reason if one wants to achieve these goals. The obligation is, then, hypothetical rather than categorical.

In less enlightened days, I argued against a model-theoretic account of validity of the kind given here.[30] One argument was to the effect that a model-theoretic account validates the inference *ex contradictione quodlibet*: $\alpha, \neg\alpha \vdash \beta$, which is not a norm of reasoning. This argument is just fallacious. A model-theoretic account may validate this argument; but equally, it may not. It depends, crucially, on what situations there are. If there are non-trivial but inconsistent situations, as there are in many logics, this will not be the case.[31]

A second argument was to the effect that a model-theoretic account cannot be right since, if it were, to know that an inference is valid we would have to know, in advance of using it, that it preserves truth in all situations; and hence it would be impossible for us to learn something new about a situation by applying a valid inference. This argument is equally, though less obviously, invalid. It confuses matters definitional with matters epistemological. We may well, and in fact do, have ways of knowing that a particular inference is valid, other than that it simply satisfies the definition. Particular cases are usually more certain than general truths. Compare: The Church/Turing Thesis provides, in effect, a definition of algorithmaticity. But we can often know that a process is algorithmic without having to write a program for a Turing machine. If we could not, the Thesis would not be refutable, which it certainly is.[32]

Finally, and further to the subject of truth-preservation: it is sometimes objected that a definition of validity on the basis of truth-preservation is too weak. What we often need of a notion of validity is that it preserve not truth, but something else, like information. Consider an inference engine for a computational database, for example. We want one which extracts the information that is implicit in the data. Truth has nothing to do with it.

This argument is also far too swift. Valid inferences preserve not just truth, but truth in a structure. Given the right way of setting things up, the situation as described in the database may well be (represented by) an appropriate structure. Structures do not have to be "large" like classical possible worlds, but may be "small", as in situation semantics. (In particular, the set of things true in a situation may be both inconsistent and complete.) A valid inference is, then, by definition, just what we want to extract the juice from the information provided by the database. Provided we choose our situations carefully, a logic of truth-preservation is also a logic of information preservation.[33]

---

[30] Priest (1979), 297.   [31] The point is made by Mortensen (1981).

[32] See Priest (1995*b*), 287 f.

[33] For example, the logic of information that Devlin gives in (1991), sect. 5.5, is exactly Dunn's four-valued truth-preservational semantics of First Degree Entailment, in disguise. For further connections between model-theoretic semantics and information, see Mares (1996).

11.12 CONCLUSION

This last claim is, of course, just a promissory note, and needs to be redeemed by a lot of hard work, specifying all the details that have only been hinted at above. The aim of this chapter has not been to present all the details of an account of validity. That is probably the work of several lifetimes! The aim has just been to provide the general form of an answer to the question of what validity is. To this extent, the slack in the definition is to its advantage. The details are to be filled in, in the most appropriate way. But despite the slack, the form of the answer is far from vacuous. There are certainly other possibilities (some of which we have briefly traversed); and the fact that this answer is possible at all is a tribute to the developments in modern model theory—of both classical and non-classical logics—of which this account can be thought of as the distilled essence.

12

Logical Pluralism

12.1 INTRODUCTION

The previous chapters in this part of the book have given us an account of the epistemology and ontology of logic. But this still leaves an important question. I said 'logic'; maybe I should have said 'logics'. Is there one logic or are there many?

Traditionally, there was only one—the logic of Aristotle and the Stoics, as melded together in the Middle Ages—and the question never arose. This century, we have seen a plethora of logics: Frege/Russell (classical) logic, intuitionism, paraconsistent logic, quantum logic. Usually, the advocates of these logics were still logical monists, in the sense that they took it that other logics were wrong. But the weight of the plethora has been too much for some people, who have decided that there is no one true logic: there are lots of things which may, with equal justification, be called logic. In logic, as in a multicultural society, pluralism must be endorsed. Is this right?[1]

The answer, as one might expect, is that it depends on what one means. There are certain senses in which the answer is clearly 'yes'. But in the case of central importance—I will explain what I take that to be in due course—I think that the answer is 'no'; and in this chapter I will defend a monist position.

I think that much of the *initial* plausibility of pluralism in this central case arises from a confusion between the various senses of the question. The first topic on the agenda is, therefore, an appropriate disambiguation. One of the important notions that requires clarification is that of rivalry between logics. For pluralism arises in a serious form when there is such a rivalry, and we are called upon to adjudicate. Can we, in such circumstances, decide for more than one candidate? The notion of rivalry will therefore be of central concern, and I will revisit the discussion of the notion in section 10.10.

A consideration of these issues in the first main part of the chapter will clear the ground for discussing serious objections to monism, which we will do in the second. This will leave a few words to be said about inductive inference in the final brief section.

---

[1] An excellent preliminary discussion of the issue can be found in Haack (1978), ch. 12. One should note, at the start, that pluralism is to be distinguished from *relativism*. Relativism equals pluralism plus the claim that each of the plurality is, in some relevant sense, equally good. Pluralists sometimes sail very close to the relativist wind though: 'There are different, equally good ways of . . . [giving an account of validity]; they are different, equally good *logics*' (Beall and Restall (2000), 478; italics in all quotes are original).

12.2   PURE AND APPLIED LOGIC

We should start by distinguishing, as we did in section 10.8, between pure and applied logic. As I noted there, there is an important analogy between logic and geometry.[2] It is now an uncontentious fact that there are many pure geometries: Euclidean, Riemannian, spherical, etc. Each is a perfectly good mathematical structure, and can be formulated as an axiom system, with standard models, etc. There is no question of rivalry between geometries at this level. The question of rivalry occurs when one applies geometries for some purpose, say to provide an account of the physical geometry of the cosmos. Then the question of which geometry is right must be faced.

In the same way, there are many pure logics. I enumerated several of these in the previous section. Each is a well-defined mathematical structure with a proof-theory, model theory, etc. There is no question of rivalry between them at this level. This can occur only when one requires a logic for application to some end. Then the question of which logic is right arises.

If one is asking about pure logics, then, pluralism is uncontentiously correct. Plurality is an issue of substance only if one is asking about applied logics. In this case, there is the potential for rivalry, and whether one should be a monist or a pluralist about this rivalry is a question that must be faced.

12.3   THEORETICAL PLURALISM

Let us turn, then, to applied logics. The first thing to note here is that pure logics can be applied for many purposes, such as simplifying electronic circuits, or analysing certain grammatical structures. And again, it is clear and uncontentious that different pure logics may be appropriate for each application. In the two examples given, for example, the appropriate logics are Boolean logic and the Lambek calculus.[3] We will have further examples, closer to home, later. Plurality is, then, an interesting issue only when we have one particular application in mind.

Fix, then, on some one application. A pure logic is applied by interpreting it in some way or other. As I argued in Chapter 10, it then becomes a *theory* of how the domain in which it is interpreted behaves; just as a pure geometry, when interpreted as a physical geometry, is a theory about space. In such a situation there may well be disputes about which theory is correct. This has certainly happened in geometry. It also happens in logic, as we shall have several occasions to observe below.

Such disputes are to be resolved in logic, as in geometry and elsewhere, by the usual criteria of theoretical evaluation, such as adequacy to the data, and theoretical virtues, such as simplicity, unity, no *ad hoc*ness, etc. We saw how in Chapter 8. The

---

[2]   Which is appealed to by many parties in the debate. See, e.g. da Costa (1997), Beall and Restall (2000).

[3]   The Lambek calculus is a sub-structural logic with a clear application to grammatical categories.

present relevance of all this is that we have the source of another kind of pluralism. Given a fixed application to some domain, there may be many different applied logics which constitute theories about the behaviour of that domain—and correspondingly, disputes about which theory is right. I will call this, for want of a better term, *theoretical pluralism*.

12.4   THE CANONICAL APPLICATION OF LOGIC

Let us now turn to the most important and traditional application of a pure logic. This is what in section 10.10 I called the *canonical application*: the application of a logic in the analysis of reasoning—which was also traditionally called 'logic', of course (just as 'geometry' was used ambiguously before Euclidean geometry and its canonical application were distinguished, to describe both). The central purpose of an analysis of reasoning is to determine what follows from what—what premises support what conclusions—and why. An argument where this is, in fact, the case is *valid*. As I discussed in Chapter 11, it is traditional to distinguish between two notions of validity, deductive and inductive. So immediately it would appear that we have a pluralism here. As to whether this is indeed the case, I will return at the end of this chapter. For most of this chapter I will focus just on deductive validity.

Before we can discuss the issue of plurality for this application, we need to recall how pure logics are applied in an analysis of reasoning. As explained in section 10.10, we reason, in the first place in the vernacular. We establish by observation that a planet moves in a certain way, and wish to know if the description of its trajectory follows from our theory of motion; or we infer what would be the case if the Butler did it, to see whether these consequences do, in fact, obtain. Premises and conclusions are formulated in a natural language. By all means, this may be a natural language augmented with technical vocabulary, such as that of mathematics. The language employed, though, is still the language of use and communication.

Pure logics, at least as standardly conceived, do not concern the vernacular at all, but are couched in terms of formal languages. A definition of validity is provided for inferences expressed in one of these. Applying this to provide an account of validity for the vernacular, as in the application of any pure mathematical structure, requires an interpretation. And in the case of logic, the interpretation is quite literally so: a translation procedure between the formal language in question and the vernacular. Such a procedure is rarely articulated at great length in logic texts. Rather, students are given hints about treating 'or' as $\vee$ (most of the time), etc., and then set loose on a bunch of exercises, through which they develop procedural knowledge. But given such a translation procedure, a pure logic provides an account of validity for vernacular inferences. A vernacular inference is valid iff its translation into the formal language is valid in the pure logic.

The result, moreover, often produces disagreement. According to some logics, 'there is an infinitude of primes' follows from 'it is not the case that there is not an infinitude of primes'; according to others, it does not. According to some logics, 'the sky is green' follows from 'the liar sentence is both true and false'; according to others, it does not. Such disagreements mean that we clearly have a case of theoretical pluralism. Is there a more serious kind of pluralism here? To address this question, let us turn to accounts of validity for formal languages.

12.5 VALIDITY

There is a plurality of formal languages employed in logic. I am not talking here of the fact that different symbols are used in different languages. The fact that '¬' is used for negation in one language, whilst '∼' is used in another, is neither here nor there: as long as each plays the role of vernacular negation (in the sense of Chapter 4) according to the appropriate translation manual, the two are, in effect, the same symbol. Rather, what is important is that one language may lack a symbol, in this sense, that another has. Thus, a modal language contains modal operators, which an extensional language lacks. Strictly speaking, then, the accounts of validity for two such languages must be different, and we have a pluralism. But this, again, is not a very interesting pluralism. For as far as the common set of symbols goes, the two accounts may be in perfect agreement; it is simply that one (or each) extends the other in some direction.

Given, then, a formal language, and a translation procedure between it and the vernacular, what should a formal theory of validity be like? I take the answer to be as explained in Chapter 11. When we reason, we reason about various situations or states of affairs. These may be actual or hypothetical. We reason to establish what holds in these situations given what we know, or assume, about them. This is truth-preservation (forward),[4] though it is not actually truth that is in question unless the situation we are reasoning about is itself actual. The *point* of deduction, then, is to give us a set of canons that preserve truth in this sense. A valid inference is therefore one such that in all the situations where the premises hold, the conclusion holds.

As noted in Chapter 11, this answer is, of course, nothing more than a gesture in the direction of an account of validity. Much remains to be done by way of spelling out what situations there are, and what it is to hold in one. And there are certainly different possibilities here: according to paraconsistent semantics, but not classical or intuitionist semantics, there are inconsistent situations. According to intuitionist semantics (and some paraconsistent semantics), but not classical semantics (and some other paraconsistent semantics), the definition of truth in a situation requires the truth conditions of negation to make reference to more than one possible world. There may therefore be different views on how to fill in the details required. But the familiar disputes about this, such as the intuitionist critique of classical logic, or the dialetheist critique of explosive logics, would seem to be cases of theoretical pluralism. Is there a more serious kind of pluralism here? So far, we have no reason to believe so.

---

[4] Conversely, we may reason to establish what fails to hold in a situation, given what we know, or assume, about what fails to hold in it. This is untruth-preservation backwards.

12.6 DOMAIN VARIATION

So let us turn to some possible reasons. These have been advocated by a number of people, and we will look at six. The first is provided by da Costa (1997).[5] Da Costa's major argument for pluralism is to the effect that reasoning about different *kinds* of things may require different logics. The kinds in question are kinds like macro-objects, quantum objects, platonic objects, mental constructions, etc. What to say about this depends on how, exactly, it is envisaged that logic will vary.

One thing that da Costa envisages is that different kinds of objects have different properties. Thus, for example, he moots the possibility that quantum objects do not have the property of self-identity, which macro-objects have. Hence, micro-objects require a non-classical logic of identity, one where $\forall x \, x = x$ is absent.

In response to this, the obvious monist reply is that since validity is truth-preservation in all situations, if there are situations in which objects may not be self-identical, then self-identity is not a logical law at all. This does not mean that when reasoning about, e.g. macro-objects one may not use the law, though. It is just a "contingent" property of certain domains, and may thus be invoked when reasoning about them. In a similar way, the intuitionist may invoke the law of excluded middle when reasoning about finite (or at least decidable) domains: this, plus intuitionist logic, gives classical logic. But the intuitionist has not changed logical allegiances. It is simply that classical validity can be recovered enthymematically, given the extra domain-specific premises.

Da Costa's pluralism is more radical than I have so far indicated, though. He envisages not only that objects of different kinds may have different logical properties, but that different logical operators may also need to be used in reasoning about different kinds of objects. Thus, for example, classical negation is appropriate for dealing with platonic objects, and intuitionist negation is appropriate for dealing with mental constructions.

But, this cannot be right. Classical and intuitionist connectives have different meanings. (Indeed, some intuitionists, such as Dummett, even claim that some classical connectives have no meaning at all). Thus, take negation as an example. Classical and intuitionist negations have different truth conditions.[6] But difference in truth conditions entails difference in meaning. Hence, the two connectives have different meanings.[7] Now, either vernacular negation is ambiguous or it is not. If it is not, then, since the different theories attribute it different meanings, they cannot both be right. We have a simple theoretical pluralism. The other possibility is that vernacular negation is ambiguous. Thus, it may be argued that vernacular negation sometimes

---

[5] A review of this in English, which documents the claims attributed to da Costa in what follows, can be found in Priest (2000*d*).

[6] Intuitionist connectives are often given provability conditions, but since an intuitionist, in effect, identifies truth and provability, these are truth conditions.

[7] One might challenge this for reasons that we will come to in sect. 12.10, and I will deal with there.

means classical negation and sometimes means intuitionist negation. But if this were right, we would have two legitimate meanings of negation, and the correct way to treat this formally would be to have two corresponding negation signs in the formal language, the translation manual telling us how to disambiguate when translating into formalese. In exactly this way, it is often argued that the English conditional is ambiguous, between the subjunctive and indicative. This does not cause us to change logics, we simply have a formal language with two conditional symbols, say $\supset$ and $>$, and use both. This is pluralism in a sense, but the sense is just one of ambiguity.

In fact, I see no cogent reason to suppose that negation is ambiguous in this sense. If the account of negation of Chapter 4 is correct, negation is unique. Indeed, negation cannot have different meanings when reasoning about different kinds of things. This is because we can reason about different kinds simultaneously. We can, for example, reason from the claim that it is not the case that a and b have some particular property in common, where a and b are of different kinds. Moreover, there are other reasons as to why vernacular negation cannot be ambiguous between intuitionist and classical negation. If it were, as I have argued, we could have two formal negations. But it is well known that in the presence of classical negation, many other important intuitionist distinctions collapse. For example, the intuitionist conditional collapses into the classical conditional.[8]

Of course, as I have already noted, the intuitionist logician can, in effect, use the full force of classical argument when reasoning about finite domains. But this is not because negation has changed its meaning. It is because they are entitled to various extra premises, such as the law of excluded middle.

12.7 CONTEXT DEPENDENCE

The next notable advocate of pluralism that we look at is Batens (1985), (1990). According to him, different logics are required, not for different domains, but in different contexts, where a context is, in a nutshell, a problem-solving situation. Two of Batens' arguments for pluralism are particularly notable.

The first, given mainly in (1990), takes it for granted that a paraconsistent logic is correct in some contexts, but argues that it cannot be correct in others (e.g. a metatheoretic one), for which classical logic is required. Hence, pluralism. Now, just as an intuitionist may use what amounts to classical logic when reasoning about finite situations, so a paraconsistent logician may use what amounts to classical logic given appropriate information about the domain. For example, sufficient information is that for all α, $(\alpha \wedge \neg\alpha) \rightarrow \perp$, where $\rightarrow$ is an appropriate detachable conditional,

---

[8] Moreover, classical negation, $\neg_C$, and intuionistic negation, $\neg_I$, become logically equivalent (see, Harris (1982))! One way to see this is to note that for both we have:

$$\frac{\alpha : \beta}{\alpha, \neg_*\beta :} \qquad \frac{\alpha, \beta :}{\alpha : \neg_*\beta}$$

where $*$ is C or I. Given $\alpha : \alpha$, a little fiddling gives $\alpha\neg_C : \neg_I\alpha$ and vice versa.

and $\bot$ is a logical constant that entails everything. This extra information, together with the base paraconsistent logic, generates classical logic.[9]

This reply might not satisfy Batens, for the following reason. As I have stressed, the meaning of a logical operator, such as negation, does not change simply in virtue of the extra information. But, Batens argues, a paraconsistent negation just cannot express certain things that need to be expressed in talking about such situations. In particular, $\neg\alpha$ cannot express the fact that α is *rejected*. What to say about this argument depends on how one interprets 'rejection', which may, in fact, mean several different things. I discussed this matter in section 6.3, so do not need to go into details here. The major sense of rejection that Batens has in mind is that to reject α is to commit oneself to something, which, in conjunction with α, produces triviality (p. 222). But a paraconsistent logician can do just that, by endorsing $(\alpha \wedge \neg\alpha) \rightarrow \bot$.

The second of Batens' arguments (given mainly in (1985)) is that, notwithstanding the above, different contexts result in different meanings for logical operators, and hence deliver different logics (p. 338 f.). The argument for meaning variance is a familiar one, of a kind employed by Kuhn and Feyerabend in the philosophy of science. The first premise is that what is accepted may vary from context to context. The second is that what is accepted (partially) determines the meanings of the words involved. It follows from these that meanings change from context to context.

Now one might say a good deal about this argument, but its central failing is that a change of what is accepted does not (necessarily) result in a change of meaning. When a Christian loses their certitude, and comes to believe that God does not exist, the word 'God' has not changed its meaning. What they come to believe is the very opposite of what they believed before. Similarly, the classical logician believes that it is not the case that it is not the case that α entails α; the intuitionist believes otherwise. It does not follow that 'it is not the case that' means something different for the two of them. If it did, they would not be in disagreement, which they most certainly are. Intuitionist and classical negation do mean different things;[10] as I have argued, the point of disagreement between the two logicians is precisely which of those two negations it is that correctly characterises vernacular negation.

12.8 LOGICAL CONSTANTS AND VARIABLES

The next three arguments we will look at are all to be found in Beall and Restall (2000), who give what is, perhaps, the most sustained defence of pluralism.[11] B&R

---

[9] See *In Contradiction*, sect. 8.5. There are less brute force ways of recovering classical logic in consistent situations. See Priest (1991*b*).

[10] If they mean anything at all, which, as I have noted, may be disputed.

[11] Page reference in what follow are to this. The position is given an extended defence in Beall and Restall (2006).

endorse an account of validity similar to that which I gave in Chapter 11;[12] but they argue for pluralism, nonetheless. The three arguments are all to the effect that the details of the account given there may be filled in in different, equally legitimate, ways.

B&R's first argument proceeds as follows. There is a strong tradition in logic of treating certain words in premises and conclusions as parameters. This is done in the semantics of first-order logic, e.g. where one treats predicates and constants as semantically variable. B&R observe that the account of validity can be parameterized in this way to give the usual model-theoretic (Tarskian) account of validity.[13] What are the consequences of this? A simple example illustrates. Consider the inference: *a* is red; hence *a* is coloured. This is valid on the unparameterized account. Any situation in which *a* is red, it is coloured (which is not to say that there might not be inconsistent situations, in which it is not coloured too). But the inference is not valid according to a parameterized definition of validity—at least if the parameters include predicates—for it is of the form: $Pa \vdash Qa$. What is at issue here is the question of what situations are to be admitted into our semantics. Are we to include, in our sweep, situations in which things can be in the extension of 'red' but not of 'coloured', etc., or are we not?

Now, it is true that the model-theoretic construction can be done in either way, parameterized or unparameterized, so giving different notions of validity. But as far as I can see, this is just another case of theoretical pluralism—or at least, B&R provide no reasons for thinking otherwise. They say that they do not think it '*fruitful* to debate which of . . .[the two accounts] is *logic*' (p. 480). I am really not sure what this means. It certainly cannot mean that there are no considerations that might persuade one to adjudicate for one theory over the other.[14] Many of the moves in this theoretical dispute are, in fact, well known.

The inference '*a* is red; hence *a* is coloured' is certainly *prima facie* valid. Hence, if the parametric account is to survive, this validity must be explained away. The standard move is to claim that the inference is, in fact, invalid, but that it *appears* to be valid because we confuse it with a valid enthymeme, with suppressed premise 'All red things are coloured', taken for granted. But this move is not very plausible when scrutinized. For if something about 'All red things are coloured' gave it the power to make an enthymeme, whose suppressed premise it was, appear valid, then the inference: 'Snow is white; hence snow is white and all red things are coloured' should equally appear valid—which it does not.

There are other reasons for being dissatisfied with the parametric account. For example, the parameterized definition of validity in effect allows the meanings of some words, but not others, to vary. But when we ask what follows from something's

---

[12] Similar, but not identical. They think of situations, essentially, as worlds—or better, as the situations of situation semantics. For me, a situation is (represented by) a structure of the kind normally thought of as an interpretation of the language.

[13] B&R appear to suggest that it is only the parameterized account that can be applied to formal languages (p. 479); this is certainly not true.

[14] B&R agree: 'One might now wonder: Is there any basis upon which to choose between these two accounts? Is there any reason you might prefer one to the other? The answer is a resounding *yes*.' (B&R, p. 480.)

being red, we are not asking about what might be the case if 'red' meant something different. That's just changing the subject. It is essential, then, that meaning change is not allowed—even of so-called logical variables.[15]

This is no place to pursue the ramifications of the dispute further. The main point for present purposes is just that parameterized validity is not real validity at all—just a false theory thereof.[16] This is not to say that the parameterized notion of validity is a useless notion. It is still true that every parametrically valid inference is valid. Hence, a conclusion that follows according to such a notion, still follows, and this may well allow us, in reasoning, to show what we need. But there is more to validity than formal validity.

12.9   CLASSES OF SITUATION

B&R's next argument is to the effect that we can obtain equally legitimate notions of logical consequence by defining validity as truth-preservation over different classes of situations. Thus, if we restrict ourselves to consistent and complete domains, classical logical consequence will result; if we take a broader class, it will not. If we include situations with empty domains we will have a free logic; otherwise not. We therefore have a plurality of validities: one for each appropriate class of situations—and all equally legitimate notions of validity.

The obvious reply to this argument is that it is only truth-preservation over *all* situations that is, strictly speaking, validity. One of the points about deductive logic is that it will work come what may: we do not have to worry about anything except the premises. As I have already observed, this is not to say that in practice one may not reason as if one were using a different, stronger, notion of validity, one appropriate to a more limited class of situations. But this is not because one has changed logical allegiances; it is because one is allowed to invoke contingent properties of the domain in question.

A possible reply here[17] is that the class of situations is so large and variegated that there are no inferences that are truth-preserving over all of them, except, possibly, the trivial $\alpha \vdash \alpha$. Hence monism is vacuous. I have never seen any persuasive argument as to why one should suppose this to be the case, however. It may well be that the intersection of the valid principles in all *pure* logics is empty, but this is beside the

---

[15] A third objection to the parametric account is that if it is to have any credibility, the distinction between logical constants and logical variables has to be drawable in some principled fashion, and I doubt that there is any such way. It is true that there is, in practice, a distinction of this kind handed down to us by tradition, which puts 'or' and 'not' on one side, and 'red' and 'coloured' on the other. But this, it seems to me, is simply an historical contingency.

[16] See, further, Read (1994*b*). It is perhaps worth noting that in the standard semantics of first-order logic, we assign predicates arbitrary extensions. Sometimes this is glossed informally as assigning each predicate a meaning. Sometimes, on the other hand, an interpretation is thought of as representing a "possible world", where the extension of each predicate, whose meaning is determined in other ways, is as assigned. These are not the same, as should now be clear. It is perhaps the confusion of these two things that lends the parameterized approach some credibility.

[17] One that, in fact, B&R (p. 490) give.

point. We are not talking about pure logics here; we are talking about applied logics, and indeed, logics applied for one particular purpose.

Moreover, I think it just false that all principles of inference fail in some situation. For example, any situation in which a conjunction holds, the conjuncts hold, simply in virtue of the meaning of ∧. Naturally, if one were allowed to vary the meanings of words as the class of situations is broadened, then this would not be the case. But when we ask about what is the case in situations where the sky is blue *and* the sun is shining, we are interested in just that: allowing 'and' to take on some other meaning is beside the point. It is certainly open to someone to claim that what I have just said gets the meaning of 'and' wrong, and that the standard truth conditions are not, in fact, delivered by its meaning. That is a substantial issue, and certainly gives rise to theoretical pluralism, but it is not germane here. As long as meanings *are* fixed, one can't vary them to dispose of valid inferences.[18]

There is another possible move that might be made at this point (of a kind that came up in another context in section 10.14). What, exactly, is the disagreement between the monist and the pluralist about here? The monist accepts that there is a core of universally correct inferences; but this may be augmented if we are reasoning about certain kinds of situations. The pluralist holds that different sorts of situations require different validities, but may accept—will accept, if the above argument is correct—that there is a core of inferences that are acceptable in all kinds of situations. What is the difference? None, it might be thought. The facts are agreed upon. What is at issue is only how to describe them.

One might argue against this duck/rabbit pluralism as follows.[19] Suppose that one is a pluralist of the kind in question. Let s be some situation about which we are reasoning; suppose that s is in different classes of situations, say, K_1 and K_2. Should one use the notion of validity appropriate for K_1 or for K_2? We cannot give the answer 'both' here. Take some inference that is valid in K_1 but not K_2, $\alpha \vdash \beta$, and suppose that we know (or assume) α holds in s; are we, or are we not entitled to accept that β does? Either we are or we are not: there can be no pluralism about this. In fact, the answer is that we are. Since s is in K_1, and the inference is truth-preserving in all situations in K_1. In other words, if we know that a situation about which we are reasoning is in class K, we are justified in reasoning with validity defined over the restricted class of situations K.[20]

---

[18] It is possible to see the argument of the previous section as a special case of the one in this. Looked at in this way, the advocate of a formal account of validity wants to include a class of situations where the meanings of non-logical constants are allowed to vary, and so where there are worlds where something is in the extension of 'red' but not of 'coloured'. If one takes this line then, it seems to me, there is no reason not to carry the process to its limit, and allow every word to change its meaning. In this case, the logical form of 'Some man is mortal' is $Qx(Ax \circ Bx)$, where $\circ$ is an arbitrary binary connective, and Q is an arbitrary monadic quantifier. If we do this, then nothing is going to come out as valid except the trivial $\alpha \vdash \alpha$. So much the worse for letting meanings change.

[19] Indeed, in the paper on which this chapter is based, I did argue in this way.

[20] Note that this raises the following possibility. Take some situation, s, that is in class K_1 and class K_2, and suppose that α is true in s. It is quite possible that, for some β, $\alpha \vdash_{K_1} \beta$ and $\alpha \vdash_{K_2} \neg\beta$, even though the consequences of α under both $\vdash_{K_1}$ and $\vdash_{K_2}$ are consistent. That is, s is an inconsistent situation, though each consequent relation exposes only part of that inconsistency.

Thus, differences in validity due to variation of the class of situations in question can be viewed from a pluralist perspective; but as I have observed, one can view it equally from a monist perspective.

12.10 INSTRUMENTALISM

B&R's final argument is that we may generate different logics by giving the truth conditions of the connectives in different ways. Thus, for example, we may give either intuitionist truth conditions or classical truth conditions. If we do the former, the result is a notion of validity that is constructive, that is, tighter than classical validity, but which it is perfectly legitimate to use for certain ends.

There are two aspects of this position that need concern us. The first was covered essentially in section 12.6. If we give different truth conditions for the connectives, we are giving the formal connectives different meanings. When we apply the logics to vernacular reasoning we are, therefore, giving different theories of the meanings of the vernacular connectives. We have a case of theoretical pluralism; and the theories cannot both be right—or if they are, we simply have a case of ambiguity, as we have already seen.

One might dispute this argument (as Restall did in discussion). Classical and intuitionist connectives do not have different meanings. Truth conditions are general and uniform. Apparently different truth conditions are just special cases. Thus, for example, the truth conditions for the connectives in a Kripke interpretation for intuitionist logic collapse into classical conditions at "classical" worlds, namely, those which access no worlds other than themselves. We do not, therefore, have connectives with different meanings. It is just that the intuitionist countenances more situations than their classical cousin.

If this move is right, then this third example of pluralism reduces to the previous one, which I have already dealt with. But I do not think it is right. For a dispute about meanings can be cashed out just as much in terms of what situations there are, as in terms of truth conditions. For example, to determine whether it is part of the meaning of 'to see' that the eyes be employed, we might consider whether there are any (maybe hypothetical) situations where someone could be described as seeing, even though they had no (functioning) eyes. One who holds that seeing involves having eyes will deny the possibility of such situations.

Exactly the same is true of the case at hand. For someone who takes classical truth conditions to govern an account of the connectives, say negation, for example, what it means to say that $\neg\alpha$ holds in a situation is just that α fails to hold there. It follows that there can be no situations where neither α nor $\neg\alpha$ holds. Suppose, for example,[21] that one thinks of a situation as a *part* of a possible world. Moreover, suppose that we have a situation of which JC is not a part. It follows that 'JC is reading' is not true of that situation. For classical negation, it will follow that 'JC is not reading' is true of that situation. It is not an option to say that neither of these two is true. The situation

[21] One of B&R's, p. 481.

cannot be "incomplete". As B&R themselves put it (p. 482), 'the classical account of negation fails *for situations*'.[22]

The second aspect of B&R's position here that we need to look at is the claim that, even if one is, say, a classical logician, one may legitimately accept the policy of restricting one's reasoning to the use of intuitionistically valid inferences, and so reason constructively, for certain ends.[23] Now this policy is certainly not intuitionism. For intuitionism justifies many mathematical principles that are classically inconsistent, and so intuitionist mathematics is not a proper part of classical mathematics. Neither is it a policy of reasoning only in accordance with principles that are constructive from a classical perspective. For this extends intuitionist logic. For example, it legitimates Markov's Principle in arithmetic: $(\forall x(A \vee \neg A) \wedge \neg \forall x \neg A) \rightarrow \exists xA$ (where the quantifiers are constructive). This is not intuitionistically valid.[24]

Nonetheless, it is certainly the case that one could decide to operate with just intuitionist logic, or, more generally, with a constructive part of one's preferred logic (assuming that that logic is not itself constructive). One could do this simply as an exercise; but more importantly, there might be a perfectly sensible *point* to doing so. A point might be provided by the fact that conclusions obtained constructively contain more information, or more computational content, than conclusions proved non-constructively. Reasoning in this way may therefore be a useful *instrumental* technique. I noted that a pure logic may be applied for many purposes, and instrumental purposes are purposes. Hence this is simply a case of applying a logic for a different end, and we have already seen that different applications may require different logics. Note, though, that it does not follow from this that conclusions obtained using non-constructive principles of inference are themselves defective in any way. The things so proved are guaranteed, in fact, to hold in the situation about which we are reasoning, by the definition of validity.

Whilst we are on the instrumental use of logics, let me give one more example of this. Inference procedures are used in science. And sometimes in science, we have a theory that we know to be incorrect, but which we use, nonetheless, for instrumental purposes. If we are doing this, then we are clearly also at liberty to use whatever inferential processes we like if they satisfy those purposes.

An example of this is as follows. The Bohr theory of the atom was a very useful theory, which made strikingly accurate empirical predictions. Its inference procedures were highly non-standard, though, involving the chunking of principles, with limited flow of information between the chunks. This can be understood in terms of a certain non-adjunctive paraconsistent reasoning strategy.[25] Now, no one ever thought that

---

[22] The case is even clearer with respect to inconsistent situations (of a kind that are also invoked in situation semantics). If one subscribes to classical negation, *no* situation can be such that α *and* ¬α hold at it. This is a very part of what negation is taken to mean.

[23] B&R, p. 485: 'The constructivism . . . [of certain mathematicians] can best be described as mathematics *pursued in the context of intuitionist logic*.'

[24] Classically, if an arithmetic predicate is decidable, and we are assured that not everything fails to satisfy it, then we can test it for each number until we find one that satisfies it. This is a perfectly good classical construction, but not an intuitionist one. See Dummett (1977), 22 f.

[25] See Brown and Priest (2004) and (forthcoming).

Bohr's theory was correct. It is commonly suggested that this is because it was inconsistent. I do not think that this is a good reason. What is a good reason, as explained
in section 9.6, is that if a truth-preserving inference mechanism had been used, the
theory would have had all sorts of empirical consequences that are not observed. The
theory, then, cannot be true. Despite this, it was an important stepping stone *en route*
to a more adequate theory. It was necessary to obtain insight into various principles
and their interaction, so that more adequate principles could be formulated. The use
of a logic that is not one of simple truth-preservation was perfectly legitimate in this
context.

A number of writers, working in the field of non-adjunctive paraconsistent logic
in particular, have argued that it may be important to have an inference engine that
preserves something other than (or as well as) truth, for certain purposes.[26] As I have
already stressed, different applications may well require different logics. State your
purpose and how it is to be achieved; then use a logic the application of which
does this.

12.11 UNDER-DETERMINATION BY THE DATA

Let us finish with one more argument for pluralism. In effect, an applied logic is,
as I have said, a theory about how its domain of application behaves. Hence, a pure
logic, when given the canonical application, provides a theory about the norms of
correct (deductive) reasoning. It may be thought that there is insufficient information
to determine which logic is the correct applied logic here; in particular, that our
intuitions about the goodness and badness of particular inferences —which provide
the data in this case—are insufficient to determine which theory is correct. Hence,
there may be a plurality of equally correct answers.

Pluralism of this kind may be argued on very general grounds, familiar from the
philosophy of science. The correct theory, it may be said, is always under-determined
by the data, which is, in any case, soft. In virtue of this, the argument sometimes
continues, the correct theory is a purely conventional matter. And we can make
whichever conventions are most convenient.

What is to be said about this? The first point is that indeterminism of the kind I
have just described is, in general, quite overrated. Adequacy to the data is just *one* of
the criteria to be employed in assessing theories. Others, such as simplicity, unity, a
low degree of *ad hoc*ness, etc., are familiar from the literature. Whilst it is clearly a
possibility of some sort that different theories may yet tie—and not just *pro tem*, but
in the long term—it is hard to come up with concrete examples of this in the history
of intellectual inquiry. At any rate, I know of no argument to suppose that this is a
real possibility in logic.

And even if it were, this is not an end of the matter. For this plurality is merely
epistemic: we just cannot tell which of the theories is the correct one. Given competing

---

[26] See, e.g. Brown (2000).

theories, as long as one is a realist about the subject matter, at most one of them can be correct, even if we cannot tell which. There is therefore no alethic pluralism.

But should we be a realist about logic? The answer, as I argued in Chapter 11, is 'yes'. Validity is determined by the class of situations involved in truth-preservation, quite independently of our theory of the matter. This answer has a certain ontological sting, of course. For, as I observed, the situations about which we reason are not all actual: many are purely hypothetical. And one must be a realist about these too. There are numerous different sorts of realism that one might endorse here, many of which are familiar from debates about the nature of possible worlds. One may take hypothetical situations to be concrete non-actual situations; abstract objects, like sets of propositions or combinations of actual components; real but non-existent objects.[27] I will not address the question of which of these account is correct here.[28] Any of them will do, as long as they provide for an independent realm of situations; and hence a determinate answer to the question of which theory is correct (even if our theories do tie, epistemically).

12.12 INDUCTIVE INFERENCE

We have now dealt with a number of important arguments for pluralism about deductive validity. Let me conclude the chapter by returning to the issue of inductive validity, to see what it adds to the picture. The situation here is complicated by the fact that there is no theoretical agreement about the nature of inductive inference, even of the limited kind that exists for deductive inference. But in section 11.9 I gave an account of what inductive validity amounts to, and I assume here that something like that is essentially right.

According to this account, situations are structured with an ordering, taken to represent normality. A most normal situation where the premises are true is then a situation where the premises are true, such that there is no situation higher in the ordering where this is so. The important point to note here is that when we reason inductively, what counts as normal is context-dependent, as pointed out in section 11.10. If we are reasoning about biological appendages, a dog with three legs is not normal; if we are reasoning about creatures' genotypes, the dog may be perfectly normal, provided that its lost leg is caused by a road accident, and not a genetic abnormality.

Now, how does this affect the issue of pluralism? First, the fact that we have two canons of inference, inductive and deductive, is not a case of pluralism. This is because, according to the above definition, all deductively valid inferences are inductively valid. (If truth is preserved in all interpretations, it is preserved in all most normal ones.) Hence, we do not have two canons of inference: we have one set of valid inferences, inside which there is a distinguished subset.

---

[27] Views of these kinds are held, concerning possible worlds, by Lewis, Stalnaker, Cresswell, and Routley, respectively.

[28] Priest (2005a), ch. 7 argues for a noneist account of worlds.

But the fact that normality is context-relative does give rise to a pluralism. What is inductively valid will depend on the normality ordering, which may vary from context to context. One might be tempted to reply here as I replied to the pluralist in section 12.9. It is still the case that there is a core of inductive inferences that are valid in all contexts, namely those that hold whatever the normality ordering. Why not call those the valid inductive inferences, the others being reducible to those enthymematically? A main answer to this is that if one conceptualizes the valid inductive inferences in this way, then there is no difference between inductive and deductive validity. The valid inductive inferences turn out to be indistinguishable from the valid deductive ones.[29] One can maintain a monism about inductive inference, but if one does, it is an entirely degenerate one.

12.13 CONCLUSION

We have now reviewed several reasons for logical pluralism, and several things that pluralism might mean. The issue of monism vs. pluralism has turned out to be a delicate one. As we have seen, there are many senses in which pluralism is uncontentiously correct. No one, for example, is going to argue about pluralism in pure logic, or theoretical pluralism in applied logic. The important, and hard, question concerns the situation with respect to the correct logic for canonical application; and I have argued that one can quite coherently view this situation from a monist perspective.

*   *   *

12.14 TO BE *AND* NOT TO BE—THAT IS THE ANSWER

The last part of this book has been concerned with the nature of logic, its status as a corrigible theory with a certain subject matter, and its claims to uniqueness. With this, our review of the natures of four central philosophical notions—truth, negation, rationality, and logic—is completed.

Many of the lessons learned are quite general; they have nothing specifically to do with dialetheism, and stand quite independently of the truth of this view. From this perspective, the upshot of the investigations is an interesting one. Consistency has often been taken to be so central to the notions in question that it has been felt that they could not operate without it. As we have seen, they can. But perhaps more importantly, the accounts of these core notions that have emerged in the discussion are not *so* different from the traditional accounts. Any of the traditional theories of truth may be allowed to stand, negation is a standard contradictory-forming operator, the view of rationality is familiar from contemporary philosophy of science, and the nature of logic has not collapsed into some faddish relativism. Perhaps the most surprising

---

[29] Just consider the degenerate ordering, where no situation compares with any other. The maximally normal models of a set of premises are then just its models.

thing, then, is how easily considerations of consistency can be detached from these notions, and so how non-integral they are to them. This makes the traditional view of the centrality of consistency to these notions even more surprising. The dead hand of Aristotle has, it would seem, weighed on the topics, preventing philosophers from applying to them the critical spirit which is their due. Even were it to be the case, then, that dialetheism turns out to be a view that, for some reason, cannot be sustained, this, at least, has come to an end.

Clearly, though, the investigations here have not been polemically innocent: the defence of dialetheism has always been running, if not in the foreground, then at least in the background.

I chose the title of this book, not simply because of its natural application to the book's contents, but because of the irony of the passage from which it comes:

> Doubt thou the stars are fire;
> Doubt that the sun doth move;
> Doubt truth to be a liar;
> But never doubt I love.

(*Hamlet*, ii. ii. 115)

The irony is twofold. That something true cannot be false is one of the things that Hamlet is holding up as certain. Unfortunately, the other things that are cited as of the same kind have turned out to be, not just uncertain, but actually false: the sun does not move—not, in the Ptolemaic sense in which Hamlet intends it; and the stars are not fire, since fire is rapid oxidation, not nuclear fusion. This is an external irony of the text. There is also an internal irony. Hamlet is saying that his love for Ophelia is even more certain than any of these certitudes. Yet, as becomes clear as the plot unfolds, his claim to love, too, is false.

Even though the quotation from which the title of this book comes appears to endorse the consistency of truth, the double irony completely reverses this. If I cannot claim Aristotle on my side, at least I can claim Shakespeare.

References

Anderson, A. R. and Belnap, N. D. (1975), *Entailment: The Logic of Relevance and Necessity*, Princeton: Princeton University Press, i.

—— —— and Dunn, J. M. (1992), *Entailment: The Logic of Relevance and Necessity*, Princeton: Princeton University Press, ii.

Anscombe, G. E. and Geach, P. (1961), *Three Philosophers*, Oxford: Blackwell.

Armour-Garb, B. and Beall, JC. (2001), 'Can Deflationists be Dieletheists?', *Journal of Philosophical Logic*, 30: 593–608.

Baldwin, T. (1991), 'The Identity Theory of Truth', *Mind*, 100: 35–52.

Barnes, J. (1967), 'The Law of Contradiction', *Philosophical Quarterly*, 19: 302–9.

—— (1979), *The Presocratic Philosophers*, London: Routledge & Kegan Paul.

—— (ed.) (1984), *The Complete Works of Aristotle*, Princeton: Princeton University Press.

Barwise, J. and Perry, J. (1983), *Situations and Attitudes*, Cambridge, Mass.: MIT Press.

Batens, D. (1985), 'Meaning, Acceptance and Dialectics', in J. C. Pitt (ed.), *Change and Progress in Modern Science*, Dordrecht: Reidel.

—— (1990), 'Against Global Paraconsistency', *Studies in Soviet Thought*, 39: 209–29.

Beall, JC. (2000), 'Is the Observable World Consistent?', *Australasian Journal of Philosophy*, 78: 113–18.

—— and Armour-Garb, B. (2003), 'Should Deflationists be Dialetheists', *Noûs*, 37: 303–24.

—— —— (eds.) (2005), *Deflationism and Paradox*, Oxford: Oxford University Press.

—— and Restall, G. (2000), 'Logical Pluralism', *Australasian Journal of Philosophy*, 78: 475–9.

—— —— (2006), *Logical Pluralism,* Oxford: Oxford University Press.

Bell, E. T. (1953), *Men of Mathematics*, London: Pelican Books.

Belnap, N. (1962), 'Tonk, Plonk and Plink', *Analysis*, 22: 130–4; repr. in Strawson (1967), 132–7.

Benacerraf, P. and Putnam, H. (eds.) (1964), *Philosophy of Mathematics: Selected Readings*, Oxford: Oxford University Press.

Borokowski, L. and Słupecki, J. (1958), 'The Logical Works of J. Łukasiewicz', *Studia Logica*, 8: 7–56.

Brady, R. (2004), 'On the Formalization of the Law of Non-Contradiction', in Priest, Beall, and Armour-Garb, ch. 2.

Brinkmann, K. (1992), 'Commentary on Gottlieb', *Proceedings of the Boston Area Colloquium in Ancient Philosophy*, 8: 199–209.

Brown, B. (1990), 'How to be a Realist about Inconsistency in Science', *Studies in History and Philosophy of Science*, 21: 281–94.

—— (1993), 'Old Quantum Theory: A Paraconsistent Approach', *Proceedings of the Philosophy of Science Association*, 2: 397–441.

—— (2000), 'Simple Natural Deduction for Weakly Aggregative Paraconsistent Logics', in D. Batens, C. Mortensen, G. Priest, and J. P. Van Bendegem (eds.), *Frontiers of Paraconsistent Logic*, Baldock: Research Studies Press, 137–48.

—— and Priest, G. (2004), 'Chunk and Permeate, a Paraconsistent Reasoning Strategy, i. The Infinitesimal Calculus', *Journal of Philosophical Logic*, 33: 379–88.

—— —— (forthcoming), 'Chunk and Permeate, a Paraconsistent Reasoning Strategy, ii. The Bohr Theory of the Atom'.

Candlish, S. (1989), 'The Truth about F. H. Bradley', *Mind*, 98: 331–48.

Campbell, R. and Sowden, L. (1985), *Paradoxes of Rationality and Cooperation: Prisoner's Dilemma and Newcomb's Problem*, Vancouver: University of British Columbia Press.

Carnap, R. (1952), 'Meaning Postulates', *Philosophical Studies*, 3: 65–73.

Castañeda, H. N. (1959), 'Arithmetic and Reality', *Australasian Journal of Philosophy*, 37: 92–107; repr. in Benacerraf and Putnam (eds.) (1964), 404–71.

Chomsky, N. (1971), 'Recent Contributions to the Theory of Innate Ideas', in J. Searle (ed.), *The Philosophy of Language*, Oxford: Oxford University Press, 121–9.

Clark, K. L. (1978), 'Negation as Failure', in H. Gallaire and J. Minker (eds.), *Logic and Data Bases*, New York: Plenum Press, 293–322.

Code, A. (1986), 'Aristotle's Investigation of a Basic Logical Principle: Which Science Investigates the Principle of Non-Contradiction?', *Canadian Journal of Philosophy*, 16: 359–70.

Cohen, S. M. (1986), 'Aristotle on the Principle of Non-Contradiction', *Canadian Journal of Philosophy*, 16: 341–57.

Crane, H. and Piantinada, T. P. (1983), 'On Seeing Reddish Green and Yellowish Blue', *Science*, 221: 1078–80.

Cresswell, M. J. (1987), 'Aristotle's Phaedo', *Australasian Journal of Philosophy*, 65: 131–55.

—— (2004), 'Aristotle on Non-Contradiction', *Theoria*, 70: 166–83.

Crocco, G., Fariñas del Cerro, L., and Herzig, A. (eds.) (1995), *Conditionals: From Philosophy to Computer Science*, Oxford: Oxford University Press.

da Costa, N. C. A. (1997), *Logique Classique et Non Classique: Essai sur les Fondements de la Logique*, Paris: Masson.

Dancy, R. M. (1975), *Sense and Contradiction in Aristotle*, Dordrecht: Reidel.

De Rijk, L. M. (2002), *Aristotle: Semantics and Ontology*, ii. The *Metaphysics. Semantics in Aristotle's Strategy of Argument*, Leiden: Brill.

Demos, R. (1917), 'A Discussion of a Certain Type of Negative Proposition', *Mind*, 26: 188–96.

Denyer, N. (1989), 'Dialetheism and Trivialisation', *Mind*, 98: 259–63.

—— (1995), 'Priest's Paraconsistent Arithmetic', *Mind*, 104: 567–75.

Devlin, K. (1991), *Logic and Information*, Cambridge: Cambridge University Press.

Dowdan, B. (1984), 'Accepting Inconsistencies from the Paradoxes', *Journal of Philosophical Logic*, 13: 125–30.

Dummett, M. (1959), 'Truth', *Proceedings of the Aristotelian Society*, 59: 141–62; repr. in Dummett (1978), ch. 1.

—— (1975a), 'The Philosophical Basis of Intuitionist Logic', in H. E. Rose and J. C. Shepherdson (eds.), *Logic Colloquium '73*, Amsterdam: North Holland, 5–40; repr. in Dummett (1978), ch. 14.

—— (1975b), 'The Justification of Deduction', *Proceedings of the British Academy*, 59: 201–32; repr. in Dummett (1978), ch. 17.

—— (1976), 'Is Logic Empirical?', in H. D. Lewis (ed.), *Contemporary British Philosophy*, 4th series, London: Allen & Unwin, 45–68; repr. in Dummett (1978), ch. 16.

—— (1977), *Elements of Intuitionism*, Oxford: Oxford University Press.

—— (1978), *Truth and Other Enigmas*, London: Duckworth.

—— (1991), *The Logical Basis of Metaphysics*, London: Duckworth.

Dunn, J. M. (1986), 'Relevance Logic and Entailment', in D. Gabbay and F. Guenthner (eds.), *Handbook of Philosophical Logic*, Dordrecht: Kluwer Academic Publishers, iii. ch. 3.

—— (1999), 'A Comparative Study of Various Model-Theoretic Treatments of Negation: A History of Formal Negation', in Gabbay and Wansing, 23–57.

Etchemendy, J. (1988), 'Tarski on Truth and Logical Consequence', *Journal of Symbolic Logic*, 53: 51–79.

——(1990), *The Concept of Logical Consequence*, Cambridge, Mass.: Harvard University Press.

Evans, G. and McDowell, J. (eds.) (1976), *Truth and Meaning; Essays in Semantics*, Oxford: Oxford University Press.

Everett, A. (1994), 'Absorbing Dialetheias', *Mind*, 103: 414–19.

Feyerabend, P. (1975), *Against Method*, London: New Left Books.

Field, H. (2003), 'A Revenge-Immune Solution to the Semantic Paradoxes', *Journal of Philosophical Logic*, 32: 139–77.

——(2005), 'Is the Liar Both True and False?', in Beall and Armour-Garb, ch. 2.

Flynt, H. (1974), 'The Apprehension of Plurality', typescript; ch. 3, 'A Provisional Axiomatic Treatment', printed in *Blueprint for a Higher Civilization*, Milan: Multhipla Edizioni, 1975, 195–200.

——(1997), 'Phenomenological Logic of Contradictions as an Outcome of Normative Everyday Logic', typescript.

Fodor, J. (1975), *The Language of Thought*, New York: Thomas Cromwell.

Frege, G. (1919), 'Negation', *Beiträge zur Philosophie des Deutschen Idealismus*, 1: 143–57; Eng. trans. repr. in P. Geach and M. Black (eds. and trans.) (1960), *Translations from the Philosophical Writings of Gottlob Frege*, Oxford: Blackwell, 117–35.

Fuhrmann, A. (1991), 'Theory Contraction through Base Contraction', *Journal of Philosophical Logic*, 20: 175–203.

——(1997), *An Essay on Contraction*, Stanford: CSLI Publications.

——(1999), 'When Hyperpropositions Meet', *Journal of Philosophical Logic*, 28: 559–74.

Furth, M. (1986), 'A Note on Aristotle's Principle of Non-Contradiction', *Canadian Journal of Philosophy*, 16: 371–81.

Gabbay, D. (1995), 'Conditional Implications and Non-Monotonic Consequence', in Crocco, Fariñas del Cerro, and Herzig (eds.), ch. 11.

——and Wansing, H. (eds.) (1999), *What is Negation?*, Dordrecht: Kluwer Academic Publishers.

Galvan, S. (1995), 'A Formalisation of Elenctic Argumentation', *Erkenntnis*, 43: 111–26.

Gärdenfors, P. (1988), *Knowledge in Flux: Modeling the Dynamics of Epistemic States*, Cambridge, Mass.: MIT Press.

Gasking, D. A. T. (1940), 'Mathematics and the World', *Australasian Journal of Philosophy*, 18: 97–116; repr. in Benacerraf and Putnam (1964), 390–403.

Geach, P. (1972), *Logic Matters*, Oxford: Blackwell.

Goddard, L. (2000), 'The Inconsistency of Aristotelian Logic?', *Australasian Journal of Philosophy*, 78: 434–7.

Goodman, N. (1979), *Fact, Fiction and Forecast*, 3rd edition, Cambridge, Mass.: Harvard University Press.

Goodstein, R. L. (1965), 'Multiple Successor Arithmetics', in J. Crossley and M. Dummett (eds.), *Formal Systems and Recursive Functions*, Amsterdam: North Holland Publishing Company, 265–71.

Gottlieb, P. (1992), 'The Principle of Non-Contradiction and Protagoras: The Strategy of Metaphysics, IV. 4', *Proceedings of the Boston Area Colloquium in Ancient Philosophy*, 8: 183–98.

Gowans, C. W. (1987), *Moral Dilemmas*, Oxford: Oxford University Press.

Gray, J. J. (1994), 'Euclidean and Non-Euclidean Geometry', in I. Grattan-Guinness (ed.), *Companion Encyclopedia of the History and Philosophy of Mathematical Sciences*, London: Routledge, sect. 7.4.

Grayling, A. C. (1997), *An Introduction to Philosophical Logic*, 3rd edition, Oxford: Blackwell.

Gregory, R. L. and Gombrich, E. H. (eds.) (1973), *Illusion in Nature and Art*, London: Duckworth.

Grim, P. (2004), 'What is a Contradiction?', in Priest, Beall, and Armour-Garb (eds.), ch. 3.

Haack, S. (1974), *Deviant Logic*, Cambridge: Cambridge University Press.

—— (1976), 'The Justification of Deduction', *Mind*, 85: 112–19.

—— (1978), *Philosophy of Logics*, Cambridge: Cambridge University Press.

Halper, E. (1984), 'Aristotle on the Extension of Non-Contradiction', *History of Philosophy Quarterly*, 1: 368–80.

Hamilton, E. and Cairns, H. (eds.) (1961), *Plato: The Collected Dialogues*, Princeton: Princeton University Press.

Hansson, S. (1997), 'Semi-Revision', *Journal of Applied and Non-Classical Logics*, 7: 151–75.

Hardin, C. L. (1988), *Color for Philosophers*, Indianapolis: Hackett Publishing Company.

Harris, J. H. (1982), 'What's so Logical about "Logical" Axioms', *Studia Logica*, 41: 159–71.

Hart, W. D. and McGinn, C. (1976), 'Knowledge and Necessity', *Journal of Philosophical Logic*, 5: 205–8.

Havas, K. (1981), 'Some Remarks on an Attempt at Formalising Dialectical Logic', *Studies in Soviet Thought*, 22: 257–64.

Hinckfuss, I. (1996), 'Instrumentalist Theories: Possibilities and Space and Time', in P. Riggs (ed.), *Natural Kinds, Laws of Nature and Scientific Methodology*, Dordrecht: Kluwer Academic Publishers, 187–209.

Horn, L. R. (1989), *A Natural History of Negation*, Chicago: University of Chicago Press.

Horwich, P. (1990), *Truth*, Oxford: Blackwell; 2nd edition, Oxford: Oxford University Press, 1998.

Howson, C. and Urbach, P. (1993), *Scientific Reasoning: The Bayesan Approach*, 2nd edition, Chicago: Open Court.

Humberstone, I. L. (1987), 'Wanting as Believing', *Canadian Journal of Philosophy*, 17: 49–62.

Irwin, T. (1977–8), 'Aristotle's Discovery of Metaphysics', *Review of Metaphysics*, 31: 210–29.

—— (1988), *Aristotle's First Principles*, Oxford: Oxford University Press.

Jeffrey, R. (1983), *The Logic of Decision*, Chicago: Chicago University Press.

Jowett, B. (ed. and trans.) (1931 edn.), *The Dialogues of Plato*, Oxford: Oxford University Press, iii.

Katsuno, H. and Satch, K. (1995), 'A Unified View of Consequence Relation, Belief Revision and Conditional Logic', in Crocco, Fariñas del Cerro, and Herzig (eds.), ch. 3.

Kemp Smith, N. (trans.) (1964), *Immanuel Kant's Critique of Pure Reason*, London: Macmillan.

Kirkham, R. L. (1992), *Theories of Truth*, Cambridge, Mass.: MIT Press.

Kirwan, C. (1993), *Aristotle; Metaphysics*, Books Γ, Δ, E, 2nd edition, Oxford: Oxford University Press.

Kneale, W. and M. (1962), *The Development of Logic*, Oxford: Oxford University Press.

Kolakowski, L. (1978), *Main Currents of Marxism*, i. *The Founders*, Oxford: Oxford University Press.

Kotarbiński, T. (1958), 'Jan Łukasiewicz's Works on the History of Logic', *Studia Logica*, 8: 57–62.

Kraus, S., Lehmann, D., and Magidor, M. (1990), 'Nonmonotonic Reasoning, Preferential Models and Cumulative Logics', *Artificial Intelligence*, 44: 167–207.

Kroon, F. (1993), 'Rationality and Epistemic Paradox', *Synthese*, 94: 377–408.

—— (2004), 'Realism and Dialetheism', in Priest, Beall, and Armour-Garb, ch. 15.

Kuhn, T. S. (1962), *The Structure of Scientific Revolutions*, Chicago: University of Chicago Press.

—— (1977), 'Objectivity, Value Judgment and Theory Choice', in *The Essential Tension*, Chicago: University of Chicago Press, ch. 13.

Lakatos, I. (1970), 'Falsification and the Methodology of Scientific Research Programmes', in I. Lakatos and A. Musgrave (eds.), *Criticism and the Growth of Knowledge*, Cambridge: Cambridge University Press, 91–196.

Laudan, L. (1977), *Progress and its Problems*, London: Routledge & Kegan Paul.

Lear, J. (1980), 'Proof by Refutation', in *Aristotle and Logical Theory*, Cambridge: Cambridge University Press, ch. 6.

—— (1988), 'The Most Certain Principle of Being', in *Aristotle; the Desire to Understand*, Cambridge: Cambridge University Press, sect. 6.4.

Leibniz, G. W. (1696), 'On Locke's Essay on Human Understanding', in A. G. Langley (ed.) (1896), *New Essays Concerning Human Understanding*, London: Macmillan, 13–20.

Levi, I. (1967), *Gambling with the Truth*, London: Routledge & Kegan Paul.

Lewis, D. K. (1973), *Counterfactuals*, Oxford: Blackwell.

—— (1982), 'Logic for Equivocators', *Noûs*, 14: 431–41.

Littman, G. (1992), 'The Irrationalist's Paradox', paper presented at meeting of the Australasian Association of Philosophy, University of Queensland.

Łukasiewicz, J. (1910), 'Über den Satz des Widerspruchs bei Aristoteles', *Bulletin International de l'Académie des Sciences de Cracovie*, 1910: 15–38; Eng. trans., by V. Wedin, 'On the Principle of Contradiction in Aristotle', *Review of Metaphysics*, 25: 485–509; re-trans. by J. Barnes as 'Aristotle on the Law of Contradiction', in J. Barnes, M. Schofield, and R. Sorabji (eds.), *Articles on Aristotle*, iii. *Metaphysics*, London: Duckworth, 1979.

—— (1930), 'Bemerkungen zu mehrwertigen Systemen des Aussagenkalküls', *Comptes Rendus des Séances de la Societé des Sciences et des Lettres de Varsovie*, 3/23: 51–77; Eng. trans., 'Philosophical Remarks on the Many-Valued Systems of Propositional Logic', in McCall (1967), ch. 3.

—— (1957), *Aristotle's Syllogistic*, Oxford: Clarendon Press.

Lycan, W. G. (1988), *Judgment and Justification*, Cambridge: Cambridge University Press.

McCall, S. (1967), *Polish Logic 1920–1939*, Oxford: Oxford University Press.

McCarty, D. (1991), 'Incompleteness in Intuitionist Mathematics', *Notre Dame Journal of Formal Logic*, 32: 323–58.

McTaggart, J. M. E. (1922), *Studies in the Hegelean Dialectic*, 2nd edition, Cambridge: Cambridge University Press.

Mares, E. (1996), 'Relevant Logic and the Theory of Information', *Synthèse*, 109: 345–60.

Martin, C. (1986), 'William's Machine', *Journal of Philosophy*, 83: 564–72.

Meyer, R. K. (1974), 'New Axiomatics for Relevant Logics, I', *Journal of Philosophical Logic*, 3: 53–86.

—— (1985), 'Boole Bights Back', paper read at the Annual Meeting of the Australasian Association of Philosophy.

—— and Routley, R. (1973), 'Classical Relevant Logics, I', *Studia Logica*, 32: 51–68.

—— —— (1974), 'Classical Relevant Logics, II', *Studia Logica*, 33: 183–94.

—— Dunn, J. M., and Routley, R. (1979), 'Curry's Paradox', *Analysis*, 39: 124–8.

Milne, P. (2004), 'Algebras of Intervals and a Logic of Conditional Assertions', *Journal of Philosophical Logic*, 33: 497–548.

Montague, R. (1974), *Formal Philosophy*, New Haven: Yale University Press.

Mortensen, C. (1981), 'A Plea for Model-Theory', *Philosophical Quarterly*, 31: 152–7.

—— (1995), *Inconsistent Mathematics*, Dordrecht: Kluwer Academic Publishers.

Nagel, E. (1944), *Naturalism and the Human Spirit*, New York: Columbia University Press.

Nerlich, G. (1976), *The Shape of Space*, Cambridge: Cambridge University Press.

Noonan, H. C. (1977), 'An Argument of Aristotle on Non-Contradiction', *Analysis*, 37: 163–9.

Norton, J. (1987), 'The Logical Inconsistency of the Old Quantum Theory of Black Body Radiation', *Philosophy of Science*, 54: 327–50.

Nuttall, J. (1978), 'Belief, Opacity and Contradiction', *Philosophical Quarterly*, 28: 353–8.

Olin, D. (2003), *Paradox*, Chesham, Bucks.: Acumen.

Parsons, T. (1984), 'Assertion, Denial, and the Liar Paradox', *Journal of Philosophical Logic*, 13: 137–52.

—— (1990), 'True Contradictions', *Canadian Journal of Philosophy*, 20: 335–53.

Pears, D. (ed.) (1972), *Russell's Logical Atomism*, London: Fontana.

Penrose, L. S. and Penrose, R. (1958), 'Impossible Objects: A Special Type of Illusion', *British Journal of Psychology*, 49: 31–5.

Poincaré, H. (n.d.), *La Science et L'Hypothèse*, Paris: Ernest Flammmarian; Eng. trans., *Science and Hypothesis*, News York: Dover Publications, 1952.

Popper, K. (1963), *Conjectures and Refutations*, London: Routledge & Kegan Paul.

Priest, G. (1979), 'Two Dogmas of Quineanism', *Philosophical Quarterly*, 29: 289–301.

—— (1980), 'Sense, Entailment and Modus Ponens', *Journal of Philosophical Logic*, 9: 415–35.

—— (1987), *In Contradiction*, Dordrecht: Martinus Nijhoff; 2nd edition, Oxford: Oxford University Press, 2006.

—— (1989a), 'Classical Logic *Aufgehoben*', in Priest, Routley, and Norman, ch. 4.

—— (1989b), '*Reductio ad Absurdum et Modus Tollendo Ponens*', in Priest, Routley, and Norman, ch. 21.

—— (1989c), 'Denyer's $ not Backed by Sterling Arguments', *Mind*, 98: 265–8.

—— (1989–90), 'Dialectic and Dialetheic', *Science and Society*, 53: 388–415.

—— (1990), 'Boolean Negation and All That', *Journal of Philosophical Logic*, 19: 201–15.

—— (1991a), 'Intensional Paradoxes', *Notre Dame Journal of Formal Logic*, 32: 193–211.

—— (1991b), 'Minimally Inconsistent *LP*', *Studia Logica*, 50: 321–31; repr. in 2nd edition of Priest (2006), ch. 16.

—— (1993a), 'Can Contradictions be True? II', *Proceedings of the Aristotelian Society*, suppl. vol., 67: 35–54.

—— (1993b), 'Another Disguise of the Same Fundamental Problems: Barwise and Etchemendy on the Liar', *Australasian Journal of Philosophy*, 71: 60–9.

—— (1994a), 'Is Arithmetic Consistent?', *Mind*, 103: 337–49.

—— (1994b), Review of V. McGee, *Truth, Vagueness and Paradox*, *Mind*, 103: 387–91.

—— (1995a), *Beyond the Limits of Thought*, Cambridge: Cambridge University Press; 2nd edition, Oxford: Oxford University Press, 2002.

—— (1995b), 'Gaps and Gluts: Reply to Parsons', *Canadian Journal of Philosophy*, 25: 57–66.

—— (1995c), 'Etchemendy and the Concept of Logical Validity', *Canadian Journal of Philosophy*, 25: 283–92.

—— (1996a), 'On Inconsistent Arithmetics: Reply to Denyer', *Mind*, 105: 649–59.

—— (1996b), 'Everett's Trilogy', *Mind*, 105: 631–47.

—— (1997a), 'Inconsistent Models of Arithmetic: I, Finite Models', *Journal of Philosophical Logic*, 26: 223–35.

—— (1997b), 'Sylvan's box: A Short Story and 10 Morals', *Notre Dame Journal of Formal Logic*, 38: 573–82; repr. in Priest (2005a), ch. 6, appendix.

—— (1998a), 'To Be *and* Not to Be—That is the Answer: Aristotle on the Law of Non-Contradiction', *Philosophiegeschichte und Logische Analyse*, 1: 91–130.

—— (1998b), 'What's so Bad about Contradictions?', *Journal of Philosophy*, 95: 410–26; repr. in Priest, Beall, and Armour-Garb (2004), ch. 1.

—— (1999a), 'What not? A Defence of a Dialetheic Account of Negation', in Gabbay and Wansing, 101–20.

—— (1999b), 'Perceiving Contradictions', *Australasian Journal of Philosophy*, 77: 439–46.

—— (1999c), 'Negation as Cancellation, and Connexivism', *Topoi*, 18: 141–8.

—— (1999d), 'Validity', in A. Varzi (ed.), *The Nature of Logic*, Stanford: CSLI Publications (*European Review of Philosophy*), iv. 183–206; abbreviated version under the same title appears in T. Childers (ed.), *The Logica Yearbook*, Prague: Institute of Philosophy, 1997, 18–25

—— (2000*a*), 'Could everything be True?', *Australasian Journal of Philosophy*, 78: 189–95.

—— (2000*b*), 'The Logic of Backwards Inductions', *Economics and Philosophy*, 16: 267–85.

—— (2000*c*), 'Inconsistent Models of Arithmetic. ii. The General Case', *Journal of Symbolic Logic*, 65: 1519–29.

—— (2000*d*), Review of N. da Costa, *Logique Classique et Non-Classique*, *Studia Logica*, 64: 435–43.

—— (2000*e*), 'Truth and Contradiction', *Philosophical Quarterly*, 50: 189–95.

—— (2001*a*), *Introduction to Non-Classical Logic*, Cambridge: Cambridge University Press.

—— (2001*b*), 'Paraconsistent Belief Revision', *Theoria*, 68: 214–28.

—— (2001*c*), 'Logic: One or Many?', in J. Woods and B. Brown (eds.), *Logical Consequences: Rival Approaches*, Oxford: Hermes Scientific Publishers, 23-38.

—— (2001*d*), 'Why it's Irrational to Believe in Consistency', in B. Brogard and B. Smith (eds.), *Rationality and Irrationality, Proceedings of the 23rd International Wittgenstein Symposium*, Vienna: öbv&hpt Verlagsgesellschaft mbh & Co, 284–93.

—— (2002*a*), 'Inconsistency and the Empirical Sciences', in J. Meheus (ed.), *Inconsistency in Science*, Dordrecht: Kluwer Academic Publishers, 119–28.

—— (2002*b*), 'Paraconsistent Logic', in D. Gabbay and F. Guenthner (eds.), *Handbook of Philosophical Logic*, 2nd edition, Dordrecht: Kluwer Academic Publishers, vi. 287–393.

—— (2002*c*), 'Rational Dilemmas', *Analysis*, 62: 11–16.

—— (2003), 'On Alternative Geometries, Arithmetics and Logics: A Tribute to Łukasiewicz', *Studia Logica*, 74: 441–68.

—— (2005a) *Towards Non-Being The Logic and Metaphysics of Intentionality*, Oxford: Oxford University Press.

—— (2005b) 'Spiking the Field Artillery', in Beall and Armour-Garb (2005), ch. 3.

—— (2007), 'Paraconsistency and Dialetheism', in D. Gabbay and J. Woods (eds.), *Handbook of the History of Logic*, Amsterdam: Elsevier. viii. ch. 3.

—— (2008), 'Beyond The Limits of Knowledge', in J. Salerno (ed.), *New Essays on the Knowability paradox*, Oxford: Oxford University Press.

—— and Routley, R. (1989*a*), 'Applications of Paraconsistent Logic', in Priest, Routley, and Norman, ch. 13.

—— —— (1989*b*), 'The Philosophical Significance and Inevitability of Paraconsistency', in Priest, Routley, and Norman, ch. 18.

—— —— and Norman, J. (eds.) (1989), *Paraconsistent Logic: Essays on the Inconsistent*, Munich: Philosophia Verlag.

—— Beall, JC., and Armour-Garb, B. (eds.) (2004), *The Law of Non-Contradiction: New Philosophical Essays*, Oxford University Press.

Prior, A. (1960), 'The Runabout Inference-Ticket', *Analysis*, 21: 38–9; repr. in Strawson (1967), 129–31.

—— (1967), 'Logic, Traditional', in P. Edwards (ed.), *Encyclopedia of Philosophy*, New York: Collier-Macmillan.

—— (1971), *Objects of Thought*, Oxford: Oxford University Press.

Putnam, H. (1962), 'It Ain't Necessarily So', *Journal of Philosophy*, 59: 658–71; repr. in. Putnam (1975), ch. 15.

Putnam, H. (1969), 'Is Logic Empirical?', in R. Cohen and M. Wartofsky (eds.), *Boston Studies in the Philosophy of Science*, Dordrecht: Reidel, v. repr. 216–41; as 'The Logic of Quantum Mechanics', in Putnam (1975), ch. 10.

—— (1975), *Mathematics, Matter and Method: Philosophical Papers*, Cambridge: Cambridge University Press, i.

—— (1976), 'There is at Least One A Priori Truth', *Erkenntnis*, 13: 153–70; repr. in *Realism and Reason: Collected Papers*, Cambridge: Cambridge University Press, 1983, iii. ch. 6.

Quine, W. V. O. (1951), 'Two Dogmas of Empiricism', *Philosophical Review*, 60: 20–43; repr. in *From a Logical Point of View*, Cambridge, Mass.: Harvard University Press, 1953, 20–46.

—— (1960), *Word and Object*, Cambridge, Mass.: MIT Press.

—— (1970), *Philosophy of Logic*, Englewood Cliffs, NJ: Prentice Hall.

—— and Ullian, J. (1970), *The Web of Belief*, New York: Random House.

Read, S. (1988), *Relevant Logic: A Philosophical Examination of Inference*, Oxford: Blackwell.

—— (1994*a*), *Thinking about Logic: An Introduction to the Philosophy of Logic*, Oxford: Oxford University Press.

—— (1994*b*), 'Formal and Material Consequence', *Journal of Philosophical Logic*, 23: 247–65.

—— (2000), 'Harmony and Autonomy in Classical Logic', *Journal of Philosophical Logic*, 29: 123–54.

Rescher, N. (1969), *Many-Valued Logic*, New York: McGraw-Hill.

—— and Brandom, R. (1980), *The Logic of Inconsistency*, Oxford: Blackwell.

Restall, G. (1999), 'Negation in Relevant Logics', in Gabbay and Wansing, 53–76.

—— (2000), *Introduction to Substructural Logic*, London: Routledge.

—— (2004), 'Laws of Non-Contradiction, Laws of Excluded Middle, and Logic', in Priest, Beall, and Armour-Garb, ch. 4.

Robinson, J. O. (1972), *The Psychology of Visual Illusion*, London: Hutchinson.

Robinson, T. M. (1987), *Heraclitus: Fragments*, Toronto: University of Toronto Press.

Ross, W. D. (1924), *Aristotle's Metaphysics*, Oxford: Oxford University Press, i.

Routley, R. and V. (1985), 'Negation and Contradiction', *Rivista Colombiana de Matemáticas*, 19: 201–31.

—— Plumwood, V., Meyer R. K., and Brady, R. (1982), *Relevant Logics and their Rivals*, Atascadero, Calif.: Ridgeview, i.

Ryle, G. (1954), 'Formal and Informal Logic', in *Dilemmas*, Cambridge: Cambridge University Press, ch. 8.

Sainsbury, M. (1994), *Paradoxes,* 2nd edition, Cambridge: Cambridge University Press.

Sartre, J. P. (1943), *L'Etre et le Néant*, Paris: Gallimard.

Schroeder-Heister, P. and Došen, K. (eds.) (1993), *Substructural Logics*, Oxford: Oxford University Press.

Selby-Bigge, L. A. (ed.) (1902), *Enquiries Concerning the Human Understanding and Concerning the Principles of Morals*, 2nd edition, Oxford: Clarendon Press.

Shepard, R. N. (1964), 'Circularity in Judgments of Relative Pitch', *Journal of the Acoustical Society of America*, 36: 2346–53.

—— (1983), 'Demonstrations of Circular Components of Pitch', *Journal of the Audio Engineering Society*, 3: 638–49.

Shoham, Y. (1988), *Reasoning about Change*, Cambridge, Mass.: MIT Press.

Slaney, J. (1990), 'A General Logic', *Australasian Journal of Philosophy*, 68: 74–88.

Slater, B. H. (1995), 'Paraconsistent Logic?', *Journal of Philosophical Logic*, 24: 451–4.

Smiley, T. J. (1993), 'Can Contradictions be True? I', *Proceedings of the Aristotelian Society*, suppl. vol. 67: 17–33.

Smith, J. M. (1988), 'Inconsistency and Scientific Reasoning', *Studies in History and Philosophy of Science*, 19: 429–45.

Sobocinski, B. (1956), 'In Memoriam Jan Łukasiewicz', *Philosophical Studies* (Dublin), 6: 3–49.

Stalnaker, R. C. (1968), 'A Theory of Conditionals', *Studies in Logical Theory* (suppl. monograph to the *American Philosophical Quarterly*), 98–112.

—— (1981), 'A Theory of Conditionals', in W. L. Harper (ed.), *Ifs*, Dordrecht: Reidel, 41–55.

Stevenson, J. (1961), 'Roundabout the Runabout Inference Ticket', *Analysis*, 21: 124–8.

Strawson, P. (1952), *Introduction to Logical Theory*, London: Methuen.

—— (ed.) (1967), *Philosophical Logic*, Oxford: Oxford University Press.

Sundholm, G. (1986), 'Proof Theory and Meaning', in D. Gabbay and F. Guenthner (eds.), *Handbook of Philosophical Logic*, Dordrecht: Kluwer Academic Publishers, iii. ch. 8.

Sylvan, R. (1999), 'What is that Item Designated Negation?', in Gabbay and Wansing, 299–324.

Tanaka, K. (1996), 'Paraconsistent Belief Revision', Hon. diss., Brisbane: University of Queensland; 'The AGM Theory and Inconsistent Belief Change', *Logique et Analyse*, 48 (2005), 113–150.

Tarski, A. (1956*a*), 'The Concept of Truth in Formalized Languages', in *Logic, Semantics, and Metamathematics*, Oxford: Oxford University Press, ch. 8.

—— (1956*b*), 'On the Concept of Logical Consequence', in *Logic, Semantics, and Metamathematics*, Oxford: Oxford University Press, ch. 16.

Tennant, N. (1987), *Anti-Realism and Logic*, Oxford: Oxford University Press.

Tenney, J. (1992), 'For Ann (Rising)', on *Selected Works, 1961–1969*, Hanover, NH: Artifact Records.

Thompson, M. (1981), 'On A Priori Truth', *Journal of Philosophy*, 78: 458–82.

Upton, T. V. (1982–3), 'Psychological and Metaphysical Dimensions of Non-Contradiction', *Review of Metaphysics*, 36: 591–606.

Van Bendegem, J. P. (1987), *Finite, Empirical Mathematics: Outline of a Model*, Gent: Rijksuniversiteit Gent.

van Fraassen, B. C. (1969), 'Facts and Tautological Entailments', *Journal of Philosophy*, 66: 477–87.

—— (1980), *The Scientific Image*, Oxford: Clarendon Press.

Vasil'év, N. (1913), 'Logica i Métalogica', *Logos*, 1–2: 53–81; Eng. trans. by V. Vasukov as 'Logic and Metalogic', *Axiomathes*, 4 (1993), 329–51.

Wason, P. C. and Johnson-Laird, P. (1972), *Psychology of Reasoning: Structure and Content*, Cambridge, Mass.: Harvard University Press.

Wedin, M. V. (1982), 'On the Range of the Principle of Non-Contradiction in Aristotle', *Logique et Analyse*, 25: 87–92.

Whitaker, C. W. A. (1995), *Aristotle's De Interpretatione: Contradiction and Dialectic*, Oxford: Clarendon Press.

Wittgenstein, L. (1978), *Remarks on the Foundations of Mathematics*, 3rd edition, Oxford: Blackwell.

Wright, C. (1983), *Frege's Conception of Numbers as Objects*, Aberdeen: Aberdeen University Press.

—— (2004), 'Intuition, Entitlement and the Epistemology of Logical Laws', *Dialectica*, 58: 155–75.

Yi, B. (2003), 'Newcome's Problem and Priest's Principle of Rational Choice', *Analysis*, 63: 237–42.

Index

geometry 155–8, 164, 173, 195
  non-Euclidean 156, 157–8, 162, 164–5, 175
globalism, and revisability 174–5
Goodman, N. 187

Hamlet (Shakespeare) 209
harmony, and Boolean negation 92–4
Hegel, G. W. F. 7, 172
Herakliteans
  and the Law of Non-Contradiction 11, 14–15, 16–17, 22, 29, 34, 36, 37, 38, 39
  and trivialism 65
Hermann grid, and trivialism 58
history of philosophy
  and dialetheism 1
  and rational belief 119–21
Horwich, P. 44, 45
Hume, D. 121

identity principle, and the Law of Non-Contradiction 33–4
In Contradiction (Priest) 19, 35, 46, 47, 125
Inclosure Schema, and rational belief 127
inconsistency 142–51
  accepting inconsistent information 147–8
  in arithmetics 159–62
  and belief-revision 3, 132–3, 134–5
  handling 146–7
  in mathematics 149–50
  and observation 142–4
  and rational belief 119, 125–9
  and truth 48–9, 50–1
  types of 144–6
  see also consistency
Indian philosophy, Nyaya school and rational belief 121
inductive validity 177, 186–90, 191
  and logical pluralism 196, 207–8
  and non-monotonic logic 189–90
  and probability 188–9
information preservation, and validity 191–2
informative semantics, and deductive validity 181
instrumentalism
  in logic 173–4
  and logical pluralism 204–6

intermediate account, of the Law of Non-Contradiction 31–2
intuitionist logic 155, 164, 172, 177, 182, 194
  and deductive validity 177, 182
  and logical pluralism 194, 197, 204
intuitionist metatheory 156
intuitionist negation 75, 76, 95, 198–9
irrational beliefs 134–5
Irrationalist's Paradox, and denial and rejection 111–12
Irwin, T. 26–7, 33

James, W. 48

Kant, I. 1, 158, 175
  Critique of Pure Reason 70–1, 157, 165
Kirwan, C. 7, 13, 16, 35, 37, 38
Kneale, W. and M. 156
Kripke, S. 23, 204
Kuhn, T. 169, 200

Lambek calculus 195
Law of Identity, and the Law of Non-Contradiction 13
LC (law of contraposition) 82, 83
LDM (Laws of De Morgan) 82, 83, 86
LDN (law of double negation) 81–2, 83
Lear, J. 27–8, 29, 32
Leibniz, G. 2, 27, 158
LEM (Law of Excluded Middle) 8, 10, 12, 35–6, 78–81, 83, 85
Levi operation, and belief revision 136
Lewis, D. K. 99
Liar Paradox
  and Boolean negation 90
  and the deflationist theory of truth 45
  and denial and rejection 111
  and the Law of Non-Contradiction 9, 40
  and rational belief 124, 126
Lindenbaum algebra 180–1
LNC (Law of Non-Contradiction) 1, 2, 7–42, 43
  Anscombe/Cresswell interpretation of 25–6, 27
  and Aristotle on substance 22–3
  and contradiction 78–81, 83, 85
  demonstration by refutation 13–16
  and the empirical sciences 149–50

Printed in Great Britain
by Amazon

48423368R10132